Tradition and Modernity

Previously Published Records of Building Bridges Seminars

The Road Ahead: A Christian-Muslim Dialogue,
Michael Ipgrave, Editor (London: Church House, 2002)

Scriptures in Dialogue: Christians and Muslims Studying the Bible and the Qur'ān Together,
Michael Ipgrave, Editor (London: Church House, 2004)

Bearing the Word: Prophecy in Biblical and Qur'ānic Perspective,
Michael Ipgrave, Editor (London: Church House, 2005)

Building a Better Bridge: Muslims, Christians, and the Common Good,
Michael Ipgrave, Editor (Washington, DC: Georgetown University Press, 2008)

Justice and Rights: Christian and Muslim Perspectives,
Michael Ipgrave, Editor (Washington, DC: Georgetown University Press, 2009)

Humanity: Texts and Contexts: Christian and Muslim Perspectives,
Michael Ipgrave and David Marshall, Editors (Washington, DC: Georgetown University Press, 2011)

Communicating the Word: Revelation, Translation, and Interpretation in Christianity and Islam,
David Marshall, Editor (Washington, DC: Georgetown University Press, 2011)

Science and Religion: Christian and Muslim Perspectives,
David Marshall, Editor (Washington, DC: Georgetown University Press, 2012)

For more information about the Building Bridges seminars, please visit:
http://berkleycenter.georgetown.edu/resources/networks/building_bridges

Tradition and Modernity

CHRISTIAN AND MUSLIM PERSPECTIVES

A record of the ninth Building Bridges seminar
Convened by the Archbishop of Canterbury
Georgetown University, Washington, DC, May 2010

DAVID MARSHALL, *Editor*

Georgetown University Press / Washington, DC

Library of Congress Cataloging-in-Publication Data

Building Bridges Seminar (9th : 2010 : Georgetown University)
Tradition and modernity : Christian and Muslim perspectives : a record of the Ninth Building Bridges Seminar, convened by the Archbishop of Canterbury, Georgetown University, Washington, D.C., May 2010 / David Marshall, editor.
p. cm.
Includes bibliographical references.
ISBN 978-1-58901-949-2 (pbk. : alk. paper)
1. Islam—Relations—Christianity. 2. Christianity and other religions—Islam. 3. Taqlid—Congresses. 4. Tradition (Theology)—Congresses. 5. Islamic modernism—Congresses. 6. Modernism (Christian theology)—Congresses. I. Marshall, David, Rev. II. Title.
BP172.B834 2010
261.2′7—dc23

2012012108

∞ This book is printed on acid-free paper meeting the requirements of the American National Standard for Permanence in Paper for Printed Library Materials.

19 18 17 16 15 14 13 12 9 8 7 6 5 4 3 2
First printing

Contents

Participants

Alparslan Açikgenç
Professor of Philosophy, Fatih University, Istanbul

Asma Afsaruddin
Professor of Islamic Studies, Department of Near Eastern Languages and Cultures, Indiana University

Abdullahi Ahmed An-Naʿim
Charles Howard Candler Professor of Law, Emory University, Atlanta, Georgia

Thomas Banchoff
Director, Berkley Center for Religion, Peace, and World Affairs, Georgetown University, Washington, DC

Vincent J. Cornell
Asa Griggs Candler Professor of Arabic and Islamic Studies, Department of Middle East and South Asian Studies, Emory University, Atlanta, Georgia

Caner Dagli
Assistant Professor of Religious Studies, College of the Holy Cross, Worcester, Massachusetts

Gavin D'Costa
Professor of Catholic Theology, University of Bristol, UK

John J. DeGioia
President, Georgetown University, Washington, DC

Waleed El-Ansary
Associate Professor of Religious Studies, University of South Carolina, Columbia, South Carolina

Stephen M. Fields
Associate Professor of Theology, Georgetown University, Washington, DC

Lucy Gardner
Tutor in Christian Doctrine, St. Stephen's House, University of Oxford, UK

SHERINE HAMDY
Assistant Professor, Department of Anthropology, Brown University, Providence, Rhode Island

HARRIET HARRIS
University Chaplain, University of Edinburgh, UK

DAVID BENTLEY HART
Eastern Orthodox theologian

PHILIP JENKINS
Edwin Erle Sparks Professor of Humanities, Pennsylvania State University

MOHAMMAD HASSAN KHALIL
Assistant Professor of Religion, University of Illinois

JOHN LANGAN
Rose Kennedy Professor of Christian Ethics, Georgetown University, Washington, DC

JOSEPH E. B. LUMBARD
Assistant Professor of Classical Islam, Brandeis University, Waltham, Massachusetts

DANIEL A. MADIGAN
Director of Graduate Studies, Department of Theology, Georgetown University, Washington, DC

MALEIHA MALIK
Professor in Law, King's College, London

JANE DAMMEN MCAULIFFE
President, Bryn Mawr College, Bryn Mawr, Pennsylvania

JOHN MILBANK
Professor in Religion, Politics and Ethics, University of Nottingham, UK

MUSTANSIR MIR
Professor of Islamic Studies, Youngstown State University, Youngstown, Ohio

SAJJAD RIZVI
Associate Professor of Islamic Intellectual History, Exeter University, UK

ABDULLAH SAEED
Sultan of Oman Professor of Arab and Islamic Studies, University of Melbourne, Australia

Lamin Sanneh
D. Willis James Professor of Missions & World Christianity and Professor of History, Yale University Divinity School, New Haven, Connecticut

Christoph Schwöbel
Professor of Systematic Theology, University of Tübingen, Germany

Recep Şentürk
Director General and Dean of Graduate Studies, Alliance of Civilizations Institute, Fatih Sultan Mehmet Vakıf University, Istanbul

Zaid Shakir
Lecturer and Scholar-in-Residence, Zaytuna Institute, California

Abdolkarim Soroush
Scholar of Islamic thought

Janet Soskice
Professor of Philosophical Theology, University of Cambridge, UK

Michael Welker
Professor of Systematic Theology, University of Heidelberg, Germany

Paul Weston
Tutor in Mission Studies and Homiletics, Ridley Hall, Cambridge, UK

Rowan Williams
Archbishop of Canterbury, Church of England

Joseph Lumbard and Abdullah Saeed were prevented from attending the seminar but their papers were presented on their behalf and are included in this volume. Paul Weston did not attend the seminar but very kindly agreed at a later stage to provide a paper on Lesslie Newbigin.

Acknowledgments

Georgetown University hosted the seminar that this volume records with its usual generous hospitality and elegant efficiency. Particular thanks are due to the president of Georgetown University, John J. DeGioia, for all his support for Building Bridges over many years. Tom Banchoff, director of the Berkley Center for Religion, Peace, and World Affairs at Georgetown University, has also provided essential support and in particular has made possible the creation of the Building Bridges website. Deven Comen, Paige Lovejoy, Chiaki Ota, and Shuang Wen took very helpful notes at the seminar's group discussions. More generally, many thanks are due to all those members of the university community who made the seminar such a success. It has once again been a pleasure to work with Richard Brown and all his colleagues at Georgetown University Press.

Introduction

DAVID MARSHALL

THIS volume is a record of the proceedings of the ninth Building Bridges seminar for Christian and Muslim scholars, convened by the Archbishop of Canterbury, Dr. Rowan Williams, and held at Georgetown University, Washington, DC, from May 25–27, 2010. The focus of this seminar on Christian and Muslim approaches to the relationship between tradition and modernity was a natural continuation of discussions at earlier Building Bridges seminars, notably on the interface between science and religion in 2009. Following an established pattern, after an opening day of public lectures, the second and third days were spent in private sessions discussing a sequence of Christian and Muslim thinkers chosen for their relevance to the theme of tradition and modernity. For each thinker a text or selection of texts provided the basis for discussion in small groups. At the end of the third day the seminar closed with a public panel discussion chaired by the Archbishop.

This book follows the structure of the seminar closely. Part I ("Surveys") consists of essays that are revised versions of the first day's lectures. Drawing on the categorization of various types of primitivism in the work of Lovejoy and Boas, Vincent Cornell explores types of primitivism in the Qur'ān and Ḥadīth before moving to the modern period to show how different forms of primitivism underpin the doctrines of Salafī Traditionalists, Salafī Modernists, Shīʿī Traditionalists, and Shīʿī Modernists. Particular reference is made to Sayyid Quṭb, Ayatollah Khomeini, and ʿAlī Sharīʿatī. Janet Soskice begins by reflecting on the nature of tradition, or "handing on," in human experience generally: "We learn from those who went before. All people are 'traditional.'" She then turns to how the idea of tradition has been debated within the Christian tradition, with particular reference to the relationship between scripture and tradition. She concludes: "To stand in a tradition is not to stand still but to stand in the deep, loamy soil that feeds further growth."

The next two essays consider the impact of modernity on forms of authority in Christianity and Islam. For Philip Jenkins, "What we see in the 21st century is not the eclipse of religious authority, but rather its unmooring from traditional institutions, and its decentralization and radical democratization." He briefly reviews the familiar story of the undermining of traditional forms of religious authority by Western forms of modernity before illustrating a range of ways in which "premodern and even ancient approaches to authority have survived and have proved astonishingly resilient." Jenkins concludes that "religious authority has a habit of resisting any number of forces that should, in theory, have been lethal to its hopes of survival." With particular reference to the history of Turkey, Recep Şentürk explores the relationship between the types of authority characterizing premodern Muslim societies and different forms of authority that have arisen more recently. He comments: "Today, the remnants of the old system exist side by side with the new forms of authority, but they are in great tension with each other." He notes the undermining of the authority of traditional religious scholars and argues that the vacuum thus created has been filled by a new class of "religious intellectuals, politicians, social activists, academics and TV celebrities." Muslim believers are now "forced to choose from among a plurality of competing options."

In the third pair of essays the theme of freedom comes to the fore. Abdullahi Ahmed An-Naʿim proposes an Islamic basis for freedom of religion and of speech. He emphasizes that "the purpose and meaning of religion that one may seek to achieve and experience must be a matter of personal, free and voluntary choice." Central to his argument is his defense of the secular state, defined as one that is "neutral regarding all religions without being hostile or indifferent to any religion"; conversely, he rejects the idea of the Islamic state as "conceptually untenable and practically counterproductive from an Islamic point of view." Other significant features of An-Naʿim's essay include his focus on Islamic approaches to apostasy and his support for the Islamic methodology of Mahmoud Mohamed Taha. David Bentley Hart contrasts modern notions of freedom in terms of "libertarian autonomy and spontaneous volition" with premodern convictions that the realization of our nature could not happen without reference to God before expounding the perspective on liberation which he finds in the very origins of Christianity, with particular reference to Pauline teaching. He argues that "in every modern demand for social and personal recognition as inherent rights, there is at least a distant echo of Paul's proclamation of the unanticipated 'free gift' found in Christ." After some discussion of slavery and the emancipation of women, Hart concludes that the task of Christian social thought must be "to enunciate a vision of freedom that neither 'idealizes away' the injustices of the past nor surrenders to the soporific nihilism of mere negative liberty."

In part II of this volume we move to a sequence of eight significant Christian and Muslim thinkers on tradition and modernity, arranged chronologically from John Henry Newman (1801–90) to Tariq Ramadan (1962–). Selections from their writings are followed by essays drawing out key themes in their thought. While some of these essays stick closely to the selected texts, others reflect more widely on the thinking of the authors in question. Different readers will naturally react variously to the selection of Christian and Muslim thinkers made here, but it is hoped that, taken altogether, they illustrate at least a reasonably representative range of approaches. Regarding the place of women in modern Christian and Islamic thought, it should be noted that whereas the selection of writings of each of the four Muslim thinkers includes examples of their approaches to the relationship between Islam and women, only one of the Christian thinkers, Elisabeth Schüssler Fiorenza, addresses the parallel theme of Christianity and women; but in her case the selected writings are entirely focused on this theme.

In the course of the seminar there was a great deal of discussion, whether responding to the broad themes of the lectures or engaging with the distinctive ideas of the different thinkers. Some of the most recurrent questions included:

- How are we to define "tradition" and "modernity"? What are the range of understandings of "tradition" in Islam and Christianity? Is "modernity" a tradition, even a religious tradition?
- How is tradition "managed"? Where is authority to interpret tradition located? Is there authority external to tradition by which it can be justified? How is legitimate development of a tradition distinguished from illegitimate? Can there be infallibility in this matter and, if so, where is it located?
- What is the relationship of scripture to tradition? Does scripture stand apart from and prior to tradition, or is it part of tradition? If part of tradition, is scripture open to criticism?
- To what extent are the approaches of Muslims and Christians to modernity influenced by a bigger historical picture dominated by belief in a past Golden Age or Utopia which believers should seek to recreate? Is tradition understood fundamentally as a deposit to be protected, or as a dynamic process stretching ahead towards future fulfilment?
- Is there a danger of Christians and Muslims holding too "gloomy" a view of modernity, failing to acknowledge its benefits? Without "modernity," it was asked, would this seminar in fact have happened?

This is by no means an exhaustive account of the many themes that were discussed over three days. Readers wishing to gain more of a sense of these discussions can access video recordings of some plenary sessions and the final seminar panel discussion on the Building Bridges website.[1]

The final word in this volume is appropriately given to the Archbishop, who convened the seminar and chaired its private sessions. In his afterword to this volume he offers his own reflections on the seminar as a whole.

Note on Translations of the Bible and the Qur'ān

When not indicated otherwise in the notes, the translations of the Qur'ān in this volume are either from M. A. S. Abdel Haleem, *The Qur'an: A New Translation* (Oxford: Oxford University Press, 2004) or are the author's own translation, and translations of the Bible are either from the New Revised Standard Version or are the author's own translation.

Note

1. http://berkleycenter.georgetown.edu/resources/networks/building ebridges.

PART I

Surveys

Tradition and History in Islam

Primitivism in Islamic Thought and Scripture

VINCENT J. CORNELL

> When the regime of the Commander of the Faithful [Aḥmad ibn Muḥammad al-Shaykh al-Mahdī] was established, he rejected imitation (*taqlīd*), increased creativity (*tawlīd*) and innovation (*ikhtirāʿ*), favored theoretical research (*qiyās al-mashāhid ʿalā al-ghāʾib*), and freed all worthy endeavors from the constraints that limited their usefulness. This resulted in numerous conquests, the exaltation of industries, the rule of civilization, subtleties of innovation and creativity, the expansion of capability, and a grandeur the like of which cannot be compared to anything achieved by his predecessors. May God prolong his days, make his achievements successful, and make his Imamate a protection for Islam! The condition of these times is of miracles beyond the limits of the human imagination. One can improve or create whatever the mind conceives, whether it is the answers to the most difficult philosophical problems or feats of engineering.[1]

THIS REMARKABLE PASSAGE was written in the late 1580s by ʿAbd al-ʿAzīz al-Fishtālī (d. 1621), the court historian of the Moroccan Sultan Aḥmad al-Manṣūr al-Dhahbī ("The Golden Conqueror," r. 1578–1603). Aḥmad al-Manṣūr's father, Muḥammad al-Shaykh al-Mahdī (d. 1557), reunited Morocco after more than a century of civil war and foreign invasion. He was a descendant of the Prophet Muḥammad and claimed for himself the caliphal titles of *amīr al-muʾminīn* (Commander of the Faithful) and imām. Aḥmad al-Manṣūr was the greatest ruler of the Saʿdian Dynasty, which dominated Morocco from 1554 to 1659. In many ways his reign was comparable to that of his contemporary, Queen Elizabeth I of Britain. Under the Saʿdians, Britain and Morocco were allies. As this passage demonstrates, Saʿdian Morocco, like Elizabethan England, encouraged both ambition and creativity. The Saʿdians welcomed merchants and adventurers from Spain, Italy, France, and the

Ottoman Empire. Iberian Jews oversaw international commerce, the state pursued a mercantilist economic policy, a fire-armed professional army maintained security, and Morocco was a place where ambitious men could "create whatever the mind conceives." There seemed to be no limit to what Aḥmad al-Manṣūr and his subjects could achieve. However, this golden age was not to last. The final major outbreak of the bubonic plague at the beginning of the seventeenth century killed the Saʿdian ruler and most of the urban elites of the country and plunged Morocco into a political, economic, and intellectual decline from which it did not recover until modern times.

Al-Fishtālī's description of Saʿdian Morocco is important because it contradicts the cliché of "the closing of the Muslim mind." This is the title of a recent book that argues that Islam is against progress and innovation.[2] This passage provides historical evidence that a premodern Muslim state could in fact foster creativity and innovation. Even today, few Western historians would admit that a progressive ethos like that of Elizabethan England could be found in the premodern Muslim world. Although the date of this text is from the early modern period, its modern sentiments make it seem as if it were written at the height of the Enlightenment.

What makes this passage seem modern? First, it rejects imitation and praises innovation, creativity, and technological change. Second, it shows the spirit of pragmatism by stating that Aḥmad al-Manṣūr "freed all worthy endeavors from the constraints that limited their usefulness." Sentiments such as these have long been considered hallmarks of modernity. Other tokens of modernity can be found in this passage as well. For example, it celebrates the ethic of well-being, which, according to some theorists, stimulates innovation and creates an aesthetic in which industrial technique is praised as art.[3] In addition, one can find signs of modernity's dynamism and acceptance of risk as well as the tendency to overturn traditional habits and rules for the sake of efficiency.[4]

Primitivism and History

The modernist ethos that characterized Saʿdian Morocco had its opponents, just as modernism has its opponents today. Historically, opposition to modernism has often been expressed through some form of primitivism. Although primitivism has existed since antiquity, antimodernists have repeatedly sought to revive this ethic since the Enlightenment. Examples of primitivism include philosophical movements such as Romanticism and religious movements such as Christian Evangelicalism. According to Arthur O. Lovejoy and George Boas, the most important theorists of primitivism, primitivism can be found in two varieties: chronological primitivism and cultural primitivism. Chronological primitivism is a theory of value that places the best condition of human life, the best state of society, or the best condition of the world at some point in the past.[5] Cultural primitivism is, in the words of Lovejoy and Boas, "the discontent of the civilized with civilization, or with some conspicuous and characteristic feature of it. It is the belief of men living in a relatively highly evolved and complex cultural condition that a life far simpler and less sophisticated in some or all respects is a more desirable life."[6]

Chronological primitivism also comes in two varieties, depending on whether one believes in the eternity of the world or the creation of the world ex nihilo. Religions such as Judaism, Christianity, and Islam, which ascribe creation to the will of God, are associated with finitist theories of primitivism. In finitist primitivism, history is viewed as a succession of events beginning at some time in the past.[7] Bilateral finitist theories assume that history has both a beginning and an end. These theories also appear in two varieties, which Lovejoy and Boas describe as follows:

> *The Theory of Undulation*: In this theory, ages and civilizations come and go, alternating from better to worse and back again; however, in the long run the human condition neither improves nor worsens but remains largely the same. History is conceived as a succession of empires or civilizations, "each of which goes through a rise, decline, and fall, after the analogy of the life-history of an individual."[8]
>
> *The Theory of Decline*: In this theory, the highest degree of excellence or happiness is assumed to have existed at the beginning of human history. This theory often appears in conjunction with the notion of a golden age and can take any one of four different forms:[9]
>
>> *The Theory of a Fall without a Subsequent Decline*: The best time was at the beginning, but after the initial fall the human condition alternates between better and worse periods, which will continue until the process is terminated by a final catastrophe, either of natural or supernatural causes.
>>
>> *The Theory of Progressive Degeneration*: The best time was at the beginning and the course of human history continues downward, in a relatively uninterrupted decline, until the process is terminated either through a direct consequence of this deterioration or by an external cause.
>>
>> *The Theory of Decline and Future Restoration*: The best time was at the beginning, but at one or more moments in history there is a restoration of primordial goodness, or happiness, or both. However, this renewal will

be cut short by a future catastrophe, which will bring the golden age or the millennium to an end.

The Three-Phase Theory of Decline: The first age was the best but subsequently, either in some past time or in the future, there will be a temporary renewal of the primordial state of excellence, after which a period of decline will ensue that lasts until the final catastrophe.

The opposite of chronological primitivism is the Theory of Ascent. This optimistic theory assumes that the least excellent or desirable phase of human history came at the beginning and that the human condition will improve until the final end of the world. The Theory of Ascent is still a form of primitivism because it assumes that in the beginning the world or human society was in a primitive state. A major premise of the Theory of Ascent is that an increase in knowledge or complexity equals an increase in value. Thus, in philosophical terms, the Theory of Evolution is one version of the Theory of Ascent. According to Lovejoy and Boas, the Theory of Ascent also comes in two varieties:[10]

The Theory of Continuous Progress: This theory holds that human history since its origin is characterized by a progressive increase or diffusion of goodness, happiness, enlightenment, or all three. It also holds that the best time is yet to come and that the human condition will continue to improve until the final catastrophe. The historical perspective of Positivism is the most famous version of this theory.

The Theory of Successive Progress and Decline: This theory holds that human progress may be arrested through deterioration caused by human nature or external events, such as natural catastrophes, invasions, or internal societal weakness. However, at some point or points in the future, human progress will be resumed, until the final end is attained.

Most premodern Muslims, like premodern Jews and Christians, believed in some form of primitivism. This is still the case for many Muslims today. Indeed, if one believes that the world begins in time, it is natural to imagine that the world should end in time as well and that the beginning is more primitive than the end. However, Lovejoy and Boas point out that the Theory of Continuous Progress, which is popular in societies that are politically or economically ascendant, is the least supportable theory of primitivism in empirical terms. Although we acknowledge that all things must pass, we tend to push this reality away from ourselves as far as possible. Perhaps the recent year 2000 hysteria and current speculations about the end of the Mayan world-cycle in 2012 are subconscious reminders of how illogical our optimism really is.

Scriptural Foundations of Islamic Primitivism

In Islam primitivism comes in both chronological and cultural varieties and can be found in the Qur'ān, the Ḥadīth, and in works of theology and history. Although Islamic primitivism is most often observed in works of history and theology, two versions of chronological primitivism can be found in the Qur'ān. The most noticeable form of primitivism in the Qur'ān is the Theory of Undulation, which characterizes the Qur'ānic view of history in general. Nations and civilizations are born, develop, and die, much like human beings. The Earth goes through a similar life cycle as well, proceeding along a predetermined path from creation to termination. The motif of undulation or fluctuation is a characteristic feature of the Qur'ānic discourse. In the Qur'ān God often speaks about things in pairs, and the complementary pairs of creation and termination, birth and death, and beginning and end are as common as those of man and woman and good and bad. The motif of alternation or undulation can be seen in the following Qur'ānic passage, which is one of many examples of this type:

> The end of all things is with your Lord. It is He who creates laughter and tears; it is He who causes life and death. It is He who created the two sexes, male and female, from a drop of ejected semen, and with Him is the Other Creation (*al-nash'at al-ukhrā*). It is He who creates wealth and contentment; He is the Lord of [the star] Sirius (*rabb al-shi'ra*) and it is He who destroyed ancient ʿAd and Thamūd, sparing no one, and before them the people of Noah, for they were most unjust and tyrannical. The overthrown cities (Sodom and Gomorrah) He also ruined, so that they were covered over. Which, then, of your Lord's blessings will you deny? (53:42–55)

Numerous verses of the Qur'ān affirm the recurrence of God's creation, whether it be the alternation of night and day; the rising and setting of the moon, the stars, and the sun; the life and death of human beings; or the rise and fall of nations: "In the creation of the heavens and the Earth and in the alternation of night and day, there are signs for people of sense" (3:190). However, while the physical world follows a pattern of undulation that is not related to divine judgment, the rise and fall of nations and civilizations is often a matter of moral desert. The purpose of history is to serve as a reminder of what happens to those who oppose God: "Is it not a matter of guidance for those who inherit the Earth after its people [are gone] that if We wished We would punish them for their sins and set a seal upon their hearts, so that they cannot hear?" (7:100). In another verse the Qur'ān states: "Many ways of life have passed away before you. So travel throughout the Earth and observe what was the outcome for the liars" (3:137).

However, despite the moral lessons to be found in the rise and fall of civilizations, there is no clear indication in the Qur'ān that the end of the world will come about as an act of divine retribution. The violence of the world's end seems unrelated to the notion of moral decline, although the Qur'ān portrays it as cataclysmic. Nevertheless, we can infer from verses that compare the life histories of human beings to that of the world that the Earth also passes through its own life history. Because of this, it is possible to see in the Qur'ān not only the Theory of Undulation but also the Theory of Progressive Degeneration. In the Qur'ānic perspective on history, an undulating or cyclical repetition of rising and falling civilizations is accompanied by the gradual degeneration of the world into exhaustion or decay. In either case, the destinies of all things are preordained: "They ask you of the Hour, when it will come to pass. Say: 'The knowledge of it is with my Lord alone. He alone will manifest it at its proper time'" (7:187).

It is not in the Qur'ān but in the Ḥadīth that we find the clearest proof-texts for Islamic primitivism. However, even here the traditions that support this perspective are sparse, despite the popularity that primitivism has enjoyed throughout Islamic history. Even more, many of the ḥadīths that express primitivism can be challenged on source-critical grounds, either because they are unsupported by other traditions or because they are anachronistic. For example, when the Prophet Muḥammad is quoted as telling Muslims to "hold fast to my Sunna and the Sunna of the Rightly Guided Caliphs after me," we may doubt the authenticity of this tradition because the term "Rightly Guided Caliphs" is a historical term from a later age.[11] In addition, from a semantic point of view, this term is clearly retrospective: "Rightly guided" in comparison to what? One of the few supports for primitivism that comes from a well-attested ḥadīth is the following:

> ['Imrān ibn Ḥusayn said:] The Prophet said, "The best people are those living in my generation, then those coming after them, and then those coming afterwards." 'Imrān said, "I do not know whether the Prophet mentioned two or three generations after your present generation." The Prophet added, "There will be some people after you, who will be dishonest and will not be trustworthy and will give witness without being asked to give witness, and will make a vow but will not fulfill their vows, and obesity will appear among them." (Ṣaḥīḥ al-Būkhārī, 3:48, 819)

This ḥadīth is a clear example of the Theory of Progressive Degeneration: the best Muslims are the first generation, and those who come after them will be worse. Another version of this ḥadīth is recounted in Ṣaḥīḥ Muslim (31:6159): "'Ā'isha reported that someone asked the Messenger of God (peace be upon him) who among the people were the best. He said: 'The generation to which I belong, then the second generation, then the third generation.'" As in the previous tradition, the earliest generation of Muslims is the best: they are more religiously observant, more virtuous, more idealistic, and more selfless in their adherence to Islam. Other traditions similarly depict the first generation of Muslims as braver and less attracted to wealth and power than their successors. Because subsequent generations are further removed from the miracle of revelation and the living example of the Prophet, they become worse until the end of time. In this perspective, the era of the Prophet Muḥammad is seen as both a golden age and a primitivist utopia. It is a golden age because the community governed by the Prophet in Medina is a paradigm for all Muslims to follow. The Qur'ān states: "Whoever opposes the Messenger after guidance has become clearly manifest to him and follows a path other than that of the believers, We shall leave him to that which he has adopted and place him in Hell; what an evil destination" (4:115). However, the prophetic community is also a primitivist utopia because it was a society of simple means but lofty goals. The Qur'ān seems to support this interpretation in the following verse: "And the foremost, the first among the Emigrants and the Helpers, and those who followed them in virtue: Allah is pleased with them as they are with Him and He has prepared for them gardens in which rivers flow beneath, abiding therein forever; this is the greatest success." (9:100)

The companions of the Prophet Muḥammad and the next two generations of Muslims are collectively known as al-Salaf al-Ṣāliḥ, "The Righteous Predecessors." This paradigmatic community has become so influential in Sunnī Islam that it is seen as defining Sunnī Islam itself. For example, one of the most disparaging terms that Salafī sectarians use against Shīʿī Muslims is al-Rawāfiḍ, "The Rejecters," because the Shīʿa are believed to reject not only the political views of the Prophet's companions but also the very tradition of Islam that they represent. In the Ḥanbalī tradition of Sunnī Islam, to belong to "the People of the Sunna and the Majority" (*Ahl al-Sunna wa al-Jamāʿa*) means to follow the example of the Salaf al-Ṣāliḥ. For Salafī Muslims like the Wahhābīs and the Ṭālibān, this means excluding both the Shīʿa and the Sufis, who are considered heretical innovators (*mubtadiʿūn*) because their doctrines supposedly differ from those of the Prophet's companions.[12]

However, if one were to ask most Sufis or Shīʿī Muslims if they follow the Salaf al-Ṣāliḥ, the Sufis would say, "Yes, of course," and the Shīʿa would say, "Maybe, depending on how you define the Salaf al-Ṣāliḥ." This is because the Sufis consider the Salaf al-Ṣāliḥ to be proto-Sufis, whereas for the Shīʿa, the "righteous predecessors" are the Imāms of the family of the Prophet and those who followed them. With respect to the primitivist ethic that lies behind the Salaf al-Ṣāliḥ paradigm, all traditionalist Muslims believe in some form of the Theory of Progressive Degeneration because both Sunnī and Shīʿī views of Islamic history assume that a period of decline followed the golden age of the Prophet. The remainder of this chapter will briefly discuss how primitivism underpins the doctrines of Salafī Traditionalists and Salafī Modernists and Shīʿī Traditionalists and Shīʿī Modernists.

Traditionalism and Modernism in Salafī Primitivism

Salafī Traditionalists are conservative by nature and see Islamic tradition as a pattern to be maintained at all costs. For example, on *Noorul-Islam*, a website from Pakistan that memorializes Mawlānā ʿAbd al-Rashīd al-Ghāzī, a religious leader and jihadist who was killed in the Pakistani assault on the Lal Masjid in Islamabad in 2007, there is a link titled, "Proofs for the Obligation to Follow the Salaf al-Ṣāliḥ."[13] Like many Salafīs, the webmasters of *Noorul-Islam* advocate the primitivist Theory of Decline and Future Restoration. This perspective is common among Islamists who call for the restoration of the caliphate or another form of Sharīʿa-based state. On this website, the traditions that are used to support the Salaf al-Ṣāliḥ paradigm are taken from *Tawḥīd of Allah's Most Beautiful Names and Lofty Attributes*, a textbook on Wahhābī doctrine by Muḥammad ibn Khalīfa al-Tamīmī, associate professor of *daʿwa* (proselytization) and *uṣūl al-dīn* (dogma) at the Islamic University of Medina.[14] This work advocates a form of traditionalism that is both reactionary and imitative. In one citation the Prophet's companion ʿAbd Allāh ibn Masʿūd (d. ca. 652) states: "We emulate and do not set precedents, we follow and do not innovate, and we will not deviate as long as we hold on to the narrations." Another citation of Ibn Masʿūd states: "Whoever amongst you seeks to adopt a path should take to the way of the dead, since the living are not safe and secure from being put to trial."

According to Wahhābī doctrine, true Muslims are those who adhere strictly to the precedents of the Salaf al-Ṣāliḥ and resist all forms of deviation or innovation. To support this view al-Tamīmī quotes ʿAbd al-Raḥmān al-Awzāʿī (d. 774), a juridical scholar of the Umayyad Dynasty: "Patiently restrict yourself to the Sunna, stop where [the predecessors[stopped, say what they say, and refrain from that which they refrained from. Traverse the path of the Salaf al-Ṣāliḥ, for indeed what was sufficient for them is sufficient for you." Another quotation states, "Knowledge is that which emanates from the Companions of Muḥammad (PBUH). As for anything else besides this, it is not knowledge." This type of epistemological traditionalism is so radical that it goes beyond chronological primitivism. Instead, it should be seen as a form of cultural primitivism, for these statements call on Muslims to emulate not only the religious interpretations of the Salaf al-Ṣāliḥ but also their personal habits.

The text of *Tawḥīd of Allah's Most Beautiful Names* can be purchased on another Salafī website called *Islamfuture*. This site also carries speeches by Anwār al-Awlakī (d. 2011), the former head of al-Qaeda in the Arabian Peninsula, and a documentary on al-Khaṭṭāb (Samīr Ṣāliḥ ʿAbdallāh al-Suwaylim), the Saudi-born jihadist and terrorist who was killed in Chechnya in 2002. The only work on the Qur'ān that *Islamfuture* recommends is *In the Shade of the Qur'ān* (*Fī Ẓilāl al-Qur'ān*) by Sayyid Quṭb (1906–66). Like Tamīmī and the Pakistani Salafīs of the Lal Masjid, Quṭb was a chronological primitivist who believed in the Theory of Decline and Future Restoration. He was also a cultural primitivist, but, unlike the Wahhābīs, he did not advocate a return to the cultural practices of the Salaf al-Ṣāliḥ. Instead, his cultural primitivism was based on idealistic notions of authenticity and purity that had more to do with European Romanticism than with traditional Islamic sources.

In contrast to the Wahhābīs, who are Salafī Traditionalists, Sayyid Quṭb was a Salafī Modernist. He was a Salafī because his view of Islam was framed in terms of the Salaf al-Ṣāliḥ paradigm. In his Islamic manifesto *Milestones* (*Maʿālim fī al-ṭarīq*), he refers to the Salaf al-Ṣāliḥ as the "Unique Qur'ānic Generation" (*jīl Qur'ānī farīd*) because "the Holy Qur'ān was the only source from which they quenched their thirst."[15] However, unlike the Salafī Traditionalists, who emphasize the chronological precedence of the Salaf al-Ṣāliḥ, Quṭb puts more emphasis on their purity. For him, their near-mystical closeness to the Prophet Muḥammad and the Qur'ān prevented their creed from being polluted by foreign cultures and ideas:

> This generation drank solely from this spring and thus attained a unique distinction in history. In later times it happened that other sources mingled with it. Other sources used by later generations included Greek philosophy and logic, ancient Persian legends and ideas, Jewish scriptures and traditions, Christian theology, and in addition to these, fragments of other religions and civilizations. These mingled with the commentaries on the Qur'ān and with scholastic theology, as they were mingled with jurisprudence and its principles. Later generations after this generation obtained their training from this mixed source, and hence the like of this generation never arose again.[16]

This passage and others like it confirm that Sayyid Quṭb's primitivism was more cultural than chronological. What is most important for him about the Salaf al-Ṣāliḥ is that their Islam was not mixed with ideas from other cultures and religions. For Quṭb the era of the Prophet and his companions cannot be recreated. Thus, Muslims must hold to those parts of the Salafī legacy that are still accessible—their pure Islamic values and their freedom from outside influences. "When a person embraced Islam during the time of the Prophet," says Quṭb, "he would immediately cut himself off from the ways of ignorance. When he stepped into the circle of Islam, he would start a new life, separating himself completely from his past life under ignorance of the Divine Law. He would look upon the deeds during his life of ignorance with mistrust and fear, with a feeling that these were impure and could not be tolerated in Islam."[17]

In chapter 8 of *Milestones*, "The Islamic Concept and Culture," Quṭb calls for an epistemological quarantine of Muslims from any form of knowledge that would mar the purity of the Salaf al-Ṣāliḥ paradigm. Modern philosophy, history, psychology, ethics, sociology, theology, and the academic study of religion—all of these disciplines are dangerous because they were not formed in the spirit of the "Unique Qur'ānic Generation." For Quṭb, the world has no common cultural or intellectual heritage. There is Islam, which is true, and all other ideologies, which are false: "Even the slightest influence from [impure sources of knowledge] can pollute the clear spring of Islam."[18] Chapter 8 of *Milestones* has had an enormous influence on Salafī thought since its publication. It was the inspiration for the "Islamization of Knowledge" ideology of the Muslim Brotherhood and Jamāʿat-i Islāmī, and its strong warnings against ideological pollution partly explain why Islamist university students tend to study engineering and the applied sciences and stay away from more theoretical and speculative pursuits.

However, despite his cultural primitivism, Quṭb saw Islam as a dynamic ideology that looked toward the future not as a fetish to be protected from all change, as with Salafī Traditionalists. The period of the Salaf al-Ṣāliḥ was both a golden age and a utopia, as the following passage from *Milestones* demonstrates:

> The society was freed from all oppression, and the Islamic order was established in which justice was God's justice and in which weighing was by God's balance. The banner of social justice was raised in the name of the One God and the name of the banner was Islam. No other name was added to it and "There is no god but Allāh" was written on it.[19]
>
> Morals were elevated, hearts and souls were purified, and with the exception of a very few cases, there was no occasion even to enforce the limits and punishments which God has prescribed; for now conscience was the law-enforcer, and the pleasure of God, the hope of divine reward, and the fear of God's anger took the place of police and punishments.
>
> Humanity was uplifted in its social order, in its morals, in all of its life, to a zenith of perfection which had never been attained before and which cannot be attained afterwards except through Islam.[20]

Even though the period of the Salaf al-Ṣāliḥ was a unique golden age, Quṭb believed that its ethic could be recreated through the establishment of Sharīʿa-based Islamic political and social order (*al-niẓām al-islāmī*). In *Basic Principles of the Islamic Worldview*, he disassociates himself from Traditionalist Islam by claiming that Islam's eternal stability lies in the principle of motion. Much like the South Asian Islamic Modernist Muḥammad Iqbāl (1877–1938), he claims that the principle of "motion within a stable framework and around a stable pivot" is fundamental to Islam.[21]

This principle allowed Quṭb to portray Islamic tradition as dynamic. For this reason, he focused more on the Qurʾān and the Sharīʿa as sources of ideology than on the Ḥadīth as a source of precedent. This is another important difference between the Salafī Modernism of Quṭb and the Salafī Traditionalism of the Wahhābīs. Much like Jamāl al-Dīn al-Afghānī (1838–97), the Shīʿī freethinker who passed himself off as a Sunnī Muslim and founded the first modern Salafī movement, Quṭb used the tropes of primitivism and the golden age to create an aura of authenticity while at the same time relying heavily on the European philosophies that he sought to prevent other Muslims from learning.

Primitivism in Shīʿī Traditionalism

The difference between the primitivism of a Salafī Traditionalist work such as Tamīmī's *Tawḥīd of Allah's Most Beautiful Names* and a Shīʿī Traditionalist work such as Ayatollah Ruhollah Khomeini's (1902–89) *Islamic Government* is striking. Although both traditions draw on Ḥadīth for their arguments, the Shīʿa extend Ḥadīth through the ninth century, up to the death of the eleventh Imām Ḥasan al-ʿAskarī in 874 CE. For the Shīʿa, the period of the imāms is considered to be an extension of the Prophetic era because the knowledge of the imāms is derived directly from the Prophet Muḥammad. Another difference is that the Shīʿa do not exhibit the same reliance on the companions of the Prophet as the Sunnīs do, and avoid figures such as Ibn Masʿūd and al-Awzāʿī, who were opponents of Shīʿism. Whereas Salafī and Shīʿī Traditionalists both adhere to the primitivist *Theory of Decline and Future Restoration*, Ayatollah Khomeini called for a pre-messianic era of justice headed by a jurist (*faqīh*), who would prepare the way for the return of the Hidden Imām or *Mahdī* (Guided One). This theory, called "Governance of the Jurist" (*wilāyat al-faqīh*), is a variant of the primitivist Three-Phase Theory of Decline. This is because the initial golden age is followed by successive attempts to recreate the just society until the advent of the Mahdī. However, despite the coming of the Mahdī, the world will end in a final cataclysm following the Qurʾānic model of entropy described earlier.

Ayatollah Khomeini was a chronological primitivist but not a cultural primitivist. His view of human nature was more like that of Hobbes than Rousseau. The "noble savage" was a concept that did not exist for him and a society of autonomous citizens was virtually unthinkable. Khomeini felt that without the benefit of guidance, "men would fall prey to corruption; the institutions, laws, customs, and ordinances of Islam would be transformed; and faith and its content would be completely changed, resulting in the corruption of all humanity."[22] Providing such guidance is the function of the prophets, who are sent by

God, and the imāms, whose divinely inspired guidance is based on their descent from the Prophet Muḥammad. Before the advent of Imām al-Mahdī, the scholars of Islamic jurisprudence are responsible for guiding the Muslim community. Khomeini takes very literally the famous ḥadīth "The scholars are the heirs to the Prophets" and discusses this tradition at length in *Islamic Government.* If the scholars are heirs to the prophets, then they are heirs to the imāms too. Thus, they act as guardians and trustees for the community, governing in place of the prophets and the imāms. Like the trustee of an orphan who has not yet come of age, they guide the Muslim community toward justice because the people cannot do so for themselves.[23] The Supreme Jurist holds the reins of government in emulation of the Prophet, for "the superiority of the learned man over the worshippers is like that of the full moon over the stars."[24]

Khomeini does not subscribe to cultural primitivism because the just society is not confined to only one place or time. In the Shīʿī conception of history there are two pristine Islamic societies: that ruled by the Prophet Muḥammad in Medina, and that ruled by the Prophet's cousin and son-in-law ʿAlī, who governed Islam from the Iraqi city of Kufa. Because Imām ʿAlī's successors formed a religious and intellectual elite, the traditions of Shīʿism are often associated with persons of advanced learning, such as Imām Jaʿfar al-Ṣādiq (d. 767). Faith and virtue in Shīʿism are not based on primitive ethics. Instead, they are principles to be established in any society and can even be found in modern nation states. Theoretically, faith and virtue can be found wherever the imām or his representatives reside, whether in a Bedouin camp, a village, or the most modern city in the world. Unlike Sayyid Quṭb, Ayatollah Khomeini never claimed that secular knowledge was necessarily inimical to virtue. The problem of the West was not its knowledge but its lack of religion and ethics.

For Shīʿī Muslims the scriptural sources of Islam are not limited to the Qurʾān, the Sunna of Muḥammad, and the consensus of the Salaf al-Ṣāliḥ. Legitimate sources of religion also include the traditions of the imāms (*ḥadīth walawī*) and human reason (*ʿaql*), which is a pillar of faith in Shīʿism. Shīʿī Traditionalism also allows an opening for dynamism in Islamic thought through the institution of the Marjāʿīyya (from *marjāʿ al-taqlīd*, "source of emulation"). In this system, the foremost religious scholar of each generation may revise the decisions of his predecessors based on his understanding of the imāms' teachings. For the Shīʿa, it is a point of pride that, unlike Sunnī Muslims, they "follow the living and not the dead."

Primitivism in Shīʿī Modernism

This opening for the revision of tradition is exploited more fully in the works of the Shīʿī Modernist ʿAlī Sharīʿatī (1933–77), the most important nonclerical thinker of revolutionary Iran. Sharīʿatī states in his book *Husayn the Heir to Adam* (1970) that Islam is not a static body of doctrines but a stream of concepts running through all of human history. Although this stream never ceases to flow, "at certain times the Prophets and their successors come to quicken the force of the current."[25] Sharīʿatī uses Heraclitus's famous metaphor of the river: one may draw water again and again from the same place, but because of the river's flow, it is never the same water. This metaphor also applies to the Shīʿī institution of the Marjāʿīyya: although every *marjāʿ al-taqlīd* draws from the same sources of tradition, the conclusions that each *marjāʿ* draws may be different. Unlike Khomeini, Sharīʿatī was heavily influenced by European ideas and mixed cultural primitivism with belief in an original utopia and golden age under Imām ʿAlī. The problem for contemporary Muslims is that they are not aware enough about this golden age to learn from its example.[26] In general, Sharīʿatī was critical of tradition. He felt that the best example that could be drawn from the Prophet and the imāms was their spiritual ethic because in most cases their actual behaviors could not be ascertained.

Sharīʿatī was more influenced by Hegel and Marx than by the Islamic sources that inspired Khomeini. In practice, his belief in the Hegelian dialectic ensured that an optimistic Theory of Ascent would supersede his cultural primitivism. The struggle between primitivism and antiprimitivism in Sharīʿatī's thought can be seen in the book *On the Sociology of Islam*. The argument of this book is based on the notion of migration, which is expressed through the biblical myth of Cain and Abel. Sharīʿatī saw pastoral life as the original state of humanity, which is exemplified by the figure of Abel. This view expresses his primitivism. However, much like Sayyid Quṭb, Sharīʿatī also believed that the purpose of the human being is to be God's vicegerent. As God's vicegerent, the spirit of God "is present in man as a potentiality, an attraction that draws him toward the summit, to the glory of the heavens; as an ascension toward the sphere of God's sovereignty and being nurtured with the attributes and characteristics of God, as far as knowledge will reach."[27] One could hardly imagine a clearer example of the antiprimitivist Theory of Ascension than this view of human potential, which Sharīʿatī himself described as combining the teachings of the Qurʾān and Pascal (1623–62).

Sharīʿatī's cultural primitivism was expressed in the notion that the first golden age was the time of Abel, "the age of a pasture-based economy, of the primitive socialism that preceded ownership." In contrast, Abel's brother Cain represents "the system of agriculture and individual or monopoly ownership." Cain's murder of his brother symbolizes humanity's fall from this utopian state. More a pastoral ideal than a true golden age, Sharīʿatī's Era of Abel is an extension of Eden. Adam and Eve are expelled from the garden but maintain a vestige of it in their pastoral way of life; their fall only becomes complete after Cain commodifies both the Garden of Eden and the pastoral life: "Abel the pastoralist was killed by Cain the landowner; the period of common ownership of the sources of production—the age of pastoralism, hunting, and fishing—the spirit of brotherhood and true faith, came to an end and was replaced by the age of agriculture and the establishment of the system of private ownership, together with religious trickery and transgression against the rights of others. Abel disappeared, and Cain came to the forefront of history, and there he still lives."[28]

Sharīʿatī's myth of Cain and Abel does not conform exactly to the primitivist trope of Fall and Subsequent Decline because the principle of movement embodied in the Fall is part of God's plan for human development. For Sharīʿatī, it is impossible for a people to advance if they stay in the same place: "There is no case on record in which a primitive tribe has become civilized and created an advanced culture without first moving from its homeland and migrating."[29] This is another example of how Sharīʿatī's thought alternates between cultural primitivism and chronological primitivism. Although Abel's pastoralists are morally better than the inhabitants of Rousseau's State of Nature, like Rousseau Sharīʿatī tempers his primitivism with the knowledge that the Fall is necessary for human society to develop its full potential.

Another vestige of cultural primitivism can be seen in Sharīʿatī's treatment of the Prophet Muḥammad. Like other Shīʿī thinkers, he tends to portray Muḥammad as a passive figure, for the most important actors in Shīʿī salvation history are the imāms. Muḥammad provides the message that the imāms put into action. For Sharīʿatī the Prophet could only have come from Arabia because "the particular geographical location of the [Arabian] Peninsula decreed that just as none of the vapors that arose over the oceans ever reached the Peninsula, so too not a trace of the surrounding civilizations ever penetrated the Peninsula."[30] This view of primitive Arabia is an example of Iranian ethnocentrism. For Sharīʿatī, the pure religion of Islam could only come from a region that was "pure" or devoid of civilization. A point similar to this has also been made by the Iranian Islamic scholar Seyyed Hossein Nasr: the tabula rasa of the "Unlettered Prophet" of Islam could only have appeared in a country that was a tabula rasa with respect to civilization.[31]

Sharīʿatī's depiction of Muḥammad as a Hegelian world-historical figure brings us back to the passage by the Moroccan historian al-Fishtālī that opens this chapter. Sharīʿatī argues in *Religion vs. Religion* that Islam came into the world as a religion of revolution, not of legitimation.[32] Thus, Muslims need to look backward only to move forward, for God wants them to seek the resources to improve their material condition and reform their practices and institutions. We can infer from this that the ultimate purpose of Sharīʿatī's primitivism is to encourage Muslims to find authentic resources of tradition that they have overlooked. For him, primitivism was not a justification for conservatism.

Unlike Ayatollah Khomeini, for Sharīʿatī tradition is not to be recovered but rediscovered.[33]

Sharīʿatī's advocacy of reform was made easier because as a Shīʿī Muslim he belonged to a messianic religious tradition whose doctrines were founded on the unacceptability of the status quo. Because Shīʿism was created as an oppositional movement, it required a theology of free will. It was also necessary to enshrine reason as a pillar of faith; without reason, one cannot freely choose which path to follow. This is not to say, however, that Shīʿism cannot become conservative or that the Shīʿī model of authority cannot lead to a dictatorship. The Islamic Republic created by Ayatollah Khomeini in Iran provides ample evidence of this tendency. However, it is still arguably true that it is easier for a Shīʿī reformer to advocate the reconfiguration of tradition than for a Sunnī reformer to do so without appearing heretical.

In general, it is easier to think of tradition as dynamic if one's perspective on history looks toward a better world. Significantly, this was also the case for sixteenth-century Morocco under the Saʿdian Sultan Aḥmad al-Manṣūr. Although Morocco is a Sunnī nation, the ideology of the sharīfs who ruled the country was founded on (Zaydī) Shīʿī political principles. Saʿdian Morocco was an innovative place where things were believed to be different, and the acceptance of change extended to the domains of politics, economics, military science, and industry, as the quotation by al Fishtālī reflects. In *Experience and Nature*, the pragmatist philosopher John Dewey stated, "[Man's] acts are trespasses on the unknown. . . . While unknown consequences flowing from the past dog the present, the future is even more unknown and perilous; the present by that fact is ominous."[34] Primitivism is one way of dealing with the "ominous present" to which Dewey refers. History, which looks back at the past from the perspective of the "ominous present," provides justification for both primitivism and progressivism. As the earlier examples of Islamic primitivism have shown, how we approach the future depends more on what we think of ourselves than on what we think of God.

Notes

1. Abū Fāris ʿAbd al-ʿAzīz al-Fishtālī, *Manāhil al-ṣafā fī maʾāthir Mawālaynā al-Sharaf*, ed. ʿAbd al-Karīm Krīm (Rabat: Ministry of Endowments, Islamic Affairs, and Culture, 1972), 209. This and all other translations from Arabic in this chapter are by Vincent Cornell.

2. Robert R. Reilly, *The Closing of the Muslim Mind: How Intellectual Suicide Created the Modern Islamist Crisis* (Wilmington, DE: Intercollegiate Studies Institute, 2010).

3. See, for example, Henri Lefebvre, *Introduction to Modernity: Twelve Preludes, September 1959–May 1961*, trans. John Moore (London: Verso, 1995), 190, 215–19; see also Jacques Ellul, *The Technological Society*, trans. John Wilkinson (New York: Alfred A. Knopf, 1964).

The passage by al-Fishtālī quoted earlier comes from a chapter that discusses Moroccan innovations in the techniques of sugar refining.

4. See, for example, Anthony Giddens, *Modernity and Self-Identity: Self and Society in the Late Modern Age* (Stanford, CA: Stanford University Press, 1991).

5. Arthur O. Lovejoy and George Boas, *Primitivism and Related Ideas in Antiquity* (Baltimore: Johns Hopkins University Press, 1935), 1.

6. Ibid., 7.

7. Ibid., 1.

8. Ibid., 2.

9. Ibid., 2–3.

10. Ibid., 3–4.

11. Because this tradition appears in the respected Ḥadīth collections of Ibn Ḥanbal, Abū Dāwūd, al-Tirmidhī, and al-Dārīmī, it is considered authentic by many Muslims, despite the historical and literary criticism given earlier. It is possible to read the phrase, "Rightly Guided Caliphs" prospectively, as referring to whichever good caliphs might reign in the future. However, there is still the problem of the anachronism of the term "caliph" itself, which most likely was not used by the Prophet Muḥammad.

12. In an October 2005 letter to Abū Muṣāb al-Zarqāwī, the al-Qaeda leader Aymān al-Ẓawāhirī counseled against killing innocent Shīʿī civilians in Iraq. However, he also left no doubt about his negative feelings toward the Shīʿa: "[Shīʿism] is a religious school based on excess and falsehood whose function is to accuse the companions of Muḥammad of heresy in a campaign against Islam, in order to free the way for a group of those who call for dialogue in the name of the hidden Mahdī who is in control of existence and is infallible in what he does." Laura Mansfield, trans., *His Own Words: A Translation of the Writings of Dr. Ayman al-Zawahiri* (Old Tappan, NJ: TLG Publications, 2006), 267.

13. "Proofs for the Obligation to Follow the Salaf Al-Salih," *Noorul-Islam*, November 26, 2007. http://noorulislam.wordpress.com/2007/11/26/proofs-for-the-obligation.

14. See "Tawhid of Allah's Most Beautiful Names and Lofty Attributes: The Belief of Ahl Al-Sunnah Wal'Jama'ah," *Islam Future → The Future for Islam*, April 28, 2010. http://islamfuture.wordpress.com/2010/04/28/. *Islamfuture* calls itself the website of "the English School of Islam" and bears the black and white jihadist "Future World Flag."

15. Sayyid Quṭb, *Milestones* (Damascus: Dār al-ʿIlm, n.d.), 16; "*Jīl Qurʾānī farīd*" is the title of the second chapter of this work in Arabic. See Sayyid Quṭb, *Maʿālim fī al-ṭarīq* (Beirut: Dār al-Shurūq, 2000), 14–23.

16. Quṭb, *Maʿālim fī al-ṭarīq*, 17.

17. Ibid., 19.

18. Ibid., 116.

19. Quṭb's description of the Islamic flag provides the model for the "Future World Flag" mentioned earlier, which is a favorite of Salafī jihadists. It is a black flag with "There is no god but God" (*Lā ilāha illā Allāh*) written on it in white Arabic letters.

20. Quṭb, *Maʿālim fī al-ṭarīq*, 30.

21. Sayyid Quṭb, *Basic Principles of the Islamic Worldview*, trans. Rami David (North Haledon, NJ: Islamic Publications International, 2006), 74; this work was written between 1960 and 1962, around the same time as *Milestones*.

22. Ruhollah Khomeini, *Islam and Revolution: Writings and Declarations of Imam Khomeini (1941–1980)*, trans. Hamid Algar (Berkeley, CA: Mizan Press, 1981), "Islamic Government," 53.

23. Ibid., 76–80.
24. Ibid., 106.
25. Introduction to ʿAlī Sharīʿatī, *On the Sociology of Islam: Lectures by Ali Shariʿati*, trans. Hamid Algar (Berkeley, CA: Mizan Press, 1979), 29.
26. Ibid., 40.
27. Ibid., 89–90.
28. Ibid., 98–99.
29. Ibid., 44.
30. Ibid., 54.
31. Seyyed Hossein Nasr, *Ideals and Realities of Islam* (1966; repr. London: Aquarian Press, 1994), 77.
32. ʿAlī Sharīʿatī, *Religion vs. Religion*, trans. Laleh Bakhtiar (Chicago: ABC International Group, 2000), 31–41.
33. These terms come from Jaroslav Pelikan, *The Vindication of Tradition* (New Haven, CT: Yale University Press, 1984), 23.
34. John Dewey, *Experience and Nature* (1925), quoted in Melvin L. Rogers, *The Undiscovered Dewey: Religion, Morality, and the Ethos of Democracy* (New York: Columbia University Press, 2009), 11.

Tradition

JANET SOSKICE

TRADITION, PUT SIMPLY, is what is handed on. The English word "tradition" derives from the Latin "to hand over, to deliver."

It may be helpful, before specifically discussing "tradition" in Christian thought, to consider how much in human life is "passed on" by others. Here are two musical examples. The first is from my own workplace—the choristers of the Jesus College chapel. I want to draw attention not to the antiquity of the particular pieces of music they sing (for they sing works both ancient and modern) but to the practice of choral singing itself. The choir is composed of young men and women as well as boys aged five to thirteen. Every year I marvel that the boys, no different from any other little boys, can perfectly perform the beautiful and complex music of Monteverdi and Brahms, Benjamin Britten and Bach, all this while being taught and led by a young choral scholar who is still only in his or her twenties. How can a group of such young people produce these wonderful sounds? Of course, if you just put twelve untrained young boys and a twenty-two-year-old on a desert island they would never come up with anything like this. But the choristers and their leader stand in a tradition in which innumerable children have gone before them. These countless generations have passed on a joint pool of knowledge and technique. It is evident if you watch the choir practice. The boys stand around their leader at the piano. He fires off a string of musical questions at them and then they are away. Singing, they look rather like a bed of seaweed in the ocean current, because the boys raise their arms fluently at frequent intervals. This, I learned, is not to ask a question but to indicate that the hand raiser knows he has made a mistake so the choir leader need not stop to correct him. Within a short time these boys can produce a performance as polished as any heard by a crowned prince at a Renaissance court. They can do so because they stand in a continuous tradition of practice and performance, and each generation of thirteen-year-old boys will give way to the next, and so on, passing on this tradition.

A second example, also musical, comes from the Islamic world. It is the African musician Ali Farka Touré and his group performing "Alla Uya" from his album, *Niafunké*.[1] Touré, who was born in 1939 and died in 2006, was one of Africa's most famous musicians and became influential on the world musical scene. His work suggests commonality between the musical traditions of his own country, Mali, and the blues tradition in the United States. In his later years he recorded from his own studio, outside Timbuktu. Of the composition "Alla Uya" his jacket notes say: "God is unique. I went to Koranic school for eight years and whether you are a believer or not when you hear this song, God is present and knows what you are thinking."

Touré's music uses traditional instruments and rhythms, and harmonizes these with elements from the blues and jazz. This piece also reflects African Muslim practices of singing songs of praise while engaged in heavy labor. The fusion of these old ways with the new forms shows the tradition is alive. Touré's performance stands, no less than that of the choir of Jesus College, in a tradition of worship and praise.

Tradition, "what is handed on," covers most broadly almost everything that makes for social and civilized life: how to build an aqueduct or a motorway or an airplane; how to bake a loaf of bread or raise a crop of wheat. We learn from those who went before. All people are "traditional." Even the most avant-garde of artists responds to what has gone before.

Turning specifically to Christian thought, the New Testament provides us with texts both hostile to traditions and insistent upon them. In Mark 7:8–9 we find Jesus being reproached by the scribes for not following the tradition of the elders. He replies: "You abandon the commandment of God, and hold to human tradition." And, "You have a fine way of rejecting the commandment of God, in order to keep your tradition!" However in 2 Thessalonians 2:15 we find Paul saying, "So then, brothers and sisters, stand firm and hold fast to the traditions that you were taught by us, either by word of mouth or by our letter."

It should not surprise us, then, that "tradition" itself—that is, the idea of tradition—has a history of debate within Christian theology. While the question of which traditions were "faithful" and to be upheld has always been of importance, the religious struggles of the sixteenth century saw an oppositional contrast drawn between tradition as such and scripture. The Protestant Reformers generally saw "tradition" as threatening to corrupt the purity of faith. Within the Church of England, too, many felt that "Scripture alone is our complete rule of faith and manners."[2] This position proved hard to hold in pure form. Even the scriptures themselves have been "handed on"—otherwise how should we possess them today? It was equally evident that there were other "genuine" and reliable traditions, going back to the earliest days of the church, which must be included as well as scripture, including for instance the Apostles' Creed, and rites or liturgies that "came down" from the apostolic church. It was impossible, in short, to put an absolute line between scripture and tradition. Even the shape of the Christian Bible as we have it, the number of the books accepted as scriptural (the canon of scripture), depends on a consensus of the early Christians, who "passed on" the teaching about the canon to us.[3]

Christianity rests on divine revelation and on the experience of the faithful community. Indeed belief in revelation presumes that God can and does disclose Godself to human beings who in turn "pass on" what has been revealed to the next generation. It is worth remembering that, prior to the invention of the printing press, this "handing on" involved the physical process of copying manuscripts.

Christianity gives a preeminent authority to scripture. Scripture is, above all, what is "handed on." With this observation in place, any crude contrast between scripture and tradition is self-defeating. The first Christians were Jews or proselytes who identified with Judaism. They received as "handed on" the scriptures of the Jewish people. But from the books of the New Testament we can see that what the first Christians experienced of Jesus caused them to reread—not reject—the Hebrew Scriptures that were their own.

This process is documented in the book of Acts. Of special interest is the story of the Ethiopian Eunuch found in Acts 8:26–40. Philip is led by God (the Spirit) to go to the road from Jerusalem to Gaza, the gateway, then as now, between Palestine and Africa. There he meets, riding in a chariot, a wealthy and highly cultured Ethiopian who is the minister for the treasury of Candace, queen of the Ethiopians. The Ethiopian appears to be a proselyte or convert to Judaism for he has traveled to Jerusalem to worship. Philip encounters him seated in his chariot reading the book of Isaiah and asks: "Do you understand what you are reading?" The Ethiopian asks Philip to join him in the chariot and explain a passage from Isaiah: "Like a sheep he was led to the slaughter . . ." "About whom," asks the Ethiopian, "does the prophet say this, about himself or about someone else?" Philip explains the venerable passage but in new terms—he starts with the good news about Jesus, that he is the promised Messiah. Presently they come to some water and the Ethiopian proposes that Philip baptize him. Again baptism is already a tradition, probably spreading to the early Christians from the practice of John the Baptist, but a tradition that is now being reconfigured by this new community. After this impromptu baptism we read that Philip was snatched away by the Spirit of the Lord.

A similar narrative, this time in the gospel of Luke, portrays two of the disciples on the way to Emmaus (Luke 24:13–35). Jesus is dead, his tomb empty and the disciples disconsolate. A stranger who falls into walking with them along the road asks them why they look so sad. They explain their disappointment at the humiliating death of one they believed to be the Messiah, and the stranger in turn admonishes them for their foolishness in failing to understand their own scriptures. It is only at supper, when the stranger blesses and breaks the bread, that they recognize him as Jesus, at which point he too disappears. This story, like that of the Ethiopian courtier, underscores the importance of what has been handed on (in this case the scriptures but also, we may note, the newer practices of baptism and of breaking of bread) but also the conviction that what has been handed on may need to be reunderstood. Herein lies the root of much debate over tradition in the Christian tradition.

Tradition, even in its more central received form of scripture, is a given but it is not static—scriptures are always open to being reread or reperformed. The process of "rereading," as we have noted, was documented in the book of Acts but is also already evident in the Hebrew Scriptures. The book of Hosea recalls for its readers the book of Exodus. The later chapters of Isaiah reread the earlier chapters in the light of exile. It appears that what is "passed on" has always been reread in the light of God's new actions in the world. But where does the rereading stop?

Christians broadly accept that revelation ceased after the period of the Apostles, but much remained unclear. One way of understanding "tradition" is to see it as the church's guided reflections on the deposit of scripture. What beliefs should be central and what practices or devotions should be excluded? Should Jewish followers of Jesus eat with Gentiles? How should they baptize? How should they "break bread" together? As to beliefs, it took two or three centuries of debate to establish the doctrine of the Trinity as Christian orthodoxy, preserving the Christian conviction that, even while they prayed to both Jesus and the Father, they worshipped but one God.

As an example of debated practice we can consider religious images, or icons. The earliest known icons of Jesus and his disciples date from the sixth century and are found at St. Catherine's monastery in Egypt's Sinai desert. These paintings are done in the realist, late Roman style familiar to us from the haunting Fayum mummy portraits of Roman Egypt, and clearly they stand in this tradition of artistry. In the eighth century debate raged over whether one could represent holy figures this way without violation of the Old Testament prohibition of images. The dispute was resolved, in the Byzantine world, after reconsideration of the doctrine of the Incarnation. Iconodules (those pro icons) argued that since Christians believe God became flesh in Christ and was visible at that time among us, he can be represented now by icons. It has been suggested that icons subsequently took on the elongated and distorted form we now associate with them to avoid idolatrous worshipping of the image.

Traditional faiths must consider what legitimately can be embraced and what must be rejected from surrounding culture. This may be practices, like that of the painting of portraits, or it may be ideas. Both Islam and Christianity, for instance, made use of Aristotle's philosophy in the early medieval period to defend belief in one Creator God while at the same time exercising caution as to just which of the philosopher's teachings could be deployed in faith's defense.

The eighteenth-century Enlightenment saw a new kind of attack on the idea of tradition. While the Reformers of the sixteenth century had pitted "mere" tradition against scripture in ways already discussed, the philosophes of the seventeenth and eighteenth centuries disparaged tradition as "blind prejudice" and without warrant as compared to pure reason. Their models for truth were mathematics and physics. Religions of all sorts fared badly under the severe intellectual diet of Enlightenment rationalism. Some religious thinkers, in order to protect a certain kind of certainty, disastrously patterned religious truth on the rigidity of mathematics.[4]

By the nineteenth century, however, scholars had seen unmistakable evidence of development and change, for instance, in the religion of Israel. It now appeared that the Jews had not always worshipped one God but had gone through a henotheistic phase where their God was the greatest among other regional gods. Furthermore, some parts of the Hebrew Scriptures were borrowed from other neighboring peoples. Psalm 104, previously credited to King David, was found by nineteenth-century explorers carved on the walls of the rock-cut tomb of the pharaoh Akhenaten at Amarna. This song had almost certainly been composed by this quirky, monotheistic pharaoh and borrowed by Hebrew scribes to praise their God. Evidences of development and change in what had been regarded as timeless truths were shocking to general Christian understanding. What can this mean for faith? How can "tradition"—that which is passed on—be subject to change?

But the new sciences of the day were in a way to provide the answer, for science could not explain itself by rigid rationalism. The nineteenth century saw the flowering of sciences of growth—biology but also geology and, of course, history. Life, it seems, is characterized by growth and change. It was with such ideas that the English theologian John Henry Newman transformed Christian thought about doctrine and tradition. Faith, he argued, is a living thing. Stressing organic growth that unfolds the true nature of a given reality, Newman argued that "to live is to change, and to be perfect is to have changed often."[5] The twentieth and twenty-first centuries have seen a renewed Aristotelianism in philosophy, in the work for instance of Alasdair MacIntyre and Charles Taylor, which stresses the process of formation, life, change—and tradition.

To stand in a tradition is not to stand still but to stand in the deep, loamy soil that feeds further growth. For Ali Farka Touré the bedrock was always his native Mali and his Muslim faith, but what he met in Paris and New York did not need to be rejected but rather transformed to praise God in new, dazzling ways.

Notes

1. At the conference, we heard this piece of music and a piece performed by the choir of Jesus College, Cambridge. I especially recommend that readers listen to Touré's song.

2. Daniel Waterland (1683–1740), from *Works*, VII; cited in Günter Biemer, *Newman on Tradition*, trans. Kevin Smyth (Freiburg: Herder, 1967), 7.

3. Different Christian denominations hold slightly different works of the Hebrew Scriptures to be canonical—for instance, the Catholic Church accepts intertestamental books such as Ecclesiasticus and Tobit, which the Anglicans regard as "apocryphal" but hold in esteem and some Protestant churches reject altogether.

4. Alasdair Macintyre has pointed out that this eighteenth-century dismissal of tradition arguably was itself an intellectual tradition and blind to the extent it was a tradition. See his *Three Rival Versions of Moral Enquiry* (London: Duckworth, 1990).

5. John Henry Newman, *An Essay on the Development of Christian Doctrine*, 8th ed. (London: Longmans, Green, and Co., 1891), 40.

Religious Authority and the Challenges of Modernity

PHILIP JENKINS

SOCIETIES LIVE by their myths. If asked about the modern history of religious authority, many Americans at least would turn to the legendary 1925 Scopes trial, the bitter confrontation between supporters and critics of Darwinian evolution, as mediated through the film *Inherit the Wind* (1960). Here, we think, reason and science ran rings around obscurantism and faith, and that victory marked the end of the Bible's credibility as an infallible source of divine wisdom. While obviously this did not mark the end of religion, it set strict limits to the scope of religion's claims, particularly in the public sphere. Religion, in this view, is a strictly private matter, and religion and science belong in different realms. In Stephen Jay Gould's phrase, they possess nonoverlapping magisteria.[1] Such a limitation also goes beyond the debate with science. If the Bible is a constructed human work that reflects a particular era, then no less culture specific are its assertions about any matter of policy or morality. The Bible in effect loses any claim to absolute authority.

I use the language of myth for many reasons, not least in linking the decline of biblical authority to Scopes, which was a far more complex and nuanced event than the popular uncreation myth holds. More generally, narratives of the decline of religious authority always raise nagging questions: Decline among whom? Where? Are we speaking of decline or of changing nature? In fact, we might offer a rather different narrative, of modernity and the challenges of religious authority. What we see in the twenty-first century is not the eclipse of religious authority but rather its unmooring from traditional institutions and its decentralization and radical democratization. And we stand at the opening stages of a rapid acceleration of this process.

The Assault of Reason

I will do no more than sketch briefly the stages by which Western forms of modernity undermined traditional forms of religious authority. In 1600, for example, Protestants and Catholics were divided over the ultimate source of authority, whether that lay in the Bible alone or in the Bible as interpreted through the church and its traditions. Political circumstances meant that challenges to religious claims emerged first in Protestant nations, especially in the Netherlands and the British Isles, and focused most directly on the Bible.

The story of the Bible's dethroning has been retold often, and its origins can be conveniently dated to the 1670s and Spinoza's *Tractatus.* Underlying the new endeavor were several principles that can be seen as fundamental aspects of modernity, especially the assumption that the Bible is a book like other books and can be subjected to the same means of examination, the same forms of analysis and criticism. Human beings can and must judge the scriptures. Christians laid claim to moral standards that allow them to perform just such criticism, and to reject or bypass those passages that fail to pass muster. This belief provided the foundation for all modern forms of liberal or progressive Christianity.

The idea of such a universal standard depended on new concepts of Natural Law, the ancient idea that all humans recognized common principles of justice that were valid in all times and places. Natural Law theory revived in the seventeenth century through the work of the Dutch polymath Hugo Grotius. Grotius, the founder of modern international law, pioneered many modern ideas concerning war and peace. He claimed that such universal principles held true even if God did not exist or did not intervene in human existence. So powerful was Natural Law, claimed Grotius, that "even the will of an omnipotent being cannot change or abrogate" it.[2]

In our own time, the idea of a universal law is revolutionary enough. It underlies all attempts to apply human rights principles across the borders of individual states, to arrest generals or heads of state for crimes against humanity, even if they had done nothing contrary to the written codes of their particular nations. But in the Enlightenment, Natural Law ideas reshaped attitudes to biblical authority. If you believed in Natural Law, rooted as it was in reason and nature, then you had an absolute standard by which to judge the biblical text. And often you found that Bible stories grossly violated the laws of nature as much as science.

Alongside Natural Law there developed in the late seventeenth century the idea of Natural Religion, the belief that reason and experience were as accurate a guide to divine truth as was scripture. If our minds reacted with horror at alleged divine commands, then we had at least as much right to put our faith in those spontaneous human feelings as in the words of scripture. God, in this view, speaks to his followers in different ways, of which revelation—scripture—is but one. Over and above the words of the text, God also wrote his law in human hearts, giving individuals the right and duty to evaluate scripture, and ultimately to choose which passages to accept, based on the dictates of reason.[3]

That idea is expressed by the title of John Toland's 1696 book, one of the core texts of the developing Enlightenment: *Christianity Not Mysterious: Or, A Treatise Shewing, That There Is Nothing in the Gospel Contrary to Reason, Nor Above It.* If the scripture contained contradictions, or if its teachings flatly violated reason, then defending those texts was in itself a crime against both reason and religion. As Toland wrote, "To believe the divinity of scripture or the sense of any passage thereof, without rational proofs, and an evident consistency, is a blamable credulity."[4] In 1730 Matthew Tindal published the most important systematic critique of biblical authority to date in his *Christianity as Old as the Creation.* (Tindal, himself a judge, was firmly rooted in Grotian thought.) Tindal stated a simple principle, "that though the literal sense of the scripture be ever so plain, yet it must not stand in competition with what our Reason tells us of the nature and perceptions of God."[5] From this perspective, Tindal felt quite able to condemn the Bible's advocacy of extirpating native peoples, the concept that we would today term genocide.

Emerging ideas of comparative anthropology also transformed notions of religious authority. The more Western societies encountered the diversity of peoples around the world, the harder it became to present the Bible or its historical narrative as unique or more advanced than its competitors. Relativism was a natural outcome. In the 1720s the sumptuous volumes of the *Religious Ceremonies and Customs of All the Peoples of the World* offered educated Westerners a picture of the diversity of religious experience and in the process became *The Book That Changed Europe.* By the nineteenth century, comparative archaeology and historical scholarship showed just where the ancient Hebrews fit into the broader picture of ancient empires and kingdoms.[6]

Meanwhile, studies of primal peoples located biblical societies in a social framework that many found disturbingly primitive. As US anthropologist James Mooney argued in 1892, the patriarchal ancestors of the biblical Hebrews "had reached about the plane of our own Navajo, but were below that of the Pueblo. Their mythologic and religious system was closely parallel."[7] If much of the Bible was the record of the barbarous tribes of ancient Israel, how could it be presented as superior to the legends and tales of the Navajo or the Cherokee? Myths are myths.

Science also played its role long before Darwin. The book of Joshua's tenth chapter contains the most glaring single violation of scientific fact in the whole

Bible, when the sun stands still over Gibeon in the heavens in order to ensure Israelite victory over the Amorites. The story only makes sense in a pre-Copernican system of astronomy, in which the sun circles the Earth. At least since the seventeenth century, infidels and radicals turned triumphantly to this passage, and the Bible's critics found new ammunition in the growing scientific evidence for the extreme age of the Earth. Darwin's theories only added to the existing indictment.

Between 1860 and 1910 the scientific and historical critique of the Bible's literal accuracy grew steadily. By 1912 defenders of that belief reorganized into the movement that came to be known as fundamentalism, which educated Westerners associated with obscurantism, ignorance, and simple fanaticism. The harder the fundamentalists campaigned, the more they seemed to be engaged in a quixotic struggle against science, progress, and the whole modern world.

Catholics, of course, founded their belief on other grounds, and some, at least since the seventeenth century, had warned Protestants not to rely so blindly on dogmatic assumptions about the Bible, for instance about the Mosaic authorship of the Pentateuch. But other forms of modern thought challenged the foundations of the Catholic model, and here too historical scholarship played its role as the Church tried to restore the values and principles of the primitive Christian community. Meanwhile, traditional Catholic concepts of authority and discipline increasingly ran up against the near-universal Western assumptions about democratic authority and popular consultation. In its effects, if not its intentions, the second Vatican Council of the 1960s gravely weakened assumptions about the power of the papacy and the hierarchy and, thus, traditional theories of religious authority.

After spending so long mocking the uncertainties of liberal Protestants, Euro-American Catholics now found themselves facing decades of struggles over papal and Episcopal authority, the grievances especially focusing on matters of sexuality and gender. One telling moment came in 1968 when the Vatican faced unprecedented criticism for the papal decision prohibiting artificial means of contraception, *Humanae vitae*. Astonishingly for anyone accustomed to centuries of Catholic history, many millions of Western Catholics found themselves disobeying an explicit papal command while continuing to regard themselves as good Catholics. Whatever the real grievances arising from the scandals surrounding sexual abuse by clergy, the affairs served to focus widespread discontent over any claims to authority vaunted by an all-male clerical elite. One common complaint in such cases was the seemingly ludicrous notion that the Church might try to deal with problem priests through its own traditions and disciplinary proceedings rather than invoking the authentic and reliable authority of therapists and secular tribunals. Religious authority was all very well, but not in cases where it might affect matters in the "real world." So if not in the pope, nor in the Bible, nor in the tradition of the Church, where in Western Christianity was one to find dependable authority in religion?

The Survival of Authority

It would be only too easy to write a history of modern religion in the West in terms of the subversion and ultimate collapse of any absolute standard of authority, whether we seek that in an infallible Bible or an authoritative church. In the Enlightenment, advanced thinkers certainly saw that as a natural evolutionary process, a rise of reason. Among his many other dubious beliefs, Thomas Jefferson firmly believed that the religion of the American future was Unitarianism, a critical questioning faith, or lack of faith, which would ideally suit an era that respected no ultimate authority beyond nature. What is wrong with this picture? I will suggest a number of ways in which premodern and even ancient approaches to authority have survived and have proved astonishingly resilient.

Traditional sources of authority are still perfectly credible for large sections of the Christian world. The first obvious point is that we are not all Unitarians: in fact, that denomination remains microscopic, as do most ultraskeptical or radically progressive versions of Christianity. Far from rejecting the Bible as a source of factual authority as well as inspiration, a great many believers cling to it quite contentedly, untroubled by critical qualms. If we just take the notions of Creation and Evolution, most surveys show a solid majority of Americans vastly preferring the Mosaic account. Depending on how the question is framed, only around a third of all Americans accept that human beings developed from earlier species of animals, and the figure would of course be lower among professed Christians. Of course, these believers do not ostensibly hold their views on faith alone, as a vast literature tries to defend Creationism in what aspires to be the language of science and intelligent design. But the consequences for belief are the same: the Bible holds good.

Europeans might tend to view such obstinacy as a manifestation of the willful ignorance of Americans, but as Grace Davie and other scholars have reminded us, in any picture of the world's religious leanings, it is secular Europe rather than faith-based America that is the bizarre outlier, the exceptional case. Very traditional concepts of biblical authority are alive and well. So well have they survived, in fact, that we really must examine closely any claims about the impact of the critical modernist assault on the Bible during the early twentieth century.[8]

Religions founded on sacred scripture inevitably tend to return to their sources, and to generate conservative views of authority. Conservative interpretations of religious authority have powerful built-in defenses that allow them to survive challenges that might seem overwhelming. This is true of any faith that bases itself upon a recognized scripture. According to a well-known pattern in the sociology of religion, every faith begins with a fiery or prophetic impulse, an urge to reject or deny the standards of the world; but over time, this impulse subsides as new generations are born into the movement. The stern independent sect morphs into a tranquil and world-accommodating church that interprets its founding documents quite liberally.

But memories of those original scriptures never entirely vanish as that new church spawns dissenters and reformers who demand a return to the imagined purity of the world depicted in scripture. If those reformers cannot transform their churches, then they must break away to form new separate institutions. Sects become churches, which in turn give birth to sects, and the process repeats itself ad infinitum. In the Christian context, movements always tend to revert to the strictest interpretations of faith, the most immediate encounters with the Bible: the Bible is always being rediscovered. As stricter and more demanding movements are more likely to attract members and grow, the market for conservative interpretations of authority always remains and (as in the US case) even gains hegemony.

Centuries of Christian faith have left a powerful inheritance in the belief that spirituality must somehow be rooted in scriptures, even if not the familiar canon. Even ostensibly scholarly attempts to reconstruct Christian history fall prey to surprisingly fundamentalist concepts of the canon and its ability to reflect the "real Jesus." The quest for the real Jesus has been a centerpiece of Western scholarship for almost two hundred years as each new generation of impartial experts has generated a series of images that look suspiciously appropriate for the period in which that quest is undertaken.

In the past thirty years, Western academic opinion finds the truest reflection of Jesus in rediscovered alternative gospels such as Thomas, together with the hypothetical gospel source Q. Yet, ironically, the liberal emphasis on restoring the presumed "early Christianity" by means of its authoritative texts bears a strong resemblance to traditional fundamentalist approaches, which are instead based on the canonical scriptures.[9]

Postmodern thought holds that no text should be privileged or authoritative because each reflects the ideological stance of a particular hegemonic group. Scholars claim a duty to challenge the received canon of approved and valued texts, whether in literature or in religion. Radical critics seek to dethrone the canonical authority of the New Testament, but in a way that substitutes an alternative range of scriptural authorities. Although these new texts are more acceptable to current tastes, they are still treated with the same kind of veneration once reserved for the Bible. Particularly with some contemporary approaches to texts such as the gospels of Thomas or Mary (or even Judas), we find what can only be described as an inverted fundamentalism, a loving consecration of the noncanonical. But, crucially, even readers who define themselves as critical and, presumably, modern in their approach still seek scriptures to validate their beliefs.

If known scriptures do not support one's desired views, then other texts must be accorded this status or, in extreme cases, invented wholesale. The history of Western new and marginal religions is littered with the creation of spurious alternative scriptures.

Traditional concepts of authority have actually gained enormously within Christianity as the faith's center of gravity has moved decisively to the Global South. Quite traditional notions of religious authority, biblical and other, also survive happily in those regions that are becoming the heartlands of the faith. Twentieth-century Christianity was decidedly a Euro-American faith. Combining Christian numbers in Europe and North America, these continents accounted for 82 percent of all believers in 1900, and even by 1970 that figure had fallen only to 57 percent. Since that point, however, change has been very marked. Today, Euro-American Christians make up 38 percent of the worldwide total, and that figure could reach a mere 27 percent by 2050. In contrast, the absolute number of African believers soared, from just 10 million in 1900 to a projected 500 million by 2015 or so, and (if projections are correct) to an astonishing billion by 2050.[10]

If we envisage the Christianity of the mid-twenty-first-century, then at least in numerical terms, we have to think of a faith located much nearer the equator. According to the World Christian Database, by far the largest share of the world's Christian population in 2050 will be African, with 32 percent of the global total. South Americans will make up 21 percent of the whole, a number that grows if we include people of Latino origin in North America. In short, well over half of all Christians alive in 2050 will be either African or Latin American.

The forms of Christianity that are flourishing in its newer heartlands tend to be conservative in their approach to the Bible, or to other forms of traditional authority. Looking at Europe or North America, we might be tempted to think that older forms of church authority are close to extinct, but such a story would be meaningless in the Global South. By 2050 the three continents of Africa, Asia, and Latin America will account for 80 percent of believers.

Cultural interactions in Global South nations actively encourage conservative and traditional understandings of religious authority. Conservative forms of Christianity have gained an ever-larger share of the world's faithful, and this predominance is unlikely to diminish. This is partly a result of the encounters with other faiths that pushed Enlightenment thinkers toward relativism. In contrast, modern-day encounters situate Global South Christians in an ongoing dialogue of faith and authority. Joel Carpenter notes how, facing the challenges of secularism, postmodernity, and changing concepts of gender, Euro-American academic theology still focuses "on European thinkers and post-Enlightenment intellectual issues. Western theologians, liberal and conservative, have been addressing the faith to an age of doubt and secularity, and to the competing salvific claims of secular ideologies."[11]

Global South Christians, in contrast, do not live in an age of doubt but must instead deal with competing claims to faith. Their views are shaped by interaction with their different neighbors and the very different issues they raise: Muslims and traditional religionists in Africa and Asia, not to mention members of the great Asian religions. The question is not authority versus doubt but rather which kind of absolute authority, and how do I know? In an age of intense competition for believers, neither side can afford to make concessions about the absolute nature of its claims to certainty and authority.

Postmodern approaches radically challenge the whole notion of religious claims being undermined by "modernity." One might in theory dismiss the force of traditional faith around the world as a consequence of ignorance or poor education, but such a view is difficult to sustain. The idea of a battle between modernity and religious authority was always deeply flawed, founded as it was on the view of the "modern" as resolutely logical, objective, and value-free rather than as a deeply ideological construct in its own right. In the past half century such a view has of course been counteracted by postmodern theories that focus absolutely on the issue of authority and claims to authority. Postmodern approaches reject all master narratives. If the Bible is the product of societies and cultures, a narrative that gains meaning from its readers, then so is modernity. Postmodern theories of reading and understanding texts make the familiar Enlightenment critique look extraordinarily dated. To say that the Gibeon story "disproves" the Bible or challenges its authority only makes sense if one holds a very crude fundamentalist interpretation of the text.

Early readings of the Bible actually look strikingly postmodern and were much less vulnerable to modernist assaults. In fact, a sensitive modern account of the Bible's authority would do well to return to the readings prevailing in the earliest Christian centuries, when allegory and typology were so much in vogue. For instance, the early Fathers commonly mocked any attempt to prove or disprove the scripture literally but rather founded its authority on the power of individual interpretation guided by the Spirit. How, for instance, should we deal with those episodes of massacre and bloodshed that so upset Tindal?

One of the pioneers of Christian Bible interpretation was the third-century Egyptian thinker Origen, for whom a straightforward literal reading of the Old Testament would have proved a real challenge to claims of authority. Origen agreed that, if literally true, the bloody tales of the old dispensation gravely undermined Christian faith. But that was only a problem if you read the stories literally, and no wise or educated person would do such a thing. Origen believed that scripture should be read on three ascending levels. Lowest in significance was the literal meaning of the text, and simple souls might well consent to remain stuck there. But more advanced believers progressed to the moral interpretation and ultimately to the spiritual level of meaning. Once you accepted this, even the Bible's darkest passages ceased to be a stumbling block for Christian faith and actually became a prime source of Christian inspiration. The scripture was consequently all but impossible to discredit by any scientific or historical analysis.[12]

Like Origen before him, Augustine saw few problems in biblical accounts of massacre precisely because they were not straightforward history. Every part of sacred scripture had to be understood in the context of the whole narrative, which culminated in Christ, and only in that context could we read any portion of the text. Rarely does Augustine press any single interpretation of a given text: a reader might prefer one meaning or another. What mattered was reading the passage holistically, as part of the Bible's overall message, rather than as a simple record of past events. "Whatever the true interpretation may be, the pious student of the Scriptures will feel certain that in the command, in the action, and in the narrative there is a purpose and a symbolic meaning."[13] Augustine acknowledges no prescribed limit to the allegorical meanings that a "pious student" can derive from the text. Anything goes, in fact, in preference to the obvious literal meaning. The reader is all.[14]

Pentecostal readings of the Bible treat the text as highly authoritative but are not vulnerable to modernist assaults. Such a comment about readership and reception would apply equally to the largest and perhaps most significant movement within contemporary Christianity, namely the Pentecostals or charismatics. Since its origins in the early twentieth century, the Pentecostal/charismatic movement now claims at least 350 million adherents worldwide, and the number grows apace.[15] Although Pentecostals vociferously proclaim the power of the Bible and biblical authority, they reject the fundamentalist tenet that God's revelation ended with the scriptures. Instead, they give high regard to prophetic, inspired, and mystical teachings, and they apply a prophetic exegesis to the scriptural text. In terms of Friedrich Schleiermacher's classic distinction of styles of Bible reading, the Pentecostal approach is feminine, based on creative intuition and immediacy with the text. As Ogbu Kalu comments, "Pentecostal hermeneutic is feminine, eschatological, organic, and helps the audience to recognize the signs of the times, and to discern what God is doing in today's world."[16]

Such an open-ended approach to authority allows believers to circumvent even the most difficult texts. When asked about biblical limitations on the role of women, one woman leader of an African Independent Church who had proclaimed herself a bishop commented succinctly that "she respects the authority of the Bible. She is also very open to God's continued revelation."[17] If liberal Christians are accused of playing fast and loose with scripture in order to pursue policies that they believe to be right—particularly in matters of sexuality—then they are not behaving too differently from churches that have the reputation of being reactionary and "fundamentalist."

The success of Pentecostalism reminds us of the huge power of charisma as a source of authority within Christianity throughout history, over and above either scripture or tradition. The success of Pentecostalism also points to another critical if underestimated form of authority within Christianity, namely, the charismatic. Pentecostal churches stand and fall by their practical manifestations of spiritual gifts, their healings and exorcisms, and in this they stand in the mainstream of Christian tradition. However much historians prize the literary and textual as authentic manifestations of faith and underplay the visionary or miraculous as folk-religion, the distinction is false. The charismatic is, and always has been, more central to the validation of authority than such accounts may suggest. For the earliest followers of Jesus—and presumably for Jesus himself—healing and exorcism were essential components of his proclamation. In his acts of healing, Jesus was not just curing individuals but trampling diabolical forces underfoot, and the signs and wonders represented visible and material tokens of Christ's victory over very real forces of evil.

Not just among Pentecostals, such promises hold true today. For millions of contemporary Catholics, too, faith stands not on the textual evidence of apostolic succession but in the long-cultivated narratives of saints and shrines, miracles and visions. Take Mary out of the picture, that accessible female face of God, and Catholic Christianity ceases to make sense in much of the world. Even in seemingly secular Europe, we today live in a golden age of pilgrimage, when more shrines operate than for centuries, and attract far more devotees than even in the pious 1950s.

Recent historical trends have revived older concepts of religious authority and have challenged the narratives of modernity. Fifty years ago it was plausible to write of absolute religious authority as having collapsed in the face of modernity. If that picture was always exaggerated, it was quite discredited by the events of the 1970s, when a general series of economic collapses around the world cast doubt on the whole postwar narrative and subverted the hitherto plausible claims of nationalism, socialism, and secularism. In every major tradition religious politics returned forcefully in the mid and late 1970s. Around the world, faith traditions long dismissed as obsolete or irrelevant acquired potent new political voices and asserted the absolute authority of scripture and tradition.

The conservative Christian movements that so radically changed US politics in the mid-1970s paralleled similar trends in very different societies—in Israel and India, Iran and Lebanon. In 1978 the accession of Pope John Paul II marked a conservative counterrevolution in the Roman Catholic Church, a development with major implications for Latin America. In their different ways, each of these events marked a socially conservative challenge to secular liberalism and to a political consensus that had held for decades. Not just in the United States, the politics of faith mattered immeasurably more in 1979 than they had in 1975, and any rational analyst would take account of those developments up to the present day.

The figures exercising this authority are commonly not accredited leaders but rather spiritual entrepreneurs who are best able to use skills of mass marketing and communication and new forms of technology. This does not mean that the nature of religious authority remains unchanged. Common to many religious systems is a crisis of traditional institutions in a world in which the laity now has access to literacy and information on a scale that would have been undreamed of just a century ago. Clergy no longer have such monopolies of information and culture while the laity has been transformed by education, mobility, and rising wealth, generating far higher expectations and self-confidence. Like regular businesses, religious institutions also have to cope with the emergence of a market in which women play a potent role, so they have somehow to accommodate tectonic shifts in assumptions about issues of gender, family, and sexuality.

Especially in Global South nations, laypeople become avid shoppers and consumers for religious styles and leaders. In turn, religious bodies know that millions of consumers are out there but that a vast number of concerns serve these consumers, who can easily redirect their business to any one of a number of competitors. Convincing claims to authority cannot necessarily rely on institutional brand loyalty. They must be constantly reasserted.

Religion thus becomes the ultimate buyers' market in which the richest prizes fall to those figures who can present their claims to authority most convincingly to the widest possible market. Among Christians, we see the extraordinarily powerful influence of Pentecostal styles of emotional worship and direct experience of spiritual gifts, together with the associated culture of healing crusades, revivals, and megachurches—the culture of spiritual spectacle, in fact. Globally, the main beneficiaries are those religious entrepreneurs and televangelists who can most creatively use the new forms of media and technology to project their charisma to unprecedented audiences.

New electronic media should have an impact on our notions of "ways of being religious" quite as substantial as the book and mass literacy did centuries ago, and in so doing will transform notions of authority. Since we live in an age of such rapid technological transformation, any commentary on contemporary media is likely to be obsolete by the time it appears. Bearing that in mind, let me be foolishly bold in projecting what the near future might hold in terms of what technology might mean for notions of authority.

Already religion and spirituality occupy a vast amount of Internet traffic. In coming decades all denominations will have to confront the issue of just how far religious experience can be conveyed through the Internet or similar remote means, and the whole language of "attendance," "participation," and even "going to church" will need careful reexamination. The electronic setting meshes very poorly with notions of authority or hierarchy since the whole ambience of the medium favors voluntarism, participation, individual choice, and "grazing" among available options. The Internet is a world that functions most naturally on a peer-to-peer basis rather than on the authoritative distribution of spiritual goods by a narrow elite. While written texts are inflexible, Internet content is endlessly malleable, and so are the truths it communicates. The medium is best suited to that kind of mix-and-match self-created religion that is sometimes called "cafeteria" faith and that is already the bane of orthodox Catholic thinkers. Nor is the highly atomized electronic culture hospitable to any attempts to impose—or even to suggest—moral absolutes. And, at least in theory, participation in Net culture takes no account of gender or sexual preference. Almost certainly, the new forms of interaction will promote a new kind of radical religious privatization much as the printed book did in its day.

Yet if familiar forms of authority are threatened, recent experience with global cable and video suggests that new structures will emerge and flourish, as immediate communication encourages the growth of global denominations and parachurch networks. In turn, these will gain importance as migration continues to reduce the significance of national boundaries. If printing and the Reformation laid the basis for modernity and Protestantism, then electronic media are eminently suited for postmodernity.

To think even more speculatively, these issues will become all the more pressing when computers break their reliance on keyboards and permit easier and more intuitive interfaces. The development cannot be more than a few years distant. Nor can it be much longer before human–machine interfaces erode the boundaries between the biological and the electronic as computers quite literally become part of our bodies.

Trying to imagine the new post-Internet religious world might be almost as hard for us as it would have been for a late medieval Catholic to have envisaged the Bible-oriented spirituality of seventeenth-century Puritanism. Literally, that was an inconceivable world to them, and imagining religious life after the Internet might be equally problematic for us. But we can safely predict that new forms of electronic media will have far-reaching effects on religious practice and the whole notion of religious authority. And religious authority has a habit of resisting any number of forces that should, in theory, have been lethal to its hopes of survival.

Notes

1. Stephen Jay Gould, *Rocks of Ages* (New York: Ballantine, 1999).

2. Christoph A. Stumpf, *The Grotian Theology of International Law* (Berlin: Walter de Gruyter, 2006).

3. Stewart J. Brown and Timothy Tackett, eds., *Enlightenment, Reawakening and Revolution 1660–1815* (New York: Cambridge University Press, 2006); and David Sorkin, *The Religious Enlightenment* (Princeton, NJ: Princeton University Press, 2008).

4. John Toland, *Christianity Not Mysterious* (London: 1702), 37; and W. Neil, "The Criticism and Theological Use of the Bible 1700–1950," in Stanley F. Greenslade, ed., *The Cambridge History of the Bible* (Cambridge: Cambridge University Press, 1975), 3:240–54.

5. Matthew Tindal, *Christianity as Old as the Creation* (1730, repr. New York: Garland, 1978), 262.

6. Lynn Hunt, Margaret C. Jacob, and Wijnand Mijnhardt, *The Book That Changed Europe* (Cambridge, MA: Belknap Press of Harvard University Press, 2010).

7. James Mooney, *The Ghost-Dance Religion and the Sioux Outbreak of 1890* (North Dighton, MA: JG Press, 1996), 290.

8. Grace Davie, *Europe: The Exceptional Case* (London: Darton, Longman & Todd, 2002).

9. Philip Jenkins, *Hidden Gospels* (New York: Oxford University Press, 2001).

10. Philip Jenkins, *The Next Christendom*, 3rd ed. (New York: Oxford University Press, 2011).

11. Quoted in Philip Jenkins, *The New Faces of Christianity* (New York: Oxford University Press, 2006), 5.

12. On Origen, see Philip Jenkins, *Laying Down the Sword* (San Francisco: HarperOne, 2011), 193–95.

13. Augustine, *Reply to Faustus*, XXII.

14. On Augustine, see Jenkins, *Laying Down the Sword*, 194–95.

15. Donald E. Miller and Tetsunao Yamamori, *Global Pentecostalism* (Berkeley: University of California Press, 2007); Allan Anderson, *Spreading Fires* (Maryknoll, NY: Orbis, 2007); and Veli-Matti Kärkkäinen, ed., *The Spirit in the World* (Grand Rapids, MI: Eerdmans, 2009).

16. Quoted in Jenkins, *New Faces of Christianity*, 12.

17. Quoted in ibid., 167.

Between Traditional and New Forms of Authority in Modern Islam

RECEP ŞENTÜRK

IF THE TRADITIONAL AUTHORITY STRUCTURE in Islam had always been polyphonic, modernization made it even more so. "Islam" means submission to God's authority alone, as expressed in the divine revelation, the Qur'ān and the Ḥadīth. Yet the authority to interpret the divine revelation is not the monopoly of a person, group, or institution. On the contrary, all Muslims, men and women, are required to study the Qur'ān and even memorize some of it.[1] The only source of authority is expertise and knowledge, which the *ʿulamāʾ*, scholars of religion, enjoyed over the centuries. Secularization, the spread of education, developments in the media, and information technology, which are briefly referred to as modernization, contributed to the further dissemination of religious knowledge and thus the rise of new authorities besides the ʿulamāʾ, based, in contrast to what had traditionally been the case, on popularity rather than expertise. Furthermore, modernization created new legitimacy mechanisms based on publicity, image-making, and marketing in the media, which had counted little in the past.

"The kings are the rulers of the people; the scholars are the rulers of the kings; and the law is the ruler of everyone." This time-honored Arabic proverb was inspired by a saying of the Prophet Muḥammad: "Nothing is more powerful than knowledge. Kings are rulers of the people but scholars [*al-ʿulamāʾ*] are the kings of the rulers."[2] However, today in most Muslim societies there is neither a king (sultan) nor the ʿulamāʾ. Even Islamic law does not exist in some Muslim societies where secularism is accepted.[3] What have changed are not only the actors but also the mechanisms by which authority is legitimized. Consequently, official and civilian attempts emerged during the last century to restructure authority and legitimacy to fill the vacuum created by the collapse of the traditional authority structure. However none of these attempts have been fully successful. Today the remnants of the old system exist side by side with the new forms of authority, but they are in great tension with each other. As neither the old nor the new prevails completely, legitimacy crises coupled with segmentation or factionalization is the best way to characterize the authority structure in the Muslim world today.

Conflicting approaches among Muslims to the question of authority, founded on the contrasting cosmologies of traditionalism and modernism, find their manifestations not only in religious thought and political theology but also in the constitutions of some Muslim countries. "Authority (sovereignty) belongs to the nation without any condition or limit." This was the motto of the founders of the Turkish Republic, which still has its place in the Turkish constitution. It meant turning the previously mentioned traditional system upside down by putting the people at the top and the rulers below, as well as excluding the caliph and ʿulamāʾ.[4] In contrast, some Muslim thinkers in Iran, in the Arab world, and in the Indian subcontinent reacted against this secularist approach during the last century and formulated another motto with the opposite idea: "authority (sovereignty) belongs to God." This idea, which also gained popularity among the masses, and which is in fact an innovation in Muslim political theology, reacting to the claim that authority belongs to the nation, has also found its place in the constitutions of such countries as Iran and Pakistan.

In addition to the changing political and cultural context, especially with the collapse of the Ottoman state and the rise of nationalism and secularism, there was another very important factor that played a significant role in the transformation of the authority structure in Muslim societies: developments in the fields of media and communication technology. At first, the rise of newspapers and magazines gave rise to the emergence of lay intellectuals besides the ʿulamāʾ class. These intellectuals did not come from madrassas, but they mastered the new media such as novels, plays, newspapers, and magazines and thus established themselves as authorities.[5] Similarly, the rise of TV and the Internet enabled the emergence of new authorities such as TV preachers and Internet sites. The formation of authority in the media and cyberspace has its own dynamics and rules, which are different from those that applied in the traditional world.

It is evident that the traditional authority system is no longer intact in the Muslim world, even in the most conservative parts. The ancient authorities either do not exist or their authority has been redefined in the process of political, social, cultural, and technological changes that the Muslim world has undergone during the last two centuries. However, it would be erroneous to say that traditional forms of authority have disappeared completely and have been replaced totally by the new forms of authority. In the following I will briefly look at the past and present authority structures in the Muslim community and will address the following questions: How did traditional authority work in

Islam? How and why was it disestablished in the process of centralization of the state power? How did it transform itself to function in a secular system in the absence of the caliphate, ʿulamāʾ, and Islamic law as well as their institutional basis? What are the factors that contributed to the transformation of authority in the Muslim world?

The Traditional Authority Structure in Islam

In this section I will briefly present the traditional authority structure in Islam prior to analyzing the present situation. This is required to be able to assess the degree of continuity and change and to identify the continuing and broken lines.

In the traditional Islamic authority structure, there was no authority speaking with the voice of God. Instead, there was a constellation of intertwined authorities: the scriptures (the Qurʾān and the Ḥadīth), the law (Sharīʿa), the community (the *umma*), the caliphate, and the ʿulamāʾ (scholars and sufis).[6] This list does not aim to reflect the hierarchy in the authority structure because the diverse actors in it constituted an integrated system—with a system of checks and balances—rather than completely subordinate, separate, or opposite authorities.

The Qurʾān and the Ḥadīth represent the divine revelation to the Prophet Muḥammad. They include normative decrees (both legal and moral) concerning a wide range of issues. The Qurʾān and the Ḥadīth are two important sources of actions in the Muslim community. Muslims make frequent references to them and invoke verses from the Qurʾān or sayings of the Prophet Muḥammad when they are about to make a decision or when they are involved in a debate. The authority of the Qurʾān and Ḥadīth is religious, legal, moral, and epistemic.

The umma was the only authority that was considered infallible (*ʿiṣma al-umma*), an authority accorded to two persons in the world: the pope and the imām in the Shīʿa school of thought. Islam, according to the Sunnī path, grants infallible authority only to the umma. The authority of the umma derives mainly from a well-known saying of the Prophet Muḥammad: "My community (*umma*) will never agree on error." The historical implementation of this authority took two significant forms: through politics and through law. First, in the political sphere the institution of *bayʿa* (the covenant or contract between the caliph and the community) was a materialization of the infallible authority of the umma. Second, in the legal sphere, the institution of *ijmāʿ* (consensus) was another form in which the infallible authority of the umma was invoked. *Ijmāʿ* could mean consensus among scholars only on a jurisprudential issue or among the Muslim community in general on a practical issue.

However, even today the infallible authority of the umma remains an undertheorized issue. Nor has it been adequately institutionalized. Through bayʿa, the infallible umma bestowed upon a single individual the fallible authority of the caliph (literally, vicegerent), which was accepted as the highest authority in Islam, encompassing both secular and religious domains.[7] In contrast, the Shīʿī school had introduced the institution of the imamate with an infallible authority. This was a fracture in the authority structure of Islam, which at the theoretical level emphasized a single highest authority leading the umma.

The term *khalīfa* (caliph) is used in two ways in Islamic discourse. First, every human being is presented by the Qurʾān (2:30) as the khalīfa of God, which gives them an authority over the rest of the creation. Second, the leader of the global Islamic community was seen as the khalīfa of the Messenger of Allah, which gave him authority over the umma. The khalīfa/caliph was *amīr al-muʾminīn*, the leader of the believers in all matters. Yet there were limits to the authority of the caliph that were well expressed in a ḥadīth stating that "there is no obedience to a creature if it involves disobedience to God." More plainly expressed, if the commands of the ruler conflicted with the divine will expressed in the Qurʾān, his subjects were required to demonstrate civil disobedience. Interestingly, the authority of the caliph did not necessarily include *ijtihād* (independent legal reasoning), which was left to the qualified ʿulamāʾ. If the caliph was not a *mujtahid*, there was thus the limitation on his authority that he could not produce a legal opinion. However, as the president of the state he was given the authority to choose which among the range of legal opinions was to be implemented as positive law in his country. The Imām in the Shīʿī school, however, had much wider authority, being infallible in his opinions and therefore requiring unconditional submission. His infallible views were above the views of the ordinary ʿulamāʾ whereas for the Sunnī school ijtihād was a fallible opinion of a fallible scholar.

The authority to exercise ijtihād, to issue fatwās, and to adjudicate legal cases belonged to the ʿulamāʾ, who were considered the heirs of the prophets. The ʿulamāʾ gained their authority from the knowledge they inherited from the prophets. The isnād and ijāza system was used to authenticate their knowledge.[8] The ʿulamāʾ represented two types of knowledge: rational (*ʿilm*) and mystical (*ʿirfān*). The method of rational knowledge was thinking (*naẓar*) while the method of mystical knowledge was seeing through the eye of the heart (*kashf*). The institutional base of the former was the madrassa while the institutional base of the latter was the *zāwiya* or Sufi lodge. While rational knowledge was the objective foundation of society, mystical knowledge provided ways to express subjective religious feelings.

The ʿulamāʾ exercised their authority over the laypeople, a category that included even the caliph if he was not also a scholar. Thus the social structure of the umma was twofold: ʿulamāʾ (scholars), who were also called the "distinguished persons" (*khawāṣṣ*), and commoners or nonscholars (*ʿawāmm*). From this perspective, the ʿulamāʾ constituted the upper class by virtue of their knowledge.

By the term ʿulamāʾ, we should not understand an organized body; instead it was a loose network of scholars with diverse interests and opinions. The ʿulamāʾ, as a group, belonged for the most part to civil society, but some of them were employed by the state, in particular in the areas of justice and education. They belonged to different schools of law and theology as well as different Sufi orders. Yet there has always been an attempt to order the ʿulamāʾ hierarchically depending on their level of knowledge and age. Consequently, the higher level ʿulamāʾ had authority over the lower level ʿulamāʾ.

The loosely organized structure of the ʿulamāʾ continued until Ottoman times. The Ottomans organized the ʿulamāʾ and integrated them within the ruling class or bureaucratic structure of the state. In the Ottoman system, the ʿulamāʾ were organized under the leadership of the Shaikhulislam as *ilmiyye* (scholars), which was a part of the *ʿaskeriyye* (ruling class), along with the *kalemiyye* (bureaucrats) and the *seyfiyye* (the army).[9]

The Ottoman Shaikhulislam, who was appointed for life by the sultan-caliphs, had authority over the spheres of justice, education, and religion.[10] Thus he can be compared to a minister of justice and education as well as the head of the constitutional or supreme court. He was also responsible for checking the compatibility with the Sharīʿa of state actions, including those of the sultan and the grand viziers. He had the right to veto any state action he deemed contrary to the Sharīʿa. Moreover, the Shaikhulislam was responsible for approving that the new sultan had all the leadership qualities required by the Sharīʿa to become caliph. He installed the new sultan on the throne through a ceremony at the shrine of Eyyub Sultan, a companion of the Prophet buried in Istanbul. Moreover, the Shaikhulislam had the power to dethrone the sultan when he decided that the sultan was no longer qualified for the position. Around one third of the Ottoman sultans were dethroned by a fatwā from the Shaikhulislam. The sultan also had the power to depose the Shaikhulislam, and did so at times.

The authority of the ʿulamāʾ was at once religious, political, moral, legal, and epistemic.[11] However, Islamic law can be characterized an "open law" in the sense that it recognized a multiplicity of authorities and a diversity of opinions instead of a single authority speaking with the voice of God. The existence of four schools of law testified to this special kind of authority structure. The authority of the ʿulamāʾ cannot be understood without taking into account this particular perspective.

The Centralization of the State and Secularization: The Disestablishment of the Traditional Authority Structure

The institutional structure of authority in Islam changed radically at the turn of the twentieth century in the process of colonization, secularization, and the rise of nationalism. Using the example of Turkey, where a top-down and authoritarian secularization policy was adopted, I will shed light on this process. I have chosen Turkey not only because it is the case most familiar to me but also because it is one of the most secularized and modernized examples. Furthermore, the abolition of the time-honored institution of the caliphate in Turkey is extremely important for understanding the ensuing changes in the authority structure of Islam.

In 1920 the Ottoman sultanate was abolished after being separated from the caliphate and the last Ottoman sultan-caliph, Mehmed VI or Vahdeddin (1861–1926), was sent into exile with his whole family. Soon after, the caliphate was also abolished in 1924 and the last caliph, Abdulmecit (1868–1944), was also sent into exile with all the members of the Ottoman dynasty. In the following years radical and swift steps were taken to secularize Turkey strictly in order to control religion completely. The office of Shaikhulislam was also abolished. The head of the newly founded directorate of religious affairs was a civil servant appointed by the government to provide religious services to the nation. The pious foundations (*awqāf*) were nationalized. Religious education was banned for several decades until the rule of the Democratic Party during the 1950s, after which religious education was offered by the secular state through the Ministry of Education. Even the word "Allāh" was banned for a while because it was Arabic; it was replaced by "Tanrı," which means God in Turkish. The *adhān* (call to prayer) was recited in Turkish for several decades. The goal of these policies was to establish a Turkish Islam.[12] To this end, the traditional dress of the ʿulamāʾ, imāms, and sufis was banned along with the fez. Wearing a Western hat was made obligatory for all male citizens after the so-called hat revolution.[13] Some of the ʿulamāʾ resisted, keeping their turbans, but they were heavily punished. Islamic seminaries, Sufi lodges, and Sufi brotherhoods were all banned. The Gregorian calendar replaced the traditional Islamic Hijrī calendar.

The new Turkish secularist ruling elite put their faith completely in positivist science and secular Western civilization, thinking that these were incompatible with religion. They took extremely seriously the claim of Auguste Comte that humanity had entered the age of science and had left religion behind. Comte's *The Catechism of Positive Religion* was translated into Turkish and was distributed by the Ministry of Education.[14] Following the positivists, the ruling secularist elite firmly believed that religion was an obstacle to progress; it was going to disappear and if it did not do so, the state should make it disappear by force and thus expedite the pace of progress. From this perspective believers were stigmatized as reactionaries and religious institutions were seen as residues of an unenlightened past. In brief, the traditional authority structure in Turkey was completely destroyed during the early decades of the Turkish republic and religion was put under the strict control of the state. Religious functionaries and prayer leaders became civil servants and religious education could be given only by the state. The result was the end of the ʿulamāʾ, Islamic seminaries, Sufi brotherhoods, Sufi lodges, and pious foundations. Islamic law was also abolished and replaced by an eclectic collection of laws from several European countries.

Secularization was understood in Turkey and the Muslim world not as giving autonomy to religion but as putting religion under the control of the state, as in the USSR and other socialist countries of the time. This system did not have any counterpart in the West although it has been falsely presented as being borrowed from France, where the church is in fact autonomous from the state. However, this Soviet or Eastern model of secularism was introduced as part of Westernization in the Muslim world. This has applied more in Muslim countries that adopted socialism, such as Syria, Tunisia, and Algeria.

The disestablishment of religious authority in Turkey can be explained by the centralization of power and the expansion of state authority into both secular and religious domains. The centralization of power and the expansion of the state took place first in Western Europe, but there religion was not integrated within the state structure. Instead, the intention was to expel religious authority from the secular domains while recognizing its autonomous authority in the religious domain. This is what is commonly known as secularization. However, in Turkey the expansion of the state did not accept any limits and subsumed the religious domain under its control as well. The rulers defended this authoritarian model of secularism by appealing to Turkish exceptionalism: that is, the special conditions of Turkey required religion to be kept under the strict control of the state.

With the disappearance of the caliphate, the ʿulamāʾ were replaced by modern academicians and intellectuals. In Turkey this was more evident than in other parts of the Muslim world. The academization of Islamic education undermined the authority of the traditional ʿulamāʾ. Yet the traditional Shīʿī authority structure, with the Imām at the top, has been able to survive until today, even gaining more power after the Iranian revolution.

Contemporary Expressions of Islamic Authority

After the demise of the caliphate, many attempts have emerged to restructure authority in the Muslim world. The leaders of the social, political, intellectual, and religious movements around the Muslim world have claimed authority for themselves, becoming the self-appointed leaders of their communities. However, their authority has not been legitimated by the traditional mechanisms associated with the ʿulamāʾ such as ijāza and isnād. Instead, new forms of legitimacy have emerged in the modern Muslim community, including such secular mechanisms as democratic elections in both political parties and religious groups. However, most of the time these leaders have derived their authority from their charisma and popularity, their role in the fight against colonialism, their service to their communities, and their critical discourse coupled with opposition to corrupt and authoritarian governments. This phenomenon is new in the Muslim world.

With the disestablishment of the caliphate, the Muslim world in general lost the highest authority, which created a great vacuum in the authority structure. There have been several unsuccessful attempts in different parts of the Muslim world from India to Egypt and Jordan to revive the caliphate. There have even been suggestions, again unsuccessful, that an institution representing all segments of the umma should take the place of the caliph.

Another vacuum was created by the disestablishment of the ʿulamāʾ, whose place has increasingly been taken by a range of academics, intellectuals, and journalists to whom, in the absence of the ʿulamāʾ, the masses have turned for guidance in religious matters. This process is evident in Turkey but also in other parts of the Muslim world. Similarly, there is a continuing vacuum created by the absence of Islamic theological seminaries (madrassas) in Turkey and elsewhere.[15] The modern university has replaced the madrassa in many countries. Ironically, in modern Muslim countries Muslim clergy graduate from secular universities. In many places the supposedly secular universities have taken over responsibility for training future imāms and muftīs. The graduates of these schools do not carry the traditional identity of the ʿulamāʾ but such modern identities as experts, academics, or civil servants. These universities give a modern diploma to their graduates instead of the traditional ijāza. Furthermore, the roles expected of them are not the same as with the traditional ʿulamāʾ. This may be seen as a shift of religious authority to new groups with modern identities and roles such as academics, intellectuals, journalists, TV preachers, and even popular singers. Today, journalists and telepreachers have enormous authority over people on religious issues, perhaps more than traditionalist scholars.

Likewise, the vacuum created by the disestablishment of *fiqh* (jurisprudence) has been filled by the social sciences. Fiqh and the modern social sciences share as their subject matter human behavior and social relations. The fiqh rules in various areas of social life have been replaced by expert opinions presented by social scientists such as economists and policymakers. A new type of knowledge is being represented by a new group of specialists.[16] While the knowledge of the

ʿulamāʾ may be characterized as "religious knowledge," the knowledge of secular academics is "knowledge about religion." However, in the Muslim world, in the absence of the distinction between seminaries and universities, academics also present their knowledge as "religious knowledge" and thus claim religious authority.

An important exception to this observation has been some of the Sufi groups (*ṭarīqa*s) which have preserved their traditional authority structures and mechanisms of legitimacy. The Sufi sheikh is still usually appointed by the previous sheikh as his successor following a tradition older than a millennium. The authority of the sheikh, which is based on a chain of masters linking him to the Prophet Muḥammad, is not provided by new mechanisms of legitimacy such as university diplomas or a majority vote in elections. These Sufi orders can be seen as civil society groups. However, some Muslim majority states impose strict restrictions on civil society, seeking to control religion and the authorities representing it and therefore usually rejecting any type of civil religious authority, whether modern or traditional. For instance, Sufi groups are banned in Turkey, Saudi Arabia, and Iran, although for contradictory reasons: in Turkey because they are backward, in Saudi Arabia because they are innovations (*bidʿa*) in Islam, and in Iran because they cannot coexist with the authority of the imām.[17] In each case the underlying political reason for banning the Sufi orders is that they have an authority structure outside the control of the state that cannot be tolerated by a totalitarian political authority.

Conclusion

The increasing expansion of the authority of the nation-state and the centralization of power are among the processes that led to secularization and the disestablishment of the traditional religious authority structure.[18] This is true for the Islamic world as a whole, although some regions are more traditional in some aspects than others. The modern nation-state subjugated religion to its control and at times even dared to get involved in religion building. It appropriated religious authority, usurping it from traditional actors whom it deemed unfit to share in the new power structure of the modern state. This is true even for the so-called Islamic states that copy the modern state structure.

It has recently been observable that European countries are also involved in creating indigenous Muslim religious authority structures under their control; this at times amounts to religion building by the state for its Muslim minority. For instance, in several European countries there are efforts to build what is called "Euro-Islam" and to educate imāms for Europe. Yet this is unprecedented in the secular European state tradition, in which religion has been given autonomy and religious education has been provided by the church only. However, with the purpose of justifying these deviations from traditional Western secular tradition, an Islam uncontrolled by the state is portrayed as a danger. The mindset of colonialism works here as the religious domain is colonized by the modern secular nation-state. Secular authorities are dangerously involved not only in who represents Islam but also in what Islam is, and they want to assume a role in determining how Islam should be and who should represent it.

One can observe that in the process of these developments, the ʿulamāʾ are increasingly losing ground. The authority of the traditional ʿulamāʾ has been challenged and undermined first by the new class of academics and intellectuals and second by popular TV preachers. Similarly, the knowledge of the ʿulamāʾ has also been challenged and undermined by modern science and philosophy. Consequently, the traditional ʿulamāʾ as a group and the traditional knowledge they represent have lost both prominence and authority in modernizing Muslim societies. The vacuum thus created has been filled by the new class of secular-educated religious intellectuals, politicians, social activists, academics, and TV celebrities. This has been an unexpected twist in the mechanisms of authority formation.

All these changes increase the polyphonic structure of Islamic culture, and thus the forms of authority in contemporary Muslim societies become ever more dispersed and diverse. Traditional authorities, who are increasingly challenged by the rise of new authorities, find themselves in competition to gain more public acceptance and support. Pluralism comes with relativism. In this context authentic religiosity emerges within an open cultural environment where a multitude of choices are available and believers are forced to choose from among a plurality of competing options.

Notes

1. During the five daily prayers, Muslims are required to recite small sections of the Qurʾān from memory. Therefore, each Muslim is required to memorize at least a few brief chapters from the Qurʾān. This establishes a direct and personal relationship between Muslims and the Word of God, the Qurʾān; the study of the divine text is thus not left entirely to the experts or theologians.

2. Quoted in Jonathan Berkey, *The Transmission of Knowledge in Medieval Cairo: A Social History* (Princeton, NJ: Princeton University Press, 1992), 4.

3. Niyazi Berkes, *The Development of Secularism in Turkey* (London: Hurst & Company, 1998).

4. Of course, this was the expression of an ideal rather than the reality as the Turkish ruling elite adopted another principle of action: "for the people, despite the people." Later it was made clear in the constitution that the nation uses its authority through the institutions

mentioned in the constitution. For a brief introduction to the history of modern Turkey, see Feroz Ahmad, *The Making of Modern Turkey* (London: Routledge and Kegan Paul, 1993).

5. Şerif Mardin, *The Genesis of Young Ottoman Thought: A Study in the Modernization of Turkish Political Ideas* (Syracuse, NY: Syracuse University Press, 2000).

6. Richard Bulliet, *Islam: The View from the Edge* (New York: Columbia University, 1994).

7. On the first emergence and usage of the term and the institution of the caliphate, see Montgomery Watt, *Islamic Political Thought* (Edinburgh: Edinburgh University Press, 1998), 32–42.

8. An *isnād* (literally, "support") linked the authority of a scholar to the Prophet Muḥammad through a continuous chain of masters. The legitimacy of a scholar was considered to depend on having a reliable and continuous isnād. An *ijāza* (literally, "permission") was a traditional diploma including a record of a chain of masters, reaching back to the Prophet Muḥammad, through whom knowledge was inherited. The ijāza was an Islamic innovation to prove the authenticity of knowledge and to bestow authority upon the graduating student. Unlike modern diplomas, it was issued by the master rather than by the school. On the social dynamics of the formation of authority in classical Islam, see Recep Şentürk, *Narrative Social Structure: Anatomy of the Hadith Transmission Network 610–1505* (Stanford, CA: Stanford University Press, 2005).

9. İsmail Hakkı Uzunçarşılı, *Osmanlı Devletinin İlmiye Teşkilatı* (Ankara: Türk Tarih Kurumu, 1965).

10. For the life of a well-known Ottoman Shaikhulislam, see Colin Imber, *Ebu's-Suʿud: The Islamic Legal Tradition* (Edinburgh: Edinburgh University Press, 1997).

11. "In Islamic law, authority—which is at once religious and moral but mostly epistemic in nature—has always encompassed the *power* to set in motion the inherent process of continuity and change." Wael B. Hallaq, *Authority, Continuity and Change in Islamic Law* (Cambridge: Cambridge University Press, 2001), ix.

12. On the discussions on building a Turkish Islam, see Yasin Aktay, *Türk Dininin Sosyolojik İmkanı* (Istanbul: İletişim, 1999).

13. Although this is widely ignored, wearing a hat is still a requirement for all Turkish citizens according to the current Turkish constitution.

14. Auguste Comte, *Pozitivizm İlmihali*, trans. Peyami Erman (Ankara: Milli Eğitim Bakanlığı, 1952).

15. The traditional madrassas, which served as Islamic seminaries, were closed and strictly banned in Turkey in 1924 as part of the Kemalist revolutions to secularize Turkey and put education completely under state control. Consequently, from 1924 till the present there have been no Islamic seminaries in Turkey and, according to the Turkish constitution, religious education can be given only by the secular state.

16. For the conflict between Islamic *fiqh* and Western social sciences in Turkey at the turn of the last century, see Recep Şentürk, "Intellectual Dependency: Late Ottoman Intellectuals between Fiqh and Social Science," *Die Welt des Islams* 47, no. 3–4 (2007): 283–318.

17. On the practice of secularism in Turkey, which has no parallel in the Western world, see Recep Şentürk, "State and Religion in Turkey: Which Secularism?" in *State and Secularism: Perspectives from Asia*, eds. Michael Heng Siam Heng and Ten Chin Liew, 319–38 (London: World Scientific, 2010).

18. On the new forms of Islamic authorities in Turkey, see Recep Şentürk, "Islamic Reformist Discourses and Intellectuals in Turkey," in *Reformist Voices of Islam: Mediating Islam and Modernity*, ed. Shireen T. Hunter, 227–46 (New York: M. E. Sharpe, 2008).

Freedoms of Speech and Religion in the Islamic Context

ABDULLAHI AHMED AN-NAʿIM

ONE PREMISE OF THIS ESSAY is that freedoms of speech and religion are necessary means for each human person to pursue what she holds as the ultimate purpose and meaning of her life. In other words, people tend to link the value of rights such as freedoms of speech and religion to the purpose for which they are asserting those rights rather than to affirm them for their independent abstract value. This does not mean that entitlement to the right should be made conditional upon satisfying some commonly preconceived purpose of free speech or authoritatively sanctioned meaning of the religion that is to be experienced by believers in any religion. But it does mean that freedoms of speech and religion are unlikely to have much meaning and relevance to the people who are supposed to exercise those rights if they are perceived to be inconsistent with the purpose for which one seeks to have the rights in the first place. We should therefore appreciate the dialectics of ends and means in defining, justifying, and practicing freedoms of speech and religion in relation to other rights and broader concerns of persons and their communities.

Another premise of this essay regarding freedom of religion in particular is that the purpose and meaning of religion that one may seek to achieve and experience must be a matter of personal, free, and voluntary choice. Since there is no logical possibility of religious belief without the equal possibility of disbelief, denying the right to disbelieve is denying the right to believe. In terms of the dialectics of ends and means emphasized earlier, the purpose and meaning of freedom *of* religion includes freedom *from* religion. Conversely, upholding freedom from religion should not be at the expense of freedom of religion. This mandate applies to dissent within religious traditions as well as between them, to protect heresy, apostasy, and freedom to propagate one's religion, all subject to appropriate safeguards. Granted that there will always be the need to mediate and negotiate competing claims, the question is how to protect and facilitate that process.

In light of these initial remarks, I will argue in this essay for the secular state, defined as one that is neutral regarding all religions without being hostile or indifferent to any religion, as the necessary location for mediating competing claims about freedom of speech and religion. Such mediation can be achieved through what I call "civic reason," which requires engaging in reasoning processes in which one gives reasons for her or his positions that all citizens can debate, accept, or reject without reference to religious beliefs as such. I also propose that constitutionalism, human rights, and citizenship are the most conducive framework for that process of civic reason.

Islam and Freedom

Islam is the monotheistic religion that the Prophet Muḥammad propagated between 610 and 632 CE, when he delivered the Qur'ān and expounded its meaning and application through what came to be known as the Sunna (Ḥadīth) of the Prophet. However, the term Sharīʿa is often used in present Islamic discourse as if it were synonymous with Islam itself, as the totality of Muslim obligations in the private, personal, religious sense, including social, political, and legal norms and institutions. This is the concept or idea of Sharīʿa, what it is supposed to represent and mean, which should not be confused with any particular conception of the content of this concept through a specific human methodology of interpretation of the Qur'ān and Sunna. It should also be emphasized that Sharīʿa principles are always derived from human interpretation of the Qur'ān and Sunna; they are what human beings can comprehend and seek to obey within their own specific historical context. Striving to know and observe Sharīʿa is always the product of the human agency of believers, a system of meaning that is constructed out of human experience and reflection, which over time evolves into a more systematic development according to an established methodology. Human reason, judgment, and experience are therefore integral to any approach to the Qur'ān and Sunna at multiple levels, ranging from centuries of accumulated experience and interpretation to the current context in which an Islamic frame of reference is invoked.

The structure and methodology known as *uṣūl al-fiqh* through which Muslims have historically understood and applied Islamic precepts as conveyed in the Qur'ān and Sunna was developed by early Muslim scholars. In its original formulations, this field of human knowledge sought to regulate the interpretation of these foundational sources in light of the historical experiences of the early generations of Muslims. It also defines and regulates the operation of juridical techniques such as *ijmāʿ* (consensus), *qiyās* (reasoning by analogy), and *ijtihād* (independent juridical reasoning). As new interpretations of Qurʾān and Sunna texts are proposed by scholars and opinion leaders through their own *ijtihād*, some of those views may be affirmed by consensus among Muslims at large and thereby become accepted in the corpus of Sharīʿa by future generations. This has always been the nature of the sources and development of Sharīʿa, as our knowledge of the texts of the Qurʾān and Sunna themselves was a result of intergenerational consensus since the seventh century. However, there is nothing in the confession of faith in Islam or its articles of belief to prevent the formation of a fresh consensus around new techniques of interpretation as well as the application of these techniques to develop new or different substantive principles and rules of Sharīʿa. Such new consensus-based techniques and principles would become part of Sharīʿa just as the traditional methodologies and interpretations became part of it in the first place.

Recalling my opening remarks about ends and means, I believe that the ultimate purpose and meaning of religion itself, and therefore of social and political or legal arrangements for protecting freedom of religion and speech, is the possibility of striving for liberation from all fear. This possibility, I believe, can be realized through knowing and being at peace with one's self, and with all beings and things. The Sunna (Ḥadīth) of the Prophet Muḥammad said "*man ʿarifa nafsahu ʿarifa rabbahu*" (he who knows himself, knows his Lord). To know God, I believe, is to be at peace with all God's creation, which requires being at peace within one's self. Islam is the means to that inner peace, in my belief and practice. Accordingly, my conception of freedom, including freedoms of speech and religion, is broader and more dynamic than the legal protection of human rights against and by the state, though such protection is necessary for realizing that broader meaning. However, such ordering of our collective life as societies and as a global human community is only one of the necessary means to the end of liberating all of us from all fear so that each of us can strive to realize our full human potential.[1]

The application of this framework to the subject at hand is that we need to organize our social and political affairs in ways that are most conducive to liberating each and every human being from fear, which is the cause of all inhibition, the father of all moral perversion and behavioral distortion. Addressing external causes of fear through the rule of law and protection of human rights is necessary to create the conditions for human beings to strive to liberate themselves from other forms and sources of fear. But devices of social and political organization are only external means to the inner processes of true and sustainable liberation, which in my belief is best achieved through religious experience and the reflection that enables us to understand and come to peace with our social and physical environment. This makes freedom of religion of paramount importance for my personal and ultimate liberation, and freedom of speech is integral to that fundamental role of religion for me.

Yet it is neither morally legitimate nor practically feasible for me to realize and enjoy these freedoms unless they are equally secured for all human beings. Indeed, my freedom of religion and speech are meaningless unless enjoyed by all others. On the one hand, religious belief must be a choice that logically requires the possibility of disbelief. On the other hand, freedom of speech must be available to all to serve my purpose in having this right. I also believe that all human rights are interdependent and complementary. For instance, a right to education enhances freedom of speech; in turn, the exercise of freedom of speech enriches educational experience. People need to be secure in their persons and property under the law to enjoy any of their human rights.

I would also suggest that the proper and sustainable exercise of all freedoms requires discretion and good judgment, self-discipline, sensitivity, and respect for the needs and feelings of other people. To have the freedom to do or refrain from doing—whether in exercising freedom of speech, religion, or any other right—does not mean that one must act or speak all the time, regardless of consequences to others. On the contrary, a right or freedom exercised recklessly or carelessly is bound to be lost or denied to the person, or to his or her community that fails to hold the person accountable for the abuse or excessive use of rights and freedoms. Moreover, the duty and ability to use our rights and freedoms properly are better instilled, nurtured, monitored, or supervised through social relationships in the family and community rather than through coercive enforcement of regulations by the state. The art of discretion, good judgment, self-discipline, responsibility, and sensitivity in exercising our rights and freedoms is acquired and promoted through socialization and social interaction. These qualities are necessary not only for the proper exercise of our rights and freedoms but also for the possibility of effective regulation by the state if that becomes necessary. It is not possible or likely for state officials and institutions to engage in coercive regulation of human behavior unless there is sufficient consensus in the society about the values to be promoted by official institutions.

Apostasy and Freedoms of Speech and Religion

There is need for Islamic reform at two levels: to transform the attitudes of Muslims regarding apostasy and related notions, and to promote the legitimacy of a secular state that does not claim to enforce Sharīʿa as state law or policy. Both aspects must be supported by an Islamic argument to make them acceptable to Muslims. It is therefore necessary to combine these two approaches by clarifying the relationship between Islam and the state while at the same time seeking to achieve fundamental reform of certain aspects of Sharīʿa because of its powerful influence on Muslims everywhere, even when it is not enforced by the state as such. There is no particular sequence or ranking in priority for these two approaches because they tend to be concurrently and mutually reinforcing. For convenience, I will first discuss the internal Islamic reform question as applied to apostasy as a challenge to both freedoms of religion and speech. The case for a secular state as framework for mediation will be presented in the following section.

The imposition of the death penalty for apostasy and related offences is not unique to Islam; it existed in Judaism and Christianity and was widely practiced under the latter in the medieval period.[2] Yet these notions have been effectively eliminated from any current Jewish or Christian discourse, and there is no possibility of imposing the death penalty for these crimes in the context of modern societies of majority Jewish or Christian population. In contrast, these notions remain entrenched in Islamic jurisprudence, and those found guilty of these offences can still be sentenced to death in countries such as Pakistan and Sudan.[3] The question I wish to address here is not simply how Islamic societies can "catch up" with Jewish and Christian societies in this regard. Rather, it is how Islamic jurisprudence can be revised on these issues as an internal Islamic imperative to preempt any possibility of penal or civil law consequences or social sanction.

There are at least two problematic aspects of the notion of apostasy in Islamic jurisprudence itself, namely, the vagueness and fluidity of the concept and the ambiguity of the basis for its legal consequences as a capital crime. The main sources of the vagueness and fluidity of the concept of apostasy relate to its definition and punishment as well as its close association with several related concepts in Islamic jurisprudence, such as unbelief (*kufr*) blasphemy (*sabb al-rasūl*), heresy (*zandaqa*), and hypocrisy (*nifāq*). However, because space does not permit discussion of all these related notions, I limit myself here to the main issue of apostasy.[4]

The Arabic word *ridda*, commonly translated as apostasy, literally means to turn back, and *murtadd*, the active participle from *irtadda*, means one who turns back. In Islamic law, *ridda* is understood to be reverting from the religion of Islam to *kufr* (unbelief) whether intentionally or by necessary implication. In other words, the vast majority of classical Muslim scholars agree that once a person becomes a Muslim by his or her free choice, there is no way by which he or she can change religion. According to those scholars, ways in which *ridda* may occur include the denial of the existence of God or the attributes of God; the denial of a particular messenger of God; the denial of a principle that is established as a matter of religion, such as the obligation to pray five times a day or fast during the month of Ramadan; declaring prohibited what is manifestly permitted (*ḥalāl*); or declaring permitted what is manifestly prohibited (*ḥarām*). But since some of these issues have always been the subject of significant and persistent disagreement among Muslim scholars, it is difficult to establish the definitive and categorical view by which all other views are to be judged.

An obvious problem with the notion of apostasy is that, while the Qur'ān repeatedly condemns apostasy as a religious sin, it does not provide any punishment for it in this life, as is seen in verses 2:217; 4:90; 5:54, 59; 16:108; and 47:25. In fact, the Qur'ān clearly contemplates situations where an apostate continues to live among the Muslim community and engages in repeated apostasy rather than being put to death the first time they commit this alleged crime. For example, verse 4:137 of the Qur'ān can be translated as follows: "Those who believed, then disbelieved, then believed, and then disbelieved [once more] and became more committed to disbelief, God will not forgive them or guide them to the righteous pathway." Nevertheless, traditional Islamic jurisprudence imposes the death penalty on the basis of some Sunna reports (Ḥadīth). According to one report, the Prophet said that the blood of a fellow Muslim should never be shed except on one of three grounds: adultery, murder, or abandoning Islam after embracing it, that is, apostasy.

The Qur'ān leaves Muslims to struggle with all these issues for themselves. It is true that they have the additional practical guidance of the Sunna, or life-model of the Prophet, but that also has its uncertainties and ambiguities. It is therefore not surprising to find major differences among Muslims on the role that actions or deeds (*a'māl*) play within the definition of belief (*īmān*). Whereas some Muslim scholars were willing to accept as sufficient an apparent confession of the faith for a person to be considered a Muslim, others insisted that professed belief must be expressed in specific actions or deeds. For those who hold the latter view, the question becomes what to do about people who claim to be Muslims but fail to act accordingly. But then who decides whether a person has acted according to the requirements of the faith, and what consequences should follow from such a determination? These debates and their violent manifestations raged from the views and actions of the Kharijites during the civil wars of the seventh century to the debates over the status of the Ahmadiyya in Pakistan since the 1950s.[5]

Since the rationalization of such persecution is alleged to be "Islamic," it is therefore necessary to challenge such violations of freedom of religion from the same Islamic perspective. An Islamic methodology that I find to be appropriate for achieving the necessary degree of reform is that proposed by Ustādh Mahmoud Mohamed Taha.[6] It is not possible to present that methodology in detail here, but it may be helpful to note its main premise and methodology of juridical reasoning (*ijtihād*). The premise of Ustādh Mahmoud's methodology is that the earlier universal message of Islam of peaceful propagation and nondiscrimination was contained in parts of the Qur'ān that were revealed in Mecca (610–22). But when the Prophet migrated with his few persecuted followers to Medina in 622, the Qur'ān had to provide for the concrete needs of the emerging community, which had to struggle for survival in an extremely harsh and violent environment. From this perspective, it is clear that traditional Sharī'a principles, like apostasy and related notions, were in fact concessions to the social and economic realities of the time and not the message Islam intended for humanity at large into the indefinite future. Since those principles were developed by early Muslim jurists applying their own method of interpretation that was not sanctioned as such in the Qur'ān or the Sunna of the Prophet, different conclusions can be drawn by applying a new methodology. This analysis, I believe, provides a coherent and systematic method of interpretation of the totality of the Qur'ān and Sunna instead of the arbitrary selectivity used by some other modern reformers who fail to explain what happens to the verses they choose to overlook.

The Secular State as Framework of Mediation of Competing Claims

I turn now to the second level of reform mentioned earlier, that of the role of the secular state (i.e., one that is neutral but not indifferent or hostile to religion) in mediating competing claims about freedoms of speech and religion. I believe that I need a secular state and the protection of my freedoms of speech and religion and other human rights in order to be a Muslim by choice and conviction, which is the only valid way of being a Muslim. My argument for this part of the proposed combination of reform is that the idea of an Islamic state to enforce Sharī'a as positive law is conceptually untenable and practically counterproductive from an Islamic point of view. This idea is untenable because once principles of Sharī'a are enacted as positive law of a state, they cease to be the religious law of Islam and become the political will of that state. In other words, given the wide diversity of opinion among classical scholars and schools of thought, in order to enact any of those principles as positive law it will be necessary to select among competing views that are regarded as equally legitimate from an Islamic perspective. Since that selection will be made by whoever happens to be in control of the state, the outcome will be political rather than religious as such. This process will be counterproductive because it will necessarily deny some Muslims their religious freedom of choice among those views.[7]

I am therefore calling for the institutional separation of religion and the state while recognizing and regulating the unavoidable connectedness of religion and politics. The aim is not to prevent religious values from influencing political behavior but rather to enable them to do so through the democratic process, just as nonbelievers may seek to advance their philosophical or ideological views. This tension between the need to separate religion from the state despite the connectedness of religion and politics can be mediated through the distinction between the state and politics. The state should be the more settled and deliberate operational side of self-governance while politics is the dynamic process of making choices among competing policy options. The state and politics may be seen as two sides of the same coin, but they cannot and should not be completely fused together.

There are many relevant aspects of the state and politics that are necessary for good constitutional governance, achieving social justice, and protection of human rights; it is not possible to discuss them all here. My focus in these brief remarks is on the secular state in the hope of contributing to clarifying its relevance to issues of free speech and religious freedom anywhere in the world, regardless of whether Muslims constitute a majority or minority of the population. One caveat to stress here is that I mean the secular state, not secularism, secularization, or related concepts and terms. I mean a state that is neutral regarding religion in particular and not neutral about all issues or matters of public policy. Another caveat is that the secular state is always inherently contextual and historical, and every society has its own experience unique to itself. The historical and contextual development of the secular state as well as persistent controversy about its meaning and practical implications continue to the present day in many parts of the world, including in countries where the state is commonly acknowledged to be secular.

The critical need to separate state and religion while regulating the interconnectedness of religion and politics requires that proposed policy or legislation must be founded on what I call civic reason, which consists of two elements.[8] First, the rationale and purpose of public policy or legislation must be based on the sort of reasoning that the generality of citizens can accept or reject, making counterproposals through public debate. Second, such reasons must be publicly and openly debated rather than being assumed to follow from the personal beliefs and motivation of citizens or officials. It is of course not possible to control the inner motivation and intentions of people's political behavior, but the objective should be to promote and encourage civic reasons and reasoning while diminishing over time the exclusive influence of personal religious beliefs.

The operation of civic reason in the negotiation of the relationship of religion and the state should be safeguarded by principles of constitutionalism, human rights, and citizenship. The consistent and institutional application of these principles ensures the ability of all citizens to participate equally and freely in the political process, and protects them against discrimination on such grounds as religion or belief. With the protection provided by such safeguards, citizens will be more likely to contribute to the formulation of public policy and legislation, including through objection to proposals made by others, in accordance with the requirements of civic reason. Religious believers, including Muslims, can make proposals emerging from their religious beliefs, provided they are also presented to others on the basis of reasons they can accept or reject.

In essence, the proposed framework seeks to establish a sustainable and legitimate theoretical and institutional structure for an ongoing process in which perceptions of Sharīʿa and its interaction with principles of constitutionalism, the secular state, and democratic governance can be negotiated and debated among different interlocutors in various societies. In all societies, Western or non-Western, constitutionalism, democracy, and the relationship between state, religion, and politics are highly contextual formations that are premised on contingent sociological and historical conditions and entrenched through specific norms of cultural legitimacy. The model proposed here combines the regulation of the relationship between Islam and politics with the separation of Islam and state as the necessary medium for negotiating the relevance of Sharīʿa to public policy and law. In this gradual and tentative process of consensus building through civic reason, various combinations of persons and groups may agree on one issue but disagree on another, and consensus-building efforts on any particular topic may fail or succeed, but none of that will be permanent and conclusive. Whatever happens to be the substantive outcome on any issue at any point in time is achieved and can change as the product of a process of civic reason based on the voluntary and free participation of all citizens. For this process to continue and thrive, it is imperative that no particular view of Sharīʿa is to be imposed coercively in the name of Islam because that would inhibit free debate and contestation.

To conclude, the position I present in this essay is premised on certain conceptions of the dynamics of ends and means of freedoms and rights, the nature of religious faith and experience. It is also based on the working definitions of Islam, modernity, and freedom presented earlier. Regarding freedoms of speech and religion from an Islamic perspective, in particular I emphasize a combination of international reform to change the attitudes of Muslims about such problematic notions as apostasy and related concepts. I also argue for a secular state as the necessary framework for mediating competing claims about freedoms of speech and religion at the domestic national level. Both types of reforms, I suggest, require religious (Islamic, in my case) justification by transforming the attitudes of believers about relevant issues, whether of particular rights such as freedom of religion, or the secular mediation of claims about the scope and regulation of freedom of religion in relation to other freedoms such as freedom of speech. We also need to appreciate the context within which such mediations happen, from the local to the global, the various actors and their agenda and limitations, and so on.

For my part as a Muslim advocate of both freedoms of religion and speech, I am also concerned with transforming Muslims' views from a principled, systematic, and methodologically coherent perspective. This transformation is both necessary and possible because every interpretation of the Qurʾān and Sunna in the past, present, or future is necessarily a product of the historical context of the Muslim society of that time and place. Thus, given the radical transformation of the political, social, and economic context of Islamic societies today, as compared to what used to prevail when traditional understandings of Sharīʿa were developed, the method of interpretation of the Qurʾān and Sunna must respond to these present realities to produce modernist formulations of Sharīʿa. This can be done, for example, by reexamining the rationale of enacting certain verses of the Qurʾān and texts of the Sunna as Sharīʿa principles and deemphasizing others as inapplicable in the context of early Islamic societies. Once it is appreciated that that selection was made by human beings rather than decreed by direct divine command, it becomes possible to reconsider the question of which texts are to be enacted today and which are to be reemphasized in the present context.

Notes

1. Mahmoud Mohamed Taha, *The Second Message of Islam* (Syracuse, NY: Syracuse University Press, 1987), 84.

2. The explicit biblical basis for the death penalty for apostasy and blasphemy can be found in Deuteronomy 13:6–9 and Leviticus 24:16, respectively.

3. On the recent imposition of the death penalty for blasphemy in Pakistan, see "Blasphemy Laws in Pakistan," *Rationalist International*, www.rationalistinternational.net/Shaikh/blasphemy_laws_in_pakistan.htm and "Dr. Shaikh Sentenced to Death," *Rationalist International*, www.rationalistinternational.net/Shaikh/2001.08.26.htm. Section 126 of the Sudan Penal Code of 1992 expressly imposes the death penalty for apostasy. But the death penalty was imposed and executed for apostasy earlier, even when the penal code did not expressly provide for it. See Abdullahi Ahmed An-Naʿim, "The Islamic Law of Apostasy and Its Modern Applicability: A Case from the Sudan," *Religion* 16 (1986): 197–223.

4. The following review of classical Islamic jurisprudence of apostasy is based on Ibn Rushd, *Bidāyat al-mujtahid*, vol. 2 (Cairo: Dār al-Fikr al-ʿArabī, n.d.); and Nuʿmān ʿAbd al-Razzāq Sāmarrāʾī, *Aḥkām al-murtad fī al-sharīʿa al-islāmīyya* (Beirut: al-Dar al-Arabiya, 1968). In English, see Shaikh Abdur Rahman, *Punishment of Apostasy in Islam* (Lahore: Institute of Islamic Culture, 1972).

5. See, for example, Martin Lau, *The Role of Islam in the Legal System of Pakistan* (Leiden: Martinus Nijhoff Publishers, 2006), 112–19.

6. See, generally, Taha, *The Second Message of Islam*; and Abdullahi Ahmed An-Naʿim, *Toward an Islamic Reformation* (Syracuse, NY: Syracuse University Press, 1990).

7. For this argument in detail, see Abdullahi Ahmed An-Naʿim, *Islam and the Secular State* (Cambridge, MA: Harvard University Press, 2008), chs. 1–3.

8. On my concept of "civic reason" and how it relates to "public reason" according to John Rawls, see ibid., 92–101.

Christianity, Modernity, and Freedom

DAVID BENTLEY HART

I

MODERNITY—to the degree that it was or is a kind of cultural project or epochal ideology—understands itself as the history of freedom. Or rather, I suppose I should say, the one grand cultural and historical narrative that we as modern persons tend to share, and that most sharply distinguishes a modern from a premodern vision of society, is the story of liberation, the story of the ascent of the individual out of the shadows of hierarchy and subsidiary identity into the light of full recognition, dignity, and autonomy. And a powerful narrative it is, whether we prefer it in the simple form embraced by the philosophes (freedom from the constraints of tradition and the discovery of an ethos obedient to universal reason), the more rigorous form of Kant (the discovery that this rational ethos is ultimately founded upon the individual's own rational autonomy), the more speculative form of Hegel (freedom as the positive achievement of the rational civil state, which creates liberty by situating it within the poetic limits of the law), the more enthusiast form of Romanticism (return to the innocent spontaneity and goodness of nature, uncorrupted by culture), the more libertarian form of that great gnostic adventure called America ("Thanks, I don't need your help"), or some eclectic mixture of all of these (which is the norm). It does not, obviously, amount to a single ideological program; rather, it gives rise to a bewildering variety of analogous but often incompatible ideologies, but it does determine what our highest or central value is, to which all other values are subordinate and in comparison to which they are always provisional.

II

It has become something of a commonplace in recent years to observe that the modern understanding of freedom differs qualitatively and rather radically from many of the more classical or medieval conceptions of freedom. According to these latter, so the story goes, true freedom is the realization of a complex nature in its proper ends, both natural and supernatural; it is the power of a thing to flourish, to become ever more fully what it is. But to think of freedom thus, one must believe not only that we possess an actual nature, which must flourish to be free, but also that there is a transcendent Good toward which that nature is oriented. To be fully free is to be joined to that end for which our natures were originally framed, and whatever separates us from that end—including even our own personal choices—is a form of bondage. We are free, that is to say, not because we can choose but only when we have chosen well. Thus ultimate liberation requires us to look to the "sun of the Good" in order to learn how to choose; but the more we emerge from illusion and caprice, and the more perfect our vision becomes, the less there is to *choose* because the will has become increasingly inalienable from its natural object, whether that object lies within or beyond itself. The power of choice, however indispensable it may be to this pilgrimage toward the Good, is nothing but the minimal condition for a freedom that can be achieved only when that power has been subsumed into the far higher power of one who is naturally "unable to sin": a paradisal state in which the consonance between desire and its proper object is so perfect that goodness is hardly even an "ethical" category any longer. Within these terms, it once made perfect sense to say that God is infinitely free because, in his infinite actuality and simplicity, he cannot be alienated from his own nature, which is the Good itself and so is "incapable" of evil.

Today, though, such language would strike most ears as a little bizarre, and even perhaps willfully perverse. What the word "freedom" has generally come to mean for most of us now, when our usage is at its most habitual and unreflective, is libertarian autonomy and spontaneous volition, the negative freedom of the unrestrained—or at least minimally restrained—individual will. If we conceive of it at all as the realization of our nature, this is only because we have already come to think of human nature primarily as free spontaneity. Thus, though many of the seminal modern narratives of liberation—Enlightenment and Romantic alike—often understood freedom as the release of an aboriginal human nature from the fetters of tradition, the modern conception of freedom achieves its most logically consistent form only when practically all constraints have come to be seen as arbitrary and extrinsic, and when the very idea of natural or intrinsic constraints has come to be regarded as an intolerable imposition upon the sovereignty of the will. In this sense, the modern notion of freedom is essentially nihilistic (using that word in its most technical and least polemical sense): it is a liberty whose intentional horizon has been purged of all prior identifiable goods—all prior objects—and one that thus lies open before the indeterminate. For us to be as free as we possibly can be, there must be nothing transcendent of the will that might command it toward ends it does not choose or even fabricate for itself, no value higher than those that the will imposes upon its world, no nature but what the will elects for itself. Thus we cannot even speak of a society ordered toward the transcendental structure of being—toward the true, the good, and the beautiful—and still be understood to be speaking about freedom. If true liberty is by definition prior to or utterly beyond nature, there can be no coherent understanding of the law as a shared mediation between individual and common good, or between a community of free souls and the Good as such. Law can be only constraint or permission, a determination of the relative preponderance of the power of the state and the license of the self, a greater or lesser aid to the realization of private ends or the suppression of conflicting desires. Thus, everything in the interval between state and self—community, affinity, natural association, all of culture—is a "lawless" realm, a sort of shared privacy or elective localism subject to the law's powers of restraint but otherwise irrelevant to the law's primary function, which is to fortify the state and regulate the individual, securing both against the claims of anything that falls outside that naked dialectic they constitute.[1]

Needless to say, perhaps, such a concept of freedom is at some level irreducibly mythical. Desire is never purely indeterminate but is always directed toward an end that is desired before it can be willed. The very first movement of the will—and any scrupulous phenomenology of action reveals this to us—is always toward some object of intention; and any distinct and finite object can appear to the intellect as desirable only because the will has already been wakened, and desire has already been evoked, by a "transcendental" object, the Good as such, the very desirability of being itself, toward which every appetite is always primordially turned. Thus an absolutely "negative liberty"—even assuming such a thing could really be created within the realm of civil law—still cannot make anyone free in the modern "pure" sense. One cannot simply choose what to desire, or choose either to desire or not to desire; and the fiction that such perfect spontaneity lies within the powers of any rational being, if truly believed, may very well leave one dangerously susceptible to any number of external manipulations or accidental "traumas" of the will. Only a wisdom that allows one to distinguish worthy ends from worthless, or to recognize the relative value of diverse desires, can actually make one in any meaningful sense free. Only the acquisition of useful constraints and powers, upon which one can reflect in relation to the Good as such, allows one consciously to act toward a meaningful end; and this, one might very well conclude, is as much a social as a personal project, which must give shape to a realm of positive law. But the modern, libertarian, mythical concept of freedom—simply by virtue of its soothing vacuity and plasticity—makes it rather difficult even to imagine what a community of "lawful freedom" might look like. And it often makes it even more difficult to notice how, veiled behind the language of mere negative liberty, certain powers and enfranchised interests (the state, capital, ideology) have largely supplanted those mediating realities of community and culture and faith in which positive law should be situated, and have taken over the task of shaping our desires for us.

III

It is also now something of a commonplace to assert that this modern understanding of what it means to be free is to a great extent a late product or indirect derivative or fortuitous metamorphosis of late scholastic voluntarism. A great deal of late medieval and early modern Christian thought, in its anxiety to protect divine action against any imputation of necessity or compulsion, either external or internal to the divine will, progressively altered the very concept of divine freedom. Divine sovereignty came to be imagined as such an abyss of pure power that God could even act in a way unrelated to his own essence; indeed, this mysterious, sublime, unimaginable, pure power—in which no creature can participate, and over against which every movement of creaturely will is as nothing at all—became in some sense the very definition of what it is for God to be God. In this way, divine liberty was progressively equated with sheer spontaneity; and, in at least one picture of God, elective *arbitrium* was elevated over rational *voluntas*. Inevitably, this understanding of freedom migrated from theology to anthropology—from God to the creature fashioned in God's image—and began to shape moral, political, and social thought. And, of course, this could lead only in the direction of an ultimate atheism, whether fully conscious or merely practical. If God's freedom is primarily his infinite power to elect what he will—if, in fact, this abyssal liberty is not only not bound to the dictates of his nature but in the most radical sense *is* his nature—and if human freedom is merely a finite instance of the same kind of liberty, then there is no ontological liaison between infinite and finite freedom. In the older model of freedom, there could not possibly be a *real* conflict between the divine and human wills because the power of the human will was understood as a finite participation in the perfect and infinite power of God's freedom, his knowledge and love of his own infinite goodness. Even sin was understood as only the misuse—the poorly aimed—operation of this imparted movement toward the Good, a disordered love still sustained by a more primordial love of the divine. In the newer model, however, the only relations possible between the divine and human wills are either conflict or surrender, embraced within an irresoluble tension between incommiscible spontaneities. Thus all genuinely modern stories of liberation, presuming as they do some version of this model of freedom, perhaps must terminate in a final rebellion against God: for he is the one intolerable rival who must be slain if humanity is ever truly to be free. Thus, much of the history of modern secularism, along with many of its humanist or collectivist or libertarian tales regarding the freedom of a humanity "come of age," might very well be regarded—from a Christian perspective—as doubly damnable: as both a rejection of the God who declares himself in all of being and as the illegitimate offspring of a degenerate theology.

One does not, incidentally, have to subscribe to what a traditional Marxist would call ideology in order to take this story seriously. One certainly need not believe that the whole of modernity was obscurely born in the darkness of monastic cells or in the flickering candlelight of scriptoria, in complete abstraction from the new material conditions that emerged in Western Europe on the threshold of the modern age. On the other hand, though, ideas are not only 'shaped by but also shape material' conditions. This story of how we came to think of freedom as we now usually do, and of why so much of modern history has been the history of conflict between different visions of liberation, is undoubtedly true, even if it is subject to countless qualifications and complications. But it is not the whole story.

IV

Christianity began not as an institution, not even as a creed, but as an event that had no proper precedent or any immediately conceivable sequel. In its earliest dawn, the gospel arrived in history as a kind of convulsive disruption of history, a subversive rejection of almost all the immemorial cultic, social, and philosophical wisdoms of the ancient world. And the event that the gospel proclaimed—the event within the event, so to speak—was the resurrection of Christ, which was neither a religious event, nor a natural event, nor even an event within the history of religion, but a moment of almost pure interruption. According to Paul, it had effectively erased all sacred, social, racial, and national boundaries, gathered into itself all divine sovereignty over history, and subdued all the spiritual agencies of the cosmos: the powers and principalities, the thrones and dominions, the "god of this world." It was a complete liberation from the constraints of elemental existence (the *stoicheia*) but also from the power of law; for even the law of Moses, holy though it was, was still only delivered by an angel, through a human mediator, in order to operate as a kind of probationary "disciplinarian" (*paidagogos*[2]), and had now been replaced by the law of love. Thus Christianity entered human consciousness not primarily as a new system of practices and observances, or as an alternative set of religious obligations, but first and foremost as apocalypse, the visionary annunciation of the Kingdom and its sudden invasion of historical and natural time alike. And, as René Girard rightly observes, the nature of this apocalypse was in a very profound sense irreligious. It was a complete reversal of perspective in the realm of the sacred, the instant in which the victim of social and religious order—whom all human wisdom has always been prepared to hand over to death as a necessary and so legitimate sacrifice—was all at once revealed as the righteous one, the innocent one, even God himself. So, in its original form the gospel was a pressing command to all persons to come forth out of the economies of society and cult and into the immediacy of that event: for the days are short. And, having thus been born in the terrible and joyous expectation of time's imminent end—its first "waking moment" utterly saturated by the knowledge that the end was near—the church was not at first quite prepared to inhabit time except in a state of something like sustained crisis. There was no obvious medium by which a people in some sense already living in history's aftermath, in a state of constant urgency, could enter history again, as either an institution, or a body of law, or even a religion. It would take some time, and some degree of adjustment of expectations, and perhaps a considerable degree of disenchantment, for so singular an irruption of the eschatological into the temporal to be recuperated into stable order again.

From the beginning, consequently, there has been a certain paradoxical tension at the very core of Christian belief. In religious terms, accommodation with and adaptation of cultic forms was possible, even within as radically novel an association as the church; and, to a large degree, it came about quite simply as a kind of natural "pseudomorphism," a crystallization of Christian cult within the religious space vacated by earlier cults, even as the church strove to generate new kinds of community within the shelter of the culturally intelligible configurations it had assumed. This was, of course, inevitable and necessary. A perfectly apocalyptic consciousness—a consciousness subsisting in a moment of pure interruption—cannot really be sustained beyond a certain, very brief period. The exigencies of material existence demanded that Christianity would in time have to become "historical" again, "cultural" again, which is to say "cultic." What began primarily as force could not endure except as structure. But, as was also inevitable, the results of this accommodation between apocalypse and cult were very frequently tragic. As a religion, Christianity has provided many guises by which the original provocation of the Christian event has been made more bearable to historical consciousness but under which it has far too often been all but entirely hidden. The religious impulse has served as the necessary vehicle by which an essentially apocalyptic awareness has been conveyed through the alien element of "fallen" time but has also frequently enough striven to suppress that awareness. The alloy, moreover, has probably always been a somewhat unstable one. At least at times it seems as if the Christian event is of its nature something too refractory and volatile—the impulse to rebellion too constitutive of its own spiritual logic—to be contained even within its own institutions. This, at least, might explain why Christianity over the centuries not only has proved so irrepressibly fissile (as all large religious traditions, to some degree, are) but has also given rise to a culture capable of the most militant atheism, and even of self-conscious nihilism. Even in its most enduring and necessary historical forms, there is an ungovernable energy within it, something that desires not to crystallize but rather to disperse itself into the future, to start always anew, more spirit than flesh or letter. As the proclamation of time's invasion by eternity, and as the seal of finality upon the annunciation of the presence of the Kingdom in and among us, the gospel of Easter must remain—within the limits of time as we know it—an event that is always yet to be fully understood.

V

All of modernity's tales of liberation, in all their variety and frequent contradictoriness, are variations within or upon or in the shadow of this very particular history. Resistance to or flight from the authority of the law—or, rather, a sense of the law's ultimate nullity—lies at the heart of the gospel. In every modern demand for social and personal recognition as inherent rights, there is at least a distant echo of Paul's proclamation of the unanticipated "free gift" found in Christ. The peculiar restlessness, the ferment, of modern Western history—great revolutions and local rebellions, the ceaseless generation of magnificent principles and insidious abstractions, politics as the interminable ideological conflict between Edenic nostalgias and eschatological optimisms, the ungovernable proliferation of ever newer "innate" rights and ever more comprehensive forms of "social justice"—belongs to the long secular aftermath of the declaration that the Kingdom has arrived in Christ, that the prince of this world has been judged and cast out, that the one who lies under the condemnation of the powers of this age has been vindicated by God and raised up as Lord. It is a sort of "oblivious memory" of Paul's message that all the powers of the present age have been subdued and death and wrath defeated not by the law—which, for all its sanctity, is impotent to set us free—but by a gift that has canceled the law's power over against us.

For the only law by which it is possible for the church truly to live is Christ's commandment that his followers must love one another; and this law of love is anarchic in its universal embrace: so much so that, in Christ, there is no longer a division between Jew and Greek, free and slave, man and woman. Paul, moreover, is adamant, even fierce: those who have been emancipated from the law's power may not now turn back to the law for shelter, on pain of subjecting themselves again to the elements of the age that is passing, and of thus excluding themselves from the age that is coming to birth.

VI

Perhaps Christian culture has always been haunted by a certain, seemingly irresoluble dilemma: the mystery of an impossible mediation between the Kingdom's charitable lawlessness (which is a higher law) and the practical necessities of social life within fallen time. Historically, the only communities that have attempted to form societies obedient to the apocalyptic consciousness of God's "anarchic" love have been monastic. Their ideal, at least, has always been to live not according to a *lex*, but to a *regula*, a sort of lawless law agreed upon by all, enforced only by gestures of love, shared service, statutes of penance and reconciliation, and the absolute rule of forgiveness. And only a precious few of these communities have succeeded to any appreciable degree, for any respectable length of time. For those, moreover, who cannot and should not retreat from the world where positive law must operate—society, the family, all the commanding heights and sheltered valleys of culture—the mediation of the law is of its nature something always imperfectly defined, always something of a hermeneutical and creative struggle, and always somewhat alien. That a truly Christian society can exist 'guided by the law of love' is more or less an article of faith—otherwise the historical venture of the church would be pointless—but its political and legal configurations are anything but obvious and are subject to constant revision, not only in response to extrinsic material developments but also on account of a certain spiritual dynamism intrinsic to the gospel. There is perhaps an admirable clarity to Islam's refusal to erect any impermeable partition between spiritual and social community, or between the prophetic and the political realms; certainly, Islam traditionally does not find itself in the predicament of trying to inhabit two frames of time simultaneously, the apocalyptic and the ordinary. But there could never be such a thing as a Christian body of law and legal interpretation analogous to Islam's Sharīʿa, not simply because of the difference of Christian cultural history from Muslim but because it would be impossible within the terms of the gospel. In a very profound sense, Christians should inhabit history not only as pilgrims but as resident aliens—or as fugitives.

VII

Of course, were it not for this essential ambiguity in the Christian approach to civil law—this inexact, tentative, conjectural, endlessly corrigible sense of how a just or free society might be cultivated in the light of the Kingdom—Western history would be missing much of its exhilarating and tragic dynamism. And this includes much of both the creativity and destructiveness of modern Western society, which is a consequence not simply of the disintegration of a "Christian cultural consensus" but of an ancient and perhaps irresoluble tension within Christian culture itself.

One sees it from the very beginning of the Christian tradition in the church's approach to the institution of slavery. On the one hand, it is doubtful that slavery could even have been recognized as an institution—as, that is, a practice entirely contingent on human custom—by pre-Christian culture, inasmuch as the latter lacked any concept of the history of sin. On the other hand, the first generations of Christians, living not only on the margins of society but at the end of days, clearly had no occasion to imagine a human society this side of the eschaton from which the institution had been deracinated. Paul's letter to Philemon is a plea to a master to recognize his slave as his brother in Christ, not his chattel, and in that sense its moral prescriptions are no less—and really somewhat more—radical than those of the Stoics; but of course it says nothing about what political or social realities should follow from the knowledge that, in Christ, the difference between slave and free had been annulled. And so, as the event of the apostolic church gradually coalesced into the institution of the imperial church, the general Christian attitude toward slavery became one of pragmatic accommodation with economic and social reality only somewhat colored by a certain apocalyptic irony—a tacit recognition that the practice was the result of the fall—which at first resulted, apart from a few significant but limited legal ameliorations, in very little. There were exceptional figures, of course, such as Gregory of Nyssa and his sister Macrina: the former produced the only ancient text still extant seeming to condemn the very institution of slavery (and on entirely theological grounds), and the latter persuaded her mother to manumit her slaves. But the typical view of educated Christians was probably that of their brother Basil of Caesarea, who regarded slavery as a regrettable necessity inasmuch as, in a fallen world, there are certain souls that cannot govern themselves justly. And, while theologians such as John Chrysostom took it for granted that a Christian master could not humiliate and beat his slaves, Augustine—always more dour—morosely recommended chastisement if it was needed to dissuade a wanton servant from injurious sin. This is understandable, perhaps. An appeal to "natural" hierarchy has always been credible within Christian culture; in the body of Christ there are many members, as the apostle said.

On the other hand, however, what has always been utterly incredible within the New Testament's picture of reality is that anyone can justly be denied the "aspect"—the face and form and dignity—given him or her in Christ (in whom there is neither slave nor free). Most good historians of the period know that the gradual disappearance of chattel slavery in Western Europe during the Middle Ages was occasioned not simply by economic and political changes (crucial though they were) but by the emergence of a wholly baptized populace and of the consequent transformation of the entirety of society into the one body of Christ, of which every member was a coheir presumptive of God's Kingdom. Of course, when chattel slavery was revived in the early modern period—the age of the nation-state, colonies, and commercial empires—there were many who attempted (quite plausibly, they thought) to defend the practice in theological terms as a stewardship of untutored souls, a kind of mission to heathens and savages, and so on. But, in the end, it was to a preponderant degree theology—and most definitely *not* economics—that carried the cause of abolition to victory (even in the one nation where the issue would be resolved finally only by war). And it is arguable that, apart from the assumptions and grammar of Christian theology, the movement would not have been intelligible.

Something similar might be said in regard to the history of the political emancipation of women. At the very least, one has to grant that, as a living cause, it was of uniquely Western provenance; and whether anything like it could have arisen in a non-Christian culture is an open question. More importantly, though, when one looks at the debates that surrounded the early campaign for women's suffrage in the press and in popular journals, one discovers that the terms of the arguments were on many occasions and to a surprising degree deeply theological and on both sides (especially in the United States). Needless to say, there were many who opposed the cause simply out of fear of change or contempt for women, but there were also many—no less adamant in their opposition—who were clearly moved by an anxiety for the organic integrity of the "body of love": they believed that the removal of the franchise from the household as a whole and its uniform extension to both sexes would, simply by introducing the divisions of political interest into the family and thereby into the whole of society, hasten the dissolution of Christian culture. And yet no argument in favor of women's suffrage was more solvent or ultimately more persuasive than the claim that the dignity conferred by Christ upon all who had been baptized into his death was apportioned without preference to men and women alike, and that therefore no Christian nation could justly relegate women to a position of only secondary dignity.[3]

VIII

All this being said, however, the fact remains that the narratives of liberation that most powerfully shape society today, whatever their remote theological antecedents or religious causes might be, presume an understanding of freedom that is not only no longer explicitly Christian but perhaps in many ways incompatible with a Christian view of the human being. And this by itself has to be taken as evidence of Christian culture's failure 'over the course of its history' to give durable form or adequate content to a vision of society that could actually translate the anarchy of Christian love into positive law or civil order. We live now under the regime of negative liberty, which is admittedly a frequently very comfortable situation to find ourselves in but which also means that we have all become the sovereign possessors of an ever emptier liberty and citizens of a social order that, on principle, does not aspire to the "paedagogy of the Good." And this, of course, means that we enjoy precisely the kind and degree of liberty that best serves the interests of state and market. It is, after all, very much at the heart of the "modern project" that both should enclose our cultural commons as thoroughly as possible while banishing to the realm of private fixations and eccentric associations any cultural forces that might prove intractable to their aims. The ideal citizen of the modern civil order is both dependent upon the state for the whole of his or her legal and social identity (the state even has the prerogative of licensing marriages) and also a wholly liberated consumer with the resources to choose whatever and as much as he or she will. Any ideas or loyalties that might dilute this dependency or inhibit this liberty must not be allowed to enter the world of law, or really even of licit public discourse; they must remain safely sequestered in the world of personal psychology.

Whatever the future of Christian social thought may be, it must begin from this situation. Its primary task, it seems to me, must be to enunciate a vision of freedom that neither "idealizes away" the injustices of the past nor surrenders to the soporific nihilism of mere negative liberty. And, as always, any worthwhile Christian theology of culture must confront, ever anew, its own baffling and fruitful and dangerous inner tension between an apocalyptic consciousness somehow "beyond the law" and the sacramental reality of a fallen world that groans in anticipation of its transformation into the Kingdom. The question of freedom for Christians must always be how to live corporately and "lawfully" within the anarchic prodigality of divine love and the light of divine goodness without attempting to collapse that tension or to flee from it to a liberty that "makes not free."

Notes

1. I would argue that even the Hegelian tradition, right or left, ultimately falls into this pattern—even Marxism, despite its best intentions—but that is a matter that can be deferred to another time.

2. The tendency to translate "*paidagogos*" in Galatians as merely the equivalent of its etymological descendent "paedagogue" is an understandable error but one that ought to be avoided.

3. I realize that the story of the women's movement is rarely told in this way, but that is because we usually tell it "backward," entirely from the perspective of early–twentieth century progressivism. One good example of what I mean (from the antisuffrage side) would be the "Editor's Table" column in the November 1853 edition of *Harper's* (although countless other examples on either side of the issue could be adduced).

PART II

Christian and Muslim Thinkers on Tradition and Modernity

John Henry Newman (1801–90)

From *An Essay on the Development of Christian Doctrine* (1845)

THE FOLLOWING ESSAY is directed towards a solution of the difficulty which has been stated,—the difficulty, as far as it exists, which lies in the way of our using in controversy the testimony of our most natural informant concerning the doctrine and worship of Christianity, viz. the history of eighteen hundred years. The view on which it is written has at all times, perhaps, been implicitly adopted by theologians, and, I believe, has recently been illustrated by several distinguished writers of the continent, such as De Maistre and Möhler: viz. that the increase and expansion of the Christian Creed and Ritual, and the variations which have attended the process in the case of individual writers and Churches, are the necessary attendants on any philosophy or polity which takes possession of the intellect and heart, and has had any wide or extended dominion; that, from the nature of the human mind, time is necessary for the full comprehension and perfection of great ideas; and that the highest and most wonderful truths, though communicated to the world once for all by inspired teachers, could not be comprehended all at once by the recipients, but, as being received and transmitted by minds not inspired and through media which were human, have required only the longer time and deeper thought for their full elucidation. This may be called the *Theory of Development of Doctrine*; and, before proceeding to treat of it, one remark may be in place.

It is undoubtedly an hypothesis to account for a difficulty; but such too are the various explanations given by astronomers from Ptolemy to Newton of the apparent motions of the heavenly bodies, and it is as unphilosophical on that account to object to the one as to object to the other. Nor is it more reasonable to express surprise, that at this time of day a theory is necessary, granting for argument's sake that the theory is novel, than to have directed a similar wonder in disparagement of the theory of gravitation, or the Plutonian theory in geology. Doubtless, the theory of the Secret and the theory of doctrinal Developments are expedients, and so is the dictum of Vincentius; so is the art of grammar or the use of the quadrant; it is an expedient to enable us to solve what has now become a necessary and an anxious problem. For three hundred years the documents and the facts of Christianity have been exposed to a jealous scrutiny; works have been judged spurious which once were received without a question; facts have been discarded or modified which were once first principles in argument; new facts and new principles have been brought to light; philosophical views and polemical discussions of various tendencies have been maintained with more or less success. Not only has the relative situation of controversies and theologies altered, but infidelity itself is in a different,—I am obliged to say in a more hopeful position,—as regards Christianity. The facts of Revealed Religion, though in their substance unaltered, present a less compact and orderly front to the attacks of its enemies now than formerly, and allow of the introduction of new inquiries and theories concerning its sources and its rise. The state of things is not as it was, when an appeal lay to the supposed works of the Areopagite, or to the primitive Decretals, or to St. Dionysius's answers to Paul, or to the Cœna Domini of St. Cyprian. The assailants of dogmatic truth have got the start of its adherents of whatever Creed; philosophy is completing what criticism has begun; and apprehensions are not unreasonably excited lest we should have a new world to conquer before we have weapons for the warfare. Already infidelity has its views and conjectures, on which it arranges the facts of ecclesiastical history; and it is sure to consider the absence of any antagonist theory as an evidence of the reality of its own. That the hypothesis, here to be adopted, accounts not only for the Athanasian Creed, but for the Creed of Pope Pius, is no fault of those who adopt it. No one has power over the issues of his principles; we cannot manage our argument, and have as much of it as we please and no more. An argument is needed, unless Christianity is to abandon the province of argument; and those who find fault with the explanation here offered of its historical phenomena will find it their duty to provide one for themselves.[1]

Moreover, an idea not only modifies, but is modified, or at least influenced, by the state of things in which it is carried out, and is dependent in various ways on the circumstances which surround it. Its development proceeds quickly or slowly, as it may be; the order of succession in its separate stages is variable; it shows differently in a small sphere of action and in an extended; it may be interrupted, retarded, mutilated, distorted, by external violence; it may be enfeebled by the effort of ridding itself of domestic foes; it may be impeded and swayed or even absorbed by counter energetic ideas; it may be coloured by the received tone of thought into which it comes, or depraved by the intrusion of foreign principles, or at length shattered by the development of some original fault within it.

But whatever be the risk of corruption from intercourse with the world around, such a risk must be encountered if a great idea is duly to be understood, and much more if it is to be fully exhibited. It is elicited and expanded by trial, and battles into perfection and supremacy. Nor does it escape the collision of opinion even in its earlier years, nor does it remain truer to itself, and with a better claim to be considered one and the same, though externally protected from vicissitude and change. It is indeed sometimes said that the stream is clearest near the spring. Whatever use may fairly be made of this image, it does not apply to the history of a philosophy or belief, which on the contrary is more equable, and purer, and stronger, when its bed has become deep, and broad, and full. It necessarily rises out of an existing state of things, and for a time savours of the soil. Its vital element needs disengaging from what is foreign and temporary, and is employed in efforts after freedom which become more vigorous and hopeful as its years increase. Its beginnings are no measure of its capabilities, nor of its scope. At first no one knows what it is, or what it is worth. It remains perhaps for a time quiescent; it tries, as it were, its limbs, and proves the ground under it, and feels its way. From time to time it makes essays which fail, and are in consequence abandoned. It seems in suspense which way to go; it wavers, and at length strikes out in one definite direction. In time it enters upon strange territory; points of controversy alter their bearing; parties rise and fall around it; dangers and hopes appear in new relations; and old principles reappear under new forms. It changes with them in order to remain the same. In a higher world it is otherwise, but here below to live is to change, and to be perfect is to have changed often.[2]

From *The Idea of a University* (1852)

[Avowed and secret unbelief]

THOUGH it cannot be denied that at the present day, in consequence of the close juxtaposition and intercourse of men of all religions, there is a considerable danger of the subtle, silent, unconscious perversion and corruption of Catholic intellects, who as yet profess, and sincerely profess, their submission to the authority of Revelation, still that danger is far inferior to what it was in one portion of the middle ages. Nay, contrasting the two periods together, we may even say, that in this very point they differ, that, in the medieval, since Catholicism was then the sole religion recognized in Christendom, unbelief necessarily made its advances under the language and the guise of faith; whereas in the present, when universal toleration prevails, and it is open to assail revealed truth (whether Scripture or Tradition, the Fathers or the "Sense of the faithful"), unbelief in consequence throws off the mask, and takes up a position over against us in citadels of its own, and confronts us in the broad light and with a direct assault. And I have no hesitation in saying (apart of course from moral and ecclesiastical considerations, and under correction of the command and policy of the Church), that I prefer to live in an age when the fight is in the day, not in the twilight; and think it a gain to be speared by a foe, rather than to be stabbed by a friend.

I do not, then, repine at all at the open development of unbelief in Germany, supposing unbelief is to be, or at its growing audacity in England; not as if I were satisfied with the state of things, considered positively, but because, in the unavoidable alternative of avowed unbelief and secret, my own personal leaning is in favour of the former. I hold that unbelief is in some shape unavoidable in an age of intellect and in a world like this, considering that faith requires an act of the will, and presupposes the due exercise of religious advantages. You may persist in calling Europe Catholic, though it is not; you may enforce an outward acceptance of Catholic dogma, and an outward obedience to Catholic precept; and your enactments may be, so far, not only pious in themselves, but even merciful towards the teachers of false doctrine, as well as just towards their victims; but this is all that you can do; you cannot bespeak conclusions which, in spite of yourselves, you are leaving free to the human will. There will be, I say, in spite of you, unbelief and immorality to the end of the world, and you must be prepared for immorality more odious, and unbelief more astute, more subtle, more bitter, and more resentful, in proportion as it is obliged to dissemble.

It is one great advantage of an age in which unbelief speaks out, that Faith can speak out too; that, if falsehood assails Truth, Truth can assail falsehood. In such an age it is possible to found a University more emphatically Catholic than could be set up in the middle age, because Truth can entrench itself carefully, and define its own profession severely, and display its colours unequivocally, by occasion of that very unbelief which so shamelessly vaunts itself. And a kindred advantage to this is the confidence which, in such an age, we can place in all who are around us, so that we need look for no foes but those who are in the enemy's camp.[3]

From *Apologia pro vita sua* (1865)

[The infallibility of the Catholic Church]

And in these latter days, in like manner, outside the Catholic Church things are tending,—with far greater rapidity than in that old time from the circumstance of the age,—to atheism in one shape or other. What a scene, what a prospect, does the whole of Europe present at this day! and not only Europe, but every government and every civilization through the world, which is under the influence of the European mind! Especially, for it most concerns us, how sorrowful, in the view of religion, even taken in its most elementary, most attenuated form, is the spectacle presented to us by the educated intellect of England, France, and Germany! Lovers of their country and of their race, religious men, external to the Catholic Church, have attempted various expedients to arrest fierce wilful human nature in its onward course, and to bring it into subjection. The necessity of some form of religion for the interests of humanity, has been generally acknowledged: but where was the concrete representative of things invisible, which would have the force and the toughness necessary to be a breakwater against the deluge? Three centuries ago the establishment of religion, material, legal, and social, was generally adopted as the best expedient for the purpose, in those countries which separated from the Catholic Church; and for a long time it was successful; but now the crevices of those establishments are admitting the enemy. Thirty years ago, education was relied upon: ten years ago there was a hope that wars would cease forever, under the influence of commercial enterprise and the reign of the useful and fine arts; but will anyone venture to say that there is anything anywhere on this earth, which will afford a fulcrum for us, whereby to keep the earth from moving onwards?

The judgment, which experience passes whether on establishments or on education, as a means of maintaining religious truth in this anarchical world, must be extended even to Scripture, though Scripture be divine. Experience proves surely that the Bible does not answer a purpose for which it was never intended. It may be accidentally the means of the conversion of individuals; but a book, after all, cannot make a stand against the wild living intellect of man, and in this day it begins to testify, as regards its own structure and contents, to the power of that universal solvent, which is so successfully acting upon religious establishments.

Supposing then it to be the Will of the Creator to interfere in human affairs, and to make provisions for retaining in the world a knowledge of Himself, so definite and distinct as to be proof against the energy of human scepticism, in such a case,—I am far from saying that there was no other way,—but there is nothing to surprise the mind, if He should think fit to introduce a power into the world, invested with the prerogative of infallibility in religious matters. Such a provision would be a direct, immediate, active, and prompt means of withstanding the difficulty; it would be an instrument suited to the need; and, when I find that this is the very claim of the Catholic Church, not only do I feel no difficulty in admitting the idea, but there is a fitness in it, which recommends it to my mind. And thus I am brought to speak of the Church's infallibility, as a provision, adapted by the mercy of the Creator, to preserve religion in the world, and to restrain that freedom of thought, which of course in itself is one of the greatest of our natural gifts, and to rescue it from its own suicidal excesses.[4]

From *Letter to the Duke of Norfolk* (1875)

[Conscience]

Conscience is not a long-sighted selfishness, nor a desire to be consistent with oneself; but it is a messenger from Him, who, both in nature and in grace, speaks to us behind a veil, and teaches and rules us by His representatives. Conscience is the aboriginal Vicar of Christ, a prophet in its informations, a monarch in its peremptoriness, a priest in its blessings and anathemas, and, even though the eternal priesthood throughout the Church could cease to be, in it the sacerdotal principle would remain and would have a sway.

Words such as these are idle empty verbiage to the great world of philosophy now. All through my day there has been a resolute warfare, I had almost said conspiracy, against the rights of conscience, as I have described it. Literature and science have been embodied in great institutions in order to put it down. Noble buildings have been reared as fortresses against that spiritual, invisible influence which is too subtle for science and too profound for literature. Chairs in Universities have been made the seats of an antagonist tradition. Public writers, day after day, have indoctrinated the minds of innumerable readers with theories subversive of its claims. As in Roman times, and in the middle age, its supremacy was assailed by the arm of physical force, so now the intellect is put in operation to sap the foundations of a power which the sword could not destroy. We are told that conscience is but a twist in primitive and untutored man; that its dictate is an imagination; that the very notion of guiltiness, which that dictate enforces, is simply irrational, for how can there possibly be freedom of will, how can there be consequent responsibility, in that infinite eternal network of cause and effect, in which we helplessly lie? and what retribution have we to fear, when we have had no real choice to do good or evil?

So much for philosophers; now let us see what is the notion of conscience in this day in the popular mind. There, no more than in the intellectual world, does "conscience" retain the old, true, Catholic meaning of the word. There too the idea, the presence of a Moral Governor is far away from the use of it, frequent and emphatic as that use of it is. When men advocate the rights of conscience, they in no sense mean the rights of the Creator, nor the duty to Him, in thought and deed, of the creature; but the right of thinking, speaking, writing, and acting, according to their judgment or their humour, without any thought of God at all. They do not even pretend to go by any moral rule, but they demand, what they think is an Englishman's prerogative, for each to be his own master in all things, and to profess what he pleases, asking no one's leave, and accounting priest or preacher, speaker or writer, unutterably impertinent, who dares to say a word against his going to perdition, if he like it, in his own way. Conscience has rights because it has duties; but in this age, with a large portion of the public, it is the very right and freedom of conscience to dispense with conscience, to ignore a Lawgiver and Judge, to be independent of unseen obligations. It becomes a licence to take up any or no religion, to take up this or that and let it go again, to go to church, to go to chapel, to boast of being above all religions and to be an impartial critic of each of them. Conscience is a stern monitor, but in this century it has been superseded by a counterfeit, which the eighteen centuries prior to it never heard of, and could not have mistaken for it, if they had. It is the right of self-will.[5]

Notes

1. John Henry Newman, *An Essay on the Development of Christian Doctrine*, 8th ed. (London: Longmans, Green, 1891), 29–31 (intro., sec. 21).
2. Ibid., 39–40 (ch. 1, sec. 6 and 7).
3. John Henry Newman, *The Idea of a University* (new impression) (London: Longmans, Green, 1921), 381–83 (part II, "University Subjects", sec. 5, "A Form of Infidelity of the Day," § 1, "Its Sentiments").
4. John Henry Newman, *Apologia pro vita sua*, new ed. (London: Longmans, Green, 1893), 243–45 (chapter 5, "Position of My Mind since 1845").
5. John Henry Newman, *A Letter Addressed to His Grace the Duke of Norfolk on Occasion of Mr. Gladstone's Recent Expostulation*, 4th ed., with a postscript (London: B. M. Pickering, 1875), 63–65 (sec. 5, "Conscience").

Newman on Revelation, Hermeneutics, and Conscience

STEPHEN M. FIELDS

I

JOHN HENRY NEWMAN (1801–90) stands undoubtedly as the most important Catholic thinker to emerge between the Council of Trent of the sixteenth century and the Second Vatican Council of 1963–65. If the first council posited Catholicism's authoritative answer to the Protestant reformers, the second rightly hails Newman as its "Father."[1] His influential essay on the development of Christian doctrine put forth a theory that made possible the council's work of expanding Catholicism's traditional teachings with fresh insights, precisely in order to perfect their meaning. Because the council provided a major impetus for the last half-century's movements in ecumenism and interreligious dialogue, it can be said without hyperbole that Newman, a convert from Anglicanism, ranks among the most important thinkers in modern history. As a sign of his genius, his charcoal portrait by Richmond still proudly occupies the most prominent position in the senior common room of Oxford's Oriel College, where between 1822 and 1845 Newman served as a fellow.

In addition to the essay on development, Newman delivered a voluminous collection of masterful sermons on pastoral themes to his Anglican and Catholic flocks and on faith and reason to Oxford University. Matthew Arnold, the noted Victorian poet and social critic, describes hearing these as an undergraduate at Balliol College. The preacher, he says, would appear, "rising into the pulpit, and then, in the most entrancing of voices, [break] the silence with words and thoughts which were a religious music."[2] Newman's best-known work remains his intellectual autobiography, *Apologia pro vita sua*, an acknowledged classic, written in 1864 to defend himself against the publicly uttered charge of deceit and hypocrisy: that, even while serving as an Anglican clergyman, he was a crypto–Roman Catholic, working to undermine the religious establishment of the British people. In response, Newman produced not only an enduring masterpiece of English prose but also a consistent hermeneutic of his life matched, perhaps, only by St Augustine's fourth-century *Confessions*. With a disarming self-disclosure, he lays bare the internal dynamics of his conscience as it makes its way through the moral dilemmas of his journey of faith. Seeking from the age of sixteen the true church of Christ, Newman explains how an honest adherent of rational coherence could move from an evangelical Christianity emphasizing predestination, through an Anglicanism grounded in its great divines of the seventeenth century, finally to rest in an allegiance to the Catholic claims of an infallible church. The irony structuring the course of this arresting human drama dovetails the theme of our seminar: "to live is to change," says Newman epigrammatically in our first selection, "and to be perfect is to have changed often."[3] History, in other words, is no barrier, prima facie, to truth.

Later in life he produced in 1870 *A Grammar of Assent*, a work of religious epistemology that charts a distinctive path between metaphysical realism and British empiricism. Having fallen under an eclipse for some years as other converts from Anglicanism gained prominence, Newman's reputation was enhanced in 1879 by his creation as a cardinal. His life's contributions achieved enduring recognition when Pope Benedict XVI beatified him in September 2010, thus placing him in the official cult of veneration of the Catholic Church.

II

In the selection included in this volume from the *Essay on the Development of Christian Doctrine* written on the eve of his conversion in 1845, Newman succinctly defines a central problem entailed in Christian revelation. As the incarnate Son of God, Christ has definitively uttered the divine word in history. Yet given the nature of the human mind, historical process is required for the ideas so uttered to be comprehended and grasped fully in their intrinsic perfection. In other words, if God has entrusted a historically conditioned revelation to humanity, then God must have both intended and anticipated the hermeneutical problems that it raises. Even when revealed ideas are committed to writing in an inspired book such as the Bible, interpretation is demanded. As Newman elsewhere opines, the Bible raises questions that it cannot answer, nor was ever intended to answer.[4] In light of this scenario, it is incumbent on Christianity to work out a theory that accounts for the historical development of religious truth.

A crucial argument against the development of doctrine concerns the risk of corruption once revealed truth comes under the influence of secular ideas. Because these can interrupt, retard, mutilate, and distort it, fideism can emerge as preferable to development. In other words, the written message, precisely as divinely revealed, can be seen as sacrosanctly immune from hermeneutical questioning. Newman responds, however, that fideism only offers an implicit argument strengthening unbelief. If revealed religion is not to be perceived as impotent to reconcile faith and reason, then it must be affirmed as following the law of our nature, which, after all, is created by the same God who utters revelation. Like a running stream, all ideas, whether religious or secular, emerge purer and stronger as they deepen and broaden from their source.[5]

III

In the passage taken from the last chapter of *Apologia*, Newman flips the coin. If reason needs its legitimate questions satisfied, it also needs the restraint that will prevent the corruption of truth. In proposing the solution of an infallible church, Newman, now a Catholic for twenty years, comments prophetically on the state of religion in the world. At his apologetic best, he is well aware of Matthew Arnold's criticism, delivered subsequently to his admiration of Newman's preaching. According to this, Newman "adopted, for all the doubts and difficulties which beset men's minds today, a solution which, to speak frankly, is impossible."[6] Newman defends his position by sharply underscoring an irony. Whereas contemporary culture is more rapidly tending toward atheism than did any former age, unbelief actually subsists as a moment within a much broader problem.[7] This is nothing less than reason's "suicidal excesses."[8] Ultimately, these, not an Archimedean point of religious truth, place humanity, pace Arnold, in an impossible situation. Once reason is untethered from faith, "aboriginal" human nature "out of joint" with its Creator's purposes will seek its salvation with relentless disappointment, in one succeeding fancy of its own invention after another, whether this be atheism, scientific induction, education, commercial enterprise, or the fine arts.[9] Newman's question, then, must strike us as both timely and timeless: If reason offers humanity only a delusional redemption, where is hope to be found?

The answer for him is clear. If different understandings of how to fill the Bible's hermeneutical gaps inevitably arise, as the history of Christian heresy and doctrine demonstrates, then it follows that only an agency endowed with a divine guarantee of truth can do justice to the Bible as God's revelation. In other words, if God is infinite truth; and if God has uttered his word for the purpose of saving humanity; then an infallible church emerges as not only probable but necessary. Otherwise, God would not be true to his own nature. The gist of this text therefore demonstrates an infallible church as the indispensable warrant of a revealed religion, even as revealed religion serves as the only salutary restraint to reason's deliberate extravagance and self-defeating delusion.

IV

Newman continues his ironic assessment of the current state of religion in the excerpt from *The Idea of a University*. This work collects a series of lectures that he gave in Dublin while serving in the early 1850s as the founding president of the Catholic University of Ireland. Here he faced the challenge of convincing the Catholic bishops that the interests of religion would be served by a university devoted not to religious catechesis but to pursuing knowledge as its own end. He thus underscores an optimism in the heart of Catholicism: that theology and all other branches of knowledge stand *utraque unum* (both as one). Because no contradiction can exist in God, from whom both revealed and natural truth spring, the work of reason unfettered by external constraint will manifest patently the superiority of faith over unbelief. Moreover, Newman opines that freedom of thought can temper immorality and remove resentment from aggressive skepticism. These views were formed in the crucible of his own bitter experience. Years of dedication to the legally established church had made it clear that the legitimate ends of religion are invariably undermined by the secular ends of the state. Motivated, for instance, by the need to balance its budget, Parliament in 1833 proposed the suppression of a number of bishops and their dioceses. Seen by Newman and his reforming friends as a "national apostasy," this constraint of government upon the Church caused the fair-minded Newman to become, in turn, sensitive to the deleterious effects of religion's strictures on independent thinking.[10]

A paradox thus arises between this sensitivity on the one hand and Newman's strong defense of the prerogatives of an infallible church on the other. Elsewhere in *Apologia*, he endeavors to resolve it. Infallibility does not aim to curtail freedom but to stem error, and that only as it corrodes the authentic content of divine revelation. Moreover, any exercise of infallibility is both preceded and succeeded by the free exercise of rational inquiry. The dialectic between the Church's teaching authority and the individual's unconstrained thinking is, for Newman, "necessary for the very life of religion." It shows Catholicism not "as a simple exhibition of religious absolutism" but as a synthesis of personal genius and communal integrity.[11]

V

Such a synthesis can find its ground in conscience, adumbrates Newman in his *Letter to the Duke of Norfolk*. Written in 1874, this work gives a riposte to

William Gladstone's attack on the First Vatican Council's definition of papal infallibility. Newman is keen to correct a false view put forth by liberalism of conscience: that it allows for "each to be his own master in all things," and hence to speak, write, and think according to his own judgment "without any thought to God." Tantamount to nothing more than "self-will," this view embodies another of reason's suicidal excesses: the assertion that conscience has "the very right and freedom . . . to dispense with" itself.[12] Against this reductive position, Newman defends conscience as "the voice of God" immanent in every person.[13] Far from locking us in solipsism, conscience, as a "sacerdotal principle," allows us to mediate between specific moral decisions and "unseen obligations" that, in justice, exert on us "the prerogative of commanding" obedience.[14] Conscience sanctions our actions by its own implicit norms, which possess a "strange, troublesome peremptoriness" that we can neither manufacture nor silence.[15] Without its voice speaking "so clearly," Newman says in *Apologia*, he "should be an atheist, or a pantheist, or a polytheist when [he] looked into the world."[16] In short, conscience is reason's own agent that regulates choice in accord with objectivity. Even if wrong, still if sincere, it may not be acted against.[17]

Yet Newman shows a balanced prudence in his assessment of the privileges of individual conscience. However quasi-divine an oracle, still its "sense of right and wrong . . . is so delicate, so fitful, so easily puzzled, obscured, and perverted . . . , so unsteady in its course that [it] is at once the highest of all teachers, yet the least luminous."[18] Moreover, it falls prey to that "vulgar spirit of [our] nature, which, at the very first rumor of a command, places itself in opposition."[19] On these accounts, conscience needs to be "sustained and completed by Revelation," precisely as infallibly discerned by the Church's magisterial office.[20] Nonetheless, in those matters that do not touch on the integrity of the divine revelation or on the grounding principles of morality, Newman sees the collision of consciences as fruitful. "Truth," he says, "is wrought out by many minds working together freely."[21]

VI

In light of this volume's theme, let us briefly conclude by offering a definition of modernity and assessing Newman's view of tradition in its light. An unfinished project still unfolding, modernity—according to Louis Dupré, the contemporary philosopher of culture—traces its origins to the fourteenth-century humanists. Dante and Petrarch, for instance, give witness to what has come to be validated as modernity's defining principle: "Mind stands in a creative relation to that physical reality on which it in other respects depends."[22] Until this time, the intelligibility of the objective world, crystallized in the notion of form, had assumed priority over the human knower.[23] Aesthetics, we notice, was essentially mimetic. Transcendence, whether understood as Plato's infinite Good, or Aristotle's Prime Mover, or a personal God, obtained in some causally necessary relation with the objective forms of the world known by the subject. With the aggressive assertion of the prerogatives of subjective ingenuity over mind's receptive assimilation of the external cosmos, a new view of skepticism was introduced. It came to be understood, not as an aberration but, as Newman himself regretfully opines, as the normal progression of reason.[24] Consequently, the modern mind finds itself embarrassed by those claims that previously emerged from its congenial reciprocity with transcendence and history.

Presciently, Newman strips a skeptical modernity of its tendency to isolate the rationalist ego. Aside from diagnosing the self-defeating results of this tendency, he also prophesies against its moral narcissism. Truth, he reminds us, is hidden when not sought. And seeking it entails a range of virtues that lead the mind outside of its own confining circularity. For instance, without trust that intelligibility is to be found in whatever it is investigating, the mind will never reach "certainty in things which at present [it] thinks trifling or irrational."[25] Without humility, which acknowledges its ignorance in the face of its questions, the mind will fall prey to bias. Without a prudent distrust in its own powers, the mind will never correct its inductive hypotheses. Accordingly, if virtue is the necessary means of the acquisition of truth, then we can see why those "of learning and ability" are so often in error, in matters both ultimate and empirical, despite their "superior intellectual endowment."[26] Education without virtue, by deludedly making the mind a self-sufficient monad, moves us ironically from one form of ignorance to another.

It is no wonder, therefore, that Newman poses a moral solution to the problem of reconciling modernity and tradition. Inspired, formed, and guided by virtue, conscience forges the link between liberty of mind and religious authority. A divine revelation, emerging in history, whose developing truth is socially discerned under an infallible sanction, restrains the solipsistic inclination of individual genius to self-will. God's word, however, can only be appropriated by trust, humility, and prudence. Nonetheless, the deeper meaning of the received tradition can be more perfectly comprehended when it enters into a dialogue with the innovative insights of questioning consciences. Although these must finally defer to magisterial dictate, without their initiative, the gaps in revelation providentially foreseen by God will nevertheless not be filled according to the temporal unfolding of his saving will. In short, Newman, understanding humanity's weakness and greatness equally, foresees no fulfillment of our species that is not as historical and social as it is supernatural.

For Further Reflection

1. Does Newman's assessment of reason and defense of infallibility take away any of the sting from Matthew Arnold's criticism that he adopts an "impossible solution"?
2. Newman posits conscience as a synthesis of freedom and authority. Today, however, can we accept as anything more than a pious metaphor his view of conscience as the "voice of God"?
3. Newman's view of history, based possibly on his own life, emphasizes homogeneity through change. Does he thereby shortchange the salutary significance of upheaval, discontinuity, caesura, and rupture in the life of religion?

Notes

1. An epithet often attributed to Pope John XXIII, who called the council.

2. Arnold quoted by W. D. White, review of Matthew Arnold, *Dissent and Dogma*, vol. 4 of *The Complete Prose Works of Matthew Arnold* (Ann Arbor: University of Michigan Press, 1968); in *Journal of the American Academy of Religion* 37 (June 1969): 193–94, at 194b.

3. John Henry Cardinal Newman, *An Essay on the Development of Christian Doctrine*, in *Conscience, Consensus and the Development of Doctrine* (New York: Doubleday, 1992), 31–384, at 75.

4. Ibid., 92.

5. Ibid., 75.

6. Arnold, in White, review, 194b.

7. John Henry Cardinal Newman, *Apologia pro vita sua* (New York: Doubleday, 1989), 321.

8. Ibid., 323.

9. Ibid., 321.

10. Ibid., 152.

11. Ibid., 328.

12. John Henry Cardinal Newman, *A Letter Addressed to His Grace the Duke of Norfolk on Occasion of Mr. Gladstone's Recent Expostulation*, in *Conscience, Consensus, and the Development of Doctrine*, 429–57, at 450.

13. Ibid., 448.

14. Ibid., 448, 449, 450.

15. John Henry Newman, *Argument from Conscience to the Existence of God*, ed. A. J. Boerkraad (Louvain: Editions Nauwelaerts, 1961), 116.

16. Newman, *Apologia*, 319.

17. Newman, citing the fourth Lateran Council (1215), *Letter to Norfolk*, 448.

18. Newman, *Letter to Norfolk*, 452.

19. Ibid., 455.

20. Ibid., 452.

21. Newman, letter to Robert Omsby (March 26, 1868), in *Letters and Diaries of John Henry Newman*, ed. C. S. Dessain et al. (Oxford: Clarendon Press, 1961–): vol. 20, 426.

22. Louis Dupré, *Passage to Modernity: An Essay in the Hermeneutics of Nature and Culture* (New Haven, CT: Yale University Press, 1993), 5–6, 249–50, 252.

23. Ibid., 18f.

24. Newman, *Apologia*, 336.

25. John Henry Newman, "Truth Hidden When Not Sought After," in *Parochial and Plain Sermons*, 8 vols. (Westminster, MD: Christian Classics, 1968), 8:185–200, at 195.

26. Ibid., 186–87.

Muḥammad ʿAbduh (1849–1905)

From *Destiny and Fate*

THE EUROPEANS BELIEVE that there is no difference between the doctrine of destiny and fate (*al-qaḍāʾ wa al-qadar*) and the doctrine of the theological school of the Predestinarians (*al-Jabrīyya*), who say that the human being is compelled absolutely in all of his acts. They imagine that with the doctrine of destiny (*al-qaḍāʾ*) Muslims see themselves as a feather floating in the air and buffeted by the wind wherever it goes. Indeed, if it were to occur to the minds of people that they have no choice in word or deed or in motion or rest, and that all of this is subject to a compelling force or a coercive power, there is no doubt that it would retard their strength and they would lose the fruits of the powers of capability and understanding that God granted them. It would also erase from their imaginations the urge to strive and earn. . . .

This is the view of a faction among the Europeans and this approach is also followed by many of the weak-minded in the East. However, I am not afraid to state: This view is false, their opinion is wrong, their conjecture is baseless, and they have imposed a lie on God and the Muslims alike. There is not a single Muslim in this present time—neither Sunnī nor Shīʿī nor Zaydī nor Ismāʿīlī, nor Wahhābī nor Khārijī—that follows the theological school of absolute predestination or believes in the ultimate denial of choice to the human will. On the contrary, every one of these Muslim sects believes that there is an element of choice (*juzʾ ikhtiyārī*) in their actions (which is called *kasb*), and that this [element of choice] is ultimately responsible for their reward or punishment. They further believe that this element of choice makes them accountable for what God has bestowed upon them, that in a like manner they are asked to follow the divine commands and prohibitions that call to every good and guide to every success, and that this element of choice is the basis of juridical responsibility (*al-taklīf al-sharʿī*), through which [God's] wisdom and justice is made complete.

Indeed there used to be among the Muslims a sect known as *al-Jabrīyya*, which taught that the human being was compelled in all of his acts by a compulsion that was not tainted by choice. . . . However, the methodology of this sect is considered by [today's] Muslims to be of no more value than the corrupt disputations of the Sophists. The leaders of this school died out in the fourth century of the Hijra and no trace of them has remained. Therefore, the doctrine of compulsion (*jabr*) cannot be considered the source of the doctrine of destiny and fate (*al-qaḍāʾ wa al-qadar*) and there is no basis for this belief on the part of the conjecturers.

The doctrine of destiny is supported by a conclusive proof and in fact the concept of the instinct (*al-fiṭra*) alludes to this. It is easy for anyone who thinks to believe that every event has a cause that is near to it in time. However, one sees in the chain of causes only [the cause] that is present to him: no one knows the full past except the one who originated the pattern [in the first place]. Thus, in the unfolding of every chain of events there is a clear opening for the determination (*taqdīr*) of [God], the Glorious, the All-Knowing. As for what the human being wills (*irādat al-insān*), this is created, just like the created moments in the chain of causation. The act of will is nothing but an effect (*athar*) produced by the human understanding (*idrāk*), whereas the understanding is a product of the mind (*al-nafs*), according to what occurs to the senses and feelings and as a response of one's instinctive nature to the needs. Even a fool (not to mention an intelligent person) understands that the powers of thought and will are part of the apparent universe (*li-ẓawāhir al-kawn*); however, [the basis of the doctrine of destiny and fate] is that the causes that one sees outwardly are effects that occur by the hand of the greatest Governor of the Universe, who originates all things according to His wisdom but makes every apparent event correspond to it as if it were independent of it, especially in the world of human [perception]. . . .

If belief in destiny and fate were separated from the inappropriate notion of compulsion the attributes of audacity and daring and the birth of courage and fortitude would follow from it, and it would lead to an upwelling of the ferocity that throbs in the hearts of lions and causes leopards to cringe in terror. It would imbue the mind with a constancy that would cause one to bear odious burdens, struggle against one's fears, and adorn the soul with generosity and liberality. It would call upon the soul to leave aside all that is dear to it; indeed, it would even charge [the soul] with the expenditure of life and to forsake the pleasures of existence! All of this is for the sake of the Truth, which calls on the mind to believe in this doctrine. . . .

God has brought exaltation to the Muslims with belief [in the doctrine of destiny and fate]. . . . The Muslims burst forth in the years of their early development to conquer and subjugate kingdoms and territories, such that minds were confounded and experts were amazed at how they conquered so many states and overpowered so many nations. Their rule spread from the Pyrenees that separate Spain and France to the Great Wall of China, despite their small numbers and lack of familiarity with different climes or variations in geography. They brought kings under their sway and brought low the Caesars and the Khusrows [of Persia] in a period of less than 80 years. Surely this must be counted among the greatest of all paranormal events and miracles! . . .

Therefore, it is our hope that the foremost scholars of the age will expend their efforts in purifying this noble doctrine from the traces of alteration (*al-bidʿ*) that have befallen it. [We hope] that they will remind the public of the precedents (*sunan*) and actions of the Righteous Predecessors (*al-Salaf al-Ṣāliḥ*) and that they will disseminate among them confirmatory [teachings] by our Imāms (may God be pleased with them), such as Shaykh al-Ghazālī and his like, to the following effect: The Divine Law (*al-sharʿ*) asks us to practice trust in God and reliance on destiny through our actions, not through idleness or laziness.[1]

From *The Theology of Unity*

[The Qurʾān forbids slavish credulity]

We must, however, believe that the Islamic religion is a religion of unity throughout. It is not a religion of conflicting principles but is built squarely on reason, while Divine revelation is its surest pillar. Whatever is other than these must be understood as contentious and inspired by Satan or political passions. The Qurʾān has cognisance of every man's deed and judges the true and the false.

The purpose of this discipline, theology, is the realisation of an obligation about which there is no dispute, namely, to know God most high in His attributes that are necessarily to be predicated of Him and to know His exaltation above all improper and impossible attribution. It is, with Him, to acknowledge His messengers with full assurance and heart-confidence, relying therein upon proof and not taking things merely upon tradition. So the Qurʾān directs us, enjoining rational procedure and intellectual enquiry into the manifestations of the universe, and, as far as may be, into its particulars, so as to come by certainty in respect of the things to which it guides. It forbids us to be slavishly credulous and for our stimulus points the moral of peoples who simply followed their fathers with complacent satisfaction and were finally involved in an utter collapse of their beliefs and their own disappearance as a community. Well is it said that traditionalism can have evil consequences as well as good and may occasion loss as well as conduce to gain. It is a deceptive thing, and though it may be pardoned in an animal is scarcely seemly in man.[2]

[Islam will have no truck with traditionalism]

Islam will have no truck with traditionalism, against which it campaigns relentlessly, to break its power over men's minds and eradicate its deep-seated influence. The underlying bases of *taqlīd* in the beliefs of the nations have been shattered by Islam.

In the same cause, it has alerted and aroused the powers of reason, out of long sleep. For whenever the rays of truth had penetrated, the temple custodians intervened with their jealous forebodings. "Sleep on, the night is pitch dark; the way is rough and the goal distant, and rest is scant and there's poor provision for the road."

Islam raised its voice against these unworthy whisperings and boldly declared that man was not created to be led by a bridle. He was endowed with intelligence to take his guidance with knowledge and to con the signs and tokens in the universe and in events. The proper role of teachers is to alert and to guide, directing men into the paths of study.

The friends of truth are those "who listen to what is said and follow its better way" (Surah 39:18) as the Qur'ān has it. It characterizes them as those who weigh all that is said, irrespective of who the speakers are, in order to follow what they know to be good and reject what gives evidence of having neither validity nor use. Islam threw its weight against the religious authorities, bringing them down from the dominance whence they uttered their commands and prohibitions. It made them answerable to those they dominated, so that these could keep an eye on them and scrutinize their claims, according to their own judgement and lights, thus reaching conclusions based on conviction, not on conjecture and delusion.

Further, Islam encouraged men to move away from their own clinging attachment to the world of their fathers and their legacies, indicting as stupid and foolish the attitude that always wants to know what the precedents say. Mere priority in time, it insisted, is not one of the signs of perceptive knowledge, nor yet of superior intelligence and capacity. Ancestor and descendant compare closely no doubt in discrimination and endowment of mind. But the latter has the advantage over his forebears in that he knows events gone by and is in a position to study and exploit their consequences as the former was not. . . .

Islam reproves the slavish imitation of the ancestors that characterizes the leaders of the religions, with their instinct to hold timidly to tradition-sanctioned ways, saying, as they do: "Nay! We will follow what we found our fathers doing" (Surah 31:21) and "We found our fathers so as a people and we will stay the same as they" (Surah 43:22).

So the authority of reason was liberated from all that held it bound and from every kind of *taqlīd* enslaving it, and thus restored to its proper dignity, to do its proper work in judgement and wisdom, always in humble submission to God alone and in conformity to His sacred law. Within its bounds there are no limits to its activity and no end to the researches it may pursue.

Hereby, and from all the foregoing, man entered fully into two great possessions relating to religion, which had for too long been denied him, namely independence of will and independence of thought and opinion. By these his humanity was perfected. By these he was put in the way of attaining that happiness which God had prepared for him in the gift of mind. A certain western philosopher of the recent past has said that the growth of civilization in Europe rested on these two principles. People were not roused to action, nor minds to vigour and speculation until a large number of them came to know their right to exercise choice and to seek out facts with their own minds. Such assurance only came to them in the sixteenth century AD—a fact which the same writer traces to the influence of Islamic culture and the scholarship of Muslim peoples in that century.[3]

[Islam's influence on the West]

From that time on [i.e., after the Crusades], there began to be much more traffic in ideas. In the west the desire for knowledge intensified and concern grew to break the entail of obscurantism. A strong resolve was generated to curb the authority of religious leaders and keep them from exceeding the proper precepts of religion and corrupting its valid meanings. It was not long after that a party made its appearance in the west calling for reform and a return to the simplicities of the faith—a reformation which included elements by no means unlike Islam. Indeed, some of the reforming groups brought their doctrines to a point closely in line with the dogma of Islam, with the exception of belief in the prophetic mission of Muhammad. Their religion was in all but name the religion of Muhammad; it differed only in the shape of worship, not in meaning or anything else.

Then it was that the nations of Europe began to throw off their bondage and reform their condition, re-ordering the affairs of their life in a manner akin to the message of Islam, though oblivious of who their real guide and leader was. So were enunciated the fundamental principles of modern civilization in which subsequent generations as compared with the peoples of earlier days have found their pride and glory.

All this was like a copious dew falling on the welcoming earth, which stirs and brings forth a glad growth of every kind. Those who had come for strife, stayed to benefit and returned to benefit others in turn. Their rulers thought that in stirring up their peoples they would find an outlet for their rancour and secure their own power. Instead they were shown up for what they were and their authority foundered. What we have shown about the nature of Islam, well enough known to every thoughtful student, is acknowledged by many scholars in western countries and they know its validity and confess that Islam has been the greatest of their mentors in attaining their present position. "God's is the final issue of all things" (Surah 22:41).[4]

[The present state of Islam]

It is said by some that if Islam truly came to call diverse peoples into one common unity . . . how does it come about that the Islamic community has been sundered into sectarian movements and broken up into groups and schools? . . .

If it was the first religion to address the rational mind, summoning it to look into the whole material universe, giving it free rein to range at will through all its secrets, saving only therein the maintenance of the faith, how is it that Muslims are content with so little and many indeed have closed and barred the door of knowledge altogether, supposing thereby that God is pleased with ignorance and a neglect of study of His marvellous handiwork? . . .

If Islam welcomes and invites enquiry into its contents, why is the Qurʾān not read except by chanting and even the majority of the educated men of religion only know it very approximately?

If Islam granted to reason and will the honour of independence, how is it that it has bound them with such chains? If it has established the principles of justice, why are the greater part of its rulers such models of tyranny? If religion eagerly anticipates the liberation of slaves, why have Muslims spent centuries enslaving the free? . . .

Those Muslims who stand on the threshold of science see their faith as a kind of old garment in which it is embarrassing to appear among men, while those who deceive themselves that they have some pretension to be religious and orthodox believers in its doctrines regard reason as a devil and science as supposition. Can we not, in the light of all this, call God, His angels and all men to witness that science and reason have no accord with this religion? . . .

All that the objection just elaborated leads to is this: a physician treated a sick man with medicine and he recovered: then the doctor himself succumbed to the disease he had been treating. In dire straits from pain and with the medicine by him in the house, he has yet no will to use it. Many of those who come to visit him or seek his ministrations or even gloat over his illness could take up the medicine and be cured, while he himself despairs of life and waits either for death or some miraculous healing.[5]

From *Tafsīr al-Manār* (Commentary on the Qur'ān)

[On Polygamy]

The following passages are taken from ʿAbduh's commentary on Qur'ān 4:3. He refers also to part of 4:129. Muhammad Abdel Haleem's translation of these Qur'ānic texts is as follows:

> "If you fear that you will not deal fairly with orphan girls, you may marry whichever [other] women seem good to you, two, three, or four. If you fear that you cannot be equitable [to them], then marry only one, or your slave(s): that is more likely to make you avoid bias." (4:3)
>
> "You will never be able to treat your wives with equal fairness, however much you may desire to do so." (4:129)

One who carefully considers these two verses [4:3 and 4:129] will understand that the permissibility of polygamy in Islam is a command that is severely restricted in scope, for it is a necessity that is based on needs whose fulfilment depends on the requirement of complete certainty in justice and security from injustice. When a person of understanding carefully considers the restriction on polygamy in this age of corruption, he will become firmly convinced that it is not possible to develop a society (*umma*) if polygamy is allowed to proliferate. This is because a house with two wives and one husband will enjoy neither peace nor order. . . .

In early Islamic times, the practice of polygamy had its benefits, the most important of which was [the development of] genealogical ties and relationships, which strengthened the solidarity of kinship (*ʿaṣabīyya*). This practice did not cause the harm then that it does now because religion was firmly established in the spirits of women and men and the enmity of a junior wife (*ḍarra*) was only against another junior wife. Today, however, ill feelings are transferred from the junior wife to her son, then to his father, and then to all of his relatives. . . . Were women to be educated with sound religious instruction, such that religion would be the supreme ruler over their hearts and would cause them to overcome their jealousy, then the practice of polygamy would be of no harm to society, for the harm of it would be limited for the most part to women alone. However, based on what we have seen and heard [in cases brought before the courts], there is no way to develop a society in which polygamy prevails. . . . When something develops into a source of corruption at a particular moment in time but has not done so before, there is no doubt about the requirement to change the ruling in conformity with the present state of affairs. What I mean is that the maxim of prevention of harm gives legal preference to public interest (*qāʿidat darʾ al-mafāsid muqaddamun ʿalā al-maṣāliḥ*). Thus, one knows for certain that out of fear of injustice, polygamy should be forbidden.[6]

Notes

1. Muḥammad ʿAbduh and Jamāl al-Dīn al-Afghānī, *al-ʿUrwa al-wuthqā* no. 7 (Beirut: Dār al-Kitāb al-ʿArabī, 1980), 89–98. This work was first published in Arabic in 1884. Translation by Vincent J. Cornell.

2. Muḥammad ʿAbduh, *The Theology of Unity*, translated from the Arabic [*Risālat al-tawḥīd*] by Isḥāq Musaʿad and Kenneth Cragg (London: George Allen & Unwin, 1966), 39–40. This work was first published in Arabic in 1897.

3. Ibid., 126–28.

4. Ibid., 149–50.

5. Ibid., 151–54.

6. Muḥammad ʿAbduh and Muḥammad Rashīd Riḍā, *Tafsīr al-Manār*, vol. 4 (Beirut: Dār al-Fikr, n.d.), 249–50. After ʿAbduh's death in 1905 his disciple Riḍā continued work on *Tafsīr al-Manār*, which was published in twelve volumes in 1927. Translation by Vincent J. Cornell.

Muḥammad ʿAbduh

A Sufi-Inspired Modernist?

VINCENT J. CORNELL

CHRONOLOGICALLY THE EARLIEST of the Muslim reformers to be discussed in this volume, Muḥammad ʿAbduh is the most ambiguous in terms of understanding the full extent of his legacy in the century since his death. With the possible exception of his teacher and political mentor Jamāl al-Dīn al-Afghānī (1838–97), he is arguably the most overinterpreted figure in modern Islamic thought. Indeed, it may be useful to think of ʿAbduh as the "Illustrated Man" of contemporary Sunnī Islam. Much as with the figure that is the frame device for Ray Bradbury's classic work of science fiction,[1] the stories that are told about ʿAbduh's theological, political, and juridical views vary significantly according to what different observers have inscribed on his body of work and even on his faith. These portrayals of ʿAbduh's motives and identity have ranged from Wilfrid Blunt's (1840–1922) acerbic comment, "I fear that he has as little faith in Islam . . . as I have in the Catholic Church," to Aziz al-Azmeh's view that he was one of the founders of modern Islamism and hence a forerunner of Sayyid Quṭb (1906–66).[2] To obscure the picture even further, in studies of Islamic reform he is almost always discussed along with his mentor al-Afghānī, such that the nominative pair "Afghānī–ʿAbduh" is nearly as ubiquitous as the pair "Muḥammad–ʿAlī." In fact, many scholars assume that Afghānī's and ʿAbduh's views were virtually identical.[3] Paradoxically, for a person whose name is so well known, there is still little clarity about his actual beliefs. An important, albeit embarrassing, reason for such misunderstanding is that few contemporary students of Islamic reform have taken the time to study the full range of ʿAbduh's writings in Arabic, which are extensive but stylistically difficult.[4]

Because of the problematical nature of ʿAbduh's legacy, a comprehensive introduction to his writings and ideas is beyond the scope of this short essay.

Therefore, in what follows I will concentrate on just one example of how his reformist theology affected his approach to the traditions of premodern Islam. This is his relationship with Sufism and related forms of Islamic mysticism. ʿAbduh's treatment of Sufism opens a new window onto how we might view the concept of "the modern" in Islam and helps clarify his rationalistic approach to Islamic theology, particularly the schools of the Muʿtazila and the Ashʿarīs.[5]

Most biographical studies of Muḥammad ʿAbduh divide his career into four major phases: (1) an "educational phase," which begins with his initial studies in Tanta starting in 1866 and culminates in his graduation from al-Azhar as an authorized scholar (*ʿālim*) in 1877; (2) a "nationalist phase," which begins when he joins the circle of students around Jamāl al-Dīn al-Afghānī in 1871, continues through his tenure as editor of the political journal *al-Waqāʿī al-Miṣrīyya* ("Egyptian Events") from 1880–82, and ends with his support of the ʿUrābī Revolt that led to the British occupation of Egypt in 1882; (3) a "Salafīyya phase," which begins with his exile with Afghānī in Paris where the two edited and published *al-ʿUrwa al-wuthqā* ("The Unbreakable Bond," 1884). This phase ends after his breakup with Afghānī and relocation to Beirut, where in 1885 he gave the lectures that formed the basis of his most famous work, *Risālat al-tawḥīd* ("The Theology of Unity," first published in 1897); and (4) a "reformist phase," which centers on his tenure as Muftī of Egypt from 1899 until his death in 1905 but also includes his involvement in the reform of Egyptian education, including his efforts to reform the al-Azhar curriculum, which began soon after his return to his native country in 1888.

While this division of ʿAbduh's complex career into four phases is useful as a sort of intellectual shorthand, it should not be forgotten that it is artificial. For example, the nationalist phase of his life never really ended: ʿAbduh was always an Egyptian nationalist, even when he advocated pan-Islamism under the tutelage of Afghānī. Similarly, his reformist phase can be traced as far back as his adolescence and even before he met Afghānī. Throughout his life he objected to the religious instruction that he received in Tanta and later at al-Azhar, whose scholars resisted even such basic reforms as standardized curricula and proctored exams. Although he liked to dress as an Azharī scholar, ʿAbduh was always ambivalent about his al-Azhar education. In the latter part of his life, during a debate about modernizing the al-Azhar curriculum, a conservative Azharī *shaykh* once admonished him not to forget that he too was a graduate of al-Azhar. To this ʿAbduh replied, "If I have a portion of true knowledge as you mention, I got it from ten years of sweeping the dirt of Azharī knowledge from my brain and to this day it is not as clean as it should be."[6] ʿAbduh's ambivalence about al-Azhar is just one of many contradictions encountered in a thorough study of his beliefs and career.

It should also be noted that when one refers to the "Salafīyya" aspect of ʿAbduh's Islamic reformism, this does not mean that he had much in common with the Muslim fundamentalists who call themselves *al-Salafīyya* today. This latter movement can be dated roughly to the year 1960 and coincides with the founding of the Muslim World League, which brought together major figures of the Wahhābī sect of Saudi Arabia and political refugees of the Muslim Brotherhood in a marriage of convenience to disseminate Salafī ideas around the globe. The connection between the "old" and "new" versions of the Salafīyya was first established by Muḥammad Rashīd Riḍā (1865–1935), ʿAbduh's Syrian disciple and editor of the journal *al-Manār* ("The Lighthouse"). Unlike ʿAbduh, Riḍā approved of the Wahhābī movement because it was based on the traditionalist epistemology of Ḥanbalism, which for Riḍā best embodied the outlook of primordial Islam. Similar views were held by Ḥasan al-Bannāʾ (1906–49), the founder of the Muslim Brotherhood, who often visited Riḍā's Salafīyya bookstore in Cairo. In his biography of ʿAbduh (1931), Riḍā portrays himself as ʿAbduh's successor and depicts his mentor's teachings as in agreement with his view of Salafism. This depiction, which was reinforced further by the publication of ʿAbduh's and Riḍā's Qurʾān commentaries together in *Tafsīr al-Manār*, has led to a number of "Six Degrees of Separation" genealogies by contemporary historians and political scientists. These scholars, such as Aziz al Azmeh, seek to link the Salafīyya of Afghānī and ʿAbduh to today's Salafīs, who in fact would be the last to view themselves as the heirs to reformers that they reject as Westernizers and heretics.

Virtually all studies of Muḥammad ʿAbduh describe him as a modernist. Although this description is largely correct, few writers have attempted to define exactly what "modernist" is supposed to mean in this context, either treating the concept as self-evident or portraying ʿAbduh as a surrogate for European ideas. For example, in his classic study *Arabic Thought in the Liberal Age*, Albert Hourani observes that after ʿAbduh's graduation from al-Azhar he taught at the modern college of Dār al-ʿUlūm (House of Sciences) and that his courses included such works as Ibn Khaldūn's *Muqaddima* (introduction to his General History) and an Arabic translation of François Guizot's *Histoire de la Civilisation en Europe* (1828). According to Hourani, ʿAbduh's use of these works meant that he was interested in the rise and fall of civilizations, which somehow prefigured his interest in the social evolutionary theories of Herbert Spencer (1820–1903).[7]

Unsubstantiated conclusions such as these merely perpetuate the suspicion, first voiced by ʿAbduh's al-Azhar professor Shaykh Muḥammad ʿIllīsh (d. 1882) and still held by today's Salafīs, that ʿAbduh's Islamic modernism was no more than a Westernized bastardization of authentic Islam.[8] However, since the trope of the rise and fall of civilizations also appears in the Qurʾān, this by itself should not be taken as evidence of ʿAbduh's lack of Islamic authenticity. The common practice of depicting ʿAbduh as a modern humanist who tried to introduce secularizing principles into Islamic thought misinterprets his actual intentions. Far from accepting the West at face value, interrogating the moral and epistemological premises of secular modernity was a major feature of ʿAbduh's reform project. Furthermore, he was highly critical of Sayyid Aḥmad Khān (1817–98) and others who were less skeptical of the West than he was. In her recent study of ʿAbduh's Islamic reformism, Samira Haj observes, "Delineating the boundaries of secularism and determining how far religion can be extricated from the domains of polity and economy without dismantling its authority altogether was a crucial issue for ʿAbduh and continues to be a crucial issue for contemporary Islamists."[9] In other words, although it is correct to say that ʿAbduh saw the principles of Islam as quintessentially modern, he also sought to prove that Islam's modernity was both non-Western and nonsecular.

ʿAbduh's attempt to find the roots of modernity in the traditions of classical Islam can be discerned in one of the least discussed aspects of his thought, his treatment of Sufism and other forms of Islamic mysticism.[10] During the latter period of his studies in Tanta and in his first years at al-Azhar, the most important influence on ʿAbduh's life was his uncle, Shaykh Darwīsh. Darwīsh was the regional head of al-Ṭarīqa al-Shādhilīyya al-Madanīyya, a reformist Sufi order that was founded by Muḥammad ibn Ḥasan al-Madanī in the early nineteenth century. As his name indicates, al-Madanī was originally from Medina but studied under the Moroccan Shādhilī master Mūlāy al-ʿArabī al-Darqāwī (1760–1823). After nine years of study under Darqāwī he established the Madanīyya Sufi order in the region of Tripoli, Libya.[11] Madanīyya Sufism was a scholarly and intellectual movement that was critical of popular religion.[12] It argued for a closer adherence to the foundational principles of Islam as taught by *al-Salaf al-Ṣāliḥ* ("the righteous predecessors"), the companions of the Prophet Muḥammad and the first two generations of their successors. The Madanīyya also stressed the importance of autonomous moral choice and required its followers to give equal attention to the doctrines and practices of Islam while eschewing *taqlīd*, blind imitation of customary practices or legal rulings.

Although most biographers have assumed that ʿAbduh learned these reformist principles from Afghānī, in fact what later came to be called "Salafī Islam" was not confined to just Wahhābī fundamentalists and Islamic modernists: Salafī principles had also been fundamental to reformist Sufism for centuries.[13] An important aspect of this doctrine was the notion of autonomous subjectivity, which has long been considered one of the hallmarks of modernity, appearing most famously in the moral philosophy of Immanuel Kant (1724–1804).[14] Thus, it is not unreasonable to suggest that ʿAbduh was in some ways a Salafī Muslim and a Muslim modernist even before he met Jamāl al-Dīn al-Afghānī and that the seeds of both his Salafism and his modernism could be found in the reformist Sufism that he learned from his uncle.

ʿAbduh continued his Sufi practices after entering al-Azhar in 1866, and continued fasting and reciting the litanies of the Madanīyya until 1871, when his uncle warned him that he was becoming too withdrawn and antisocial. Significantly, this directive to come back to the world was given to ʿAbduh just before he became a disciple of Jamāl al-Dīn al-Afghānī. For all intents and purposes, Afghānī replaced Shaykh Darwīsh as a spiritual father and mentor for ʿAbduh. This aspect of their relationship was proven in 1963, when the University of Tehran published a collection of Afghānī's personal papers, including a letter from ʿAbduh.[15] It seems that as a token of gratitude to Afghānī, ʿAbduh replaced the doctrines and practices of Madanīyya Sufism with Shīʿī theosophy (*ʿirfān*) and the mystical philosophy of Abū ʿAlī ibn Sīnā (Avicenna, d. 1036), subjects that were important to the Shaikhi sect of Shīʿism to which Afghānī belonged.[16]

ʿAbduh's first major treatise, *Risālat al-wāridāt fī sirr al-tajallīyāt* (Treatise on Mystical Inspirations in the Secret of Divine Manifestations), contains an amalgamation of Sufi ideas that he learned from his uncle and *ʿirfān* concepts that he learned from Afghānī. Originally written in 1874 but not published until 1925, some two decades after his death, this work has proved vexing to anti-Sufi Salafīs such as ʿAbduh's disciple and first editor, Rashīd Riḍā, and his second editor and biographer, Muḥammad ʿImāra. Both writers sought to preserve ʿAbduh's reputation as a rationalist reformer who was critical of Sufism.[17] In fact, ʿImāra excluded this work from the supposedly "complete" collection of ʿAbduh's writings that he published in 1972, on the grounds that it was actually written by Afghānī.[18] Riḍā was not able to resort to such subterfuge because ʿAbduh himself asked him to publish this work shortly before he died.[19] However, to minimize its effects Riḍā changed the title to *Risālat al-wāridāt fī naẓarīyat al-mutakallimīn wa al-ṣūfīyya fī al-falsafa al-ilāhīyya* (Treatise on Mystical Inspirations in the Debates between the Theologians and the Sufis on Metaphysical Philosophy). This gave the impression that the work was a collection of notes from Afghānī's lessons rather than an expression of ʿAbduh's own thinking.[20] According to Riḍā, ʿAbduh's interest in both Sufism and Shīʿī *ʿirfān* was nothing more than a youthful flirtation.

As a treatise on mystical theology, *Risālat al-wāridāt* relies heavily on the concept of the Oneness of Existence (*waḥdat al-wujūd*) associated with the Andalusian Sufi and theologian Muḥyīʾ al-Dīn ibn ʿArabī (d. 1240). It is also influenced by the Illuminationist (*ishrāqī*) mysticism of Shihāb al-Dīn al-Suhrawardī (d. 1191), and the metaphysics of the philosopher Ibn Sīnā and the Shīʿī theosophist Mullā Ṣadra (d. 1640). ʿAbduh's forward to the work describes

Jamāl al-Dīn al-Afghānī as the personification of the Perfect Man (*al-insān al-kāmil*) in a way that is consistent with the doctrines of the school of Ibn ʿArabī and of Shaikhi Shīʿism. Shaikhism, which was a doctrinal forerunner of Bābism and Bahaism, was considered heretical by the majority Imāmī Shīʿa of Iran. The "Fourth Pillar" of Shaikhi doctrine taught that there was always in the world a Perfect Man who could guide humanity in the absence of the Twelfth Imām. Shaikhism also taught that the Qurʾān mystically encompassed an infinite variety of meanings and was thus always open to new interpretations.[21]

Riḍā was partly correct in his dismissal of *Risālat al-wāridāt* because it clearly contains notions that ʿAbduh abandoned later in life. These include his view of Afghānī as the Perfect Man and his reliance on Wujūdī metaphysics instead of mainstream Sunnī theology or Kalām. However, the work also contains much that remained with ʿAbduh throughout his life, such as his reliance on Ibn Sīnā's proofs for God's existence and in particular the concept of the Necessarily Existent (*wājib al-wujūd*). This latter concept, along with Ibn Sīnā's three proofs for the existence of God (the proofs from necessity, causality, and ontology), appear prominently in ʿAbduh's most famous theological treatise, *Risālat al-tawḥīd* (The Theology of Unity).[22]

The clearest example of continuity between *Risālat al-wāridāt* and *Risālat al-tawḥīd* (as well as the theological articles that ʿAbduh published in the journal *al-ʿUrwa al-wuthqā*) is in his defense of Ashʿarī theology. This defense of Ashʿarism is also in general agreement with Sufi theology, which bases its notion of the miracles of saints (*kharq al-ʿāda*, literally, "ripping custom asunder") on Ashʿarī ontology. In the following passage from *Risālat al-wāridāt*, ʿAbduh distinguishes between God's actions and human actions by alluding to the Ashʿarī concept of *kasb*, "acquisition." He states: "There is no contradiction between [divine and human actions] in reality. God is acting, just as his servant is acting. His servant is acting, for the Lord is acting. Being in all its levels is thus free to choose."[23] In the article "Destiny and Fate" (*al-Qaḍā wa al-qadar*) in the political newspaper *al-ʿUrwa al-wuthqā*, ʿAbduh similarly equates the Ashʿarī concept of *kasb* with an "element of choice" (*juzʾ ikhtiyārī*) that preserves both divine voluntarism and human responsibility.[24] Because the human actor acquires free choice from God at the same time that God wills her actions, the individual retains moral responsibility for her acts and thus cannot claim to be coerced by predestination. The concept of choice (*ikhtiyār*), which is not part of classical Ashʿarism but is found in Imāmī Shīʿī theology, made it easier to avoid the trap of predestination by focusing increased attention on the human portion of the created act.

ʿAbduh's seemingly "anti-Sufi" actions while serving as mufti of Egypt, such as banning the works of Ibn ʿArabī, have led some observers to conclude (with considerable help from Rashīd Riḍā) that he ended his life as an opponent of

Sufism. However, on closer examination one finds that this was not the case and that he never repudiated all of the ideas that are to be found in *Risālat al-wāridāt.* Neither did he renounce his long association with the Madanīyya Sufi order. As a modern reformer, ʿAbduh's objections were not with mysticism per se but with certain aspects of popular religion that were associated with Egyptian Sufism but which, to his mind, were not essential to Sufi doctrine. These accretions of popular religion included belief in the miracles of saints. At the end of *Risālat al-tawḥīd* ʿAbduh confirms the possibility of saintly miracles, remarking that the idea "would not give rise to much controversy among intelligent thinking people."[25] However, at the same time he stresses that there is no obligation to believe in the miracles of saints and that all Muslims are free to deny "proofs" of miracles, even if they are confirmed by consensus.

To conclude, it is most accurate to say that ʿAbduh was a Salafī Sufi just as he was a Salafī reformer and that, contrary to most scholarly opinion, he was as much a traditionalist as he was a modernist. His approach to Sufism, like his approach to the traditions of Islam in general, was to focus on the essential and to set aside issues of secondary importance. Like many scholars before him, he was concerned lest the Muslim masses be confused by doctrines that they could not understand. In fact, this paternalistic attitude was the very reason he gave as a Muftī for banning the books of Ibn ʿArabī. Also like other scholars before him, he was concerned about the social effects of local customs and popular religion and felt that the application of reason through education would cure the lassitude and ignorance that prevented Muslims from taking their rightful place among the progressive peoples of the world. His uncle Shaykh Darwīsh and the reformist Sufis of the premodern period also shared the same goals. This suggests that many of the contradictions noted by contemporary scholars in ʿAbduh's combination of modernism and traditionalism were more apparent than real.

For Further Reflection

1. According to a recent study, ʿAbduh "attempted to address the problems of Egypt through Islam, creating in the process a certain synthesis of Islam and of modern thought, though that was modern in terms of the nineteenth century, not of the twentieth or twenty-first. The emphasis was more on the modern than on Islam, and the synthesis did not prove to be a lasting one."[26] Is this a fair assessment of ʿAbduh's project?
2. How does the author's discussion of ʿAbduh's approach to Sufism help us better understand ʿAbduh's attempts to relate Islam to the modern world?

3. How might a more thorough understanding of ʿAbduh's critical stance toward both Islamic tradition and Western modernity open new possibilities for an interreligious approach to these concepts?

Notes

1. Ray Bradbury, *The Illustrated Man* (New York: Doubleday, 1951).

2. For Blunt's statement, see Albert Hourani, *Arabic Thought in the Liberal Age, 1798–1939* (Cambridge: Cambridge University Press, 1983), 141; on the connection between ʿAbduh and Islamism, see Aziz Al-Azmeh, "Islamist Revivalism and Western Ideologies," History Workshop Journal 32 (Autumn 1991): 44–52.

3. For example, Malcolm H. Kerr, following the lead of ʿAbduh's disciple Muḥammad Rashīd Riḍā (1865–1935), states, "It is fruitless to try to separate the ideas of ʿAbduh from those of Jamāl al-Dīn in the articles of *al-ʿUrwa al-wuthqā*." According to Kerr, "ʿAbduh's function was to supply the [Arabic] language for his master's thought." However, Kerr also notes that the ideas expressed in the article "Destiny and Fate," excerpts from which are included in the present volume, "are substantially similar to those found in ʿAbduh's own *Risālat al-tawḥīd*, and in this instance there is no reason to abstain from associating ʿAbduh fully with them." Kerr, *Islamic Reform: The Political and Legal Theories of Muḥammad ʿAbduh and Rashīd Riḍā* (Berkeley: University of California Press; and London: Cambridge University Press, 1966), 113n19.

4. A purportedly definitive collection of ʿAbduh's works was published in the 1970s by Muḥammad ʿImāra. SeeʿImāra, *al-Aʿmāl al-kāmila li-l-Imām Muḥammad ʿAbduh*, 5 vols. (Beirut: al-Muʾassasa al-ʿarabīyya li-l-dirāsat wa al-nashr, 1972–74). However, despite its title, this work is not complete. As discussed in the following, ʿAbduh's first major treatise was excluded as inauthentic by ʿImāra because it contained mystical content and was heavily influenced by Sufism, *falsafa*, and Shīʿism. Many later treatments of ʿAbduh's oeuvre (including Malcom Kerr's) were also influenced by Rashīd Riḍā's self-serving biography, *Taʾrīkh al-Ustādh al-Imām al-Shaykh Muḥammad ʿAbduh*, 3 vols. (Cairo: Maṭbaʿat al-Manār, 1924–31).

5. See Mark Sedgwick, *Muhammad Abduh* (Oxford: One World, 2010) for a good and very readable survey of ʿAbduh's life and career.

6. Samira Haj, *Reconfiguring Islamic Tradition: Reform, Rationality, and Modernity* (Stanford, CA: Stanford University Press, 2009), 237n89.

7. Hourani, *Arabic Thought*, 132; Hourani, like many other Western scholars, saw Ibn Khaldūn (d. 1406) as ahead of his time because of his supposedly modern attempt to ground universal history in an explicit theoretical perspective.

8. The term "bastardization" is Samira Haj's. See *Reconfiguring Islamic Tradition*, 80.

9. Ibid., 68–69.

10. The best discussion to date of ʿAbduh's Sufism and mystical thought can be found in Oliver Scharbrodt, "The Salafiyya and Sufism: Muḥammad ʿAbduh and his *Risālat al-Wāridāt* (Treatise on Mystical Inspirations)," *Bulletin of the School of Oriental and African Studies* 70, no. 1 (2007): 89–115.

11. See Martin Lings, *A Sufi Saint of the Twentieth Century: Sheikh Aḥmad al-ʿAlawī, His Spiritual Heritage and Legacy* (Berkeley: University of California Press, 1973), 70–71; see

also R. S. O'Fahey, *Enigmatic Saint: Aḥmad ibn Idrīs and the Idrīsī Tradition* (Evanston, IL: Northwestern University Press, 1990), 71.

12. Sedgwick, *Muhammad Abduh*, 4–5.

13. For a discussion of what I have termed "the *salaf al-ṣāliḥ* paradigm" in reformist Sufism, see Vincent J. Cornell, *Realm of the Saint: Power and Authority in Moroccan Sufism* (Austin: University of Texas Press, 1998), 17–18. The second half of the book discusses the Jazūlīyya Sufi order, a major Moroccan Sufi–Salafī reformist movement of the fifteenth and sixteenth centuries.

14. For an excellent study of this concept as it culminates in Kant, see J. B. Schneewind, *The Invention of Autonomy: A History of Modern Moral Philosophy* (Cambridge: Cambridge University Press, 1998).

15. Scharbrodt, "Salafīyya and Sufism," 96; see also, I. Afshar and A. Mahdawī eds., *Majmūʿa-yi asānīd u madārīk chap nashūdā dār barāyi Sayyid Jamāl al-Dīn mashhūr ba Afghānī* (Tehran: University of Tehran, 1963).

16. On Afghānī's background in Shaikhi Shīʿism, see Nikki R. Keddie, *Sayyid Jamāl ad-Dīn "al-Afghānī": A Political Biography* (Berkeley: University of California Press, 1972), 19–21.

17. This negative attitude toward Sufism was also shared by B. Michel and M. Abdel Razik, the editors of the French edition and translation of ʿAbduh's *Risālat al-tawḥīd* (also published in 1925). Knowing nothing at the time of Afghānī's Shaikhi Shīʿism, they state in the introduction to this work that Afghānī led ʿAbduh into "a new world, which was no longer that of mystic dreams but that of realities." See Keddie, *Sayyid Jamāl ad-Dīn "al-Afghani,"* 88.

18. Scharbrodt, "Salafīyya and Sufism," 96.

19. Ibid., 112.

20. Ibid., 95.

21. Ibid., 98; Scharbrodt does not recognize the Shaikhi influence in these passages but sees them instead as a reflection of Ibn ʿArabī's teachings. On Shaikhi doctrines, see Keddi, *Sayyid Jamāl al-Dīn "al-Afghānī,"* 20–21. When Keddie was doing the research on her book and working through Afghānī's papers, she found texts that Afghānī had copied from the founder of Shaikhism, Shaykh Aḥmad Aḥsā'ī (1753–1826), and his successor, Ḥajjī Muḥammad Karīm Khān Qajar Kirmānī (1809–70).

22. Scharbrodt, "Salafīyya and Sufism," 99; see also, Muḥammad ʿAbduh, *The Theology of Unity*, trans. Isḥāq Musaʿad and Kenneth Cragg (1966; repr., Selangor, Malaysia: Islamic Book Trust, 2004), ch. 3, "The Principles of the Necessarily Existing," 45–52.

23. Scharbrodt, "Salafīyya and Sufism," 110; and Muḥammad ʿAbduh, *Risālat al-wāridāt* (Cairo: al-Manār, 1925), 21; Scharbrodt misinterprets the meaning of this passage. Instead of seeing it as an expression of the Ashʿarī theology of acquisition, he incorrectly sees it as an expression of Ibn ʿArabī's notion of *waḥdat al-wujūd* (oneness of existence). I have changed the text of Scharbrodt's translation slightly to improve its English syntax.

24. See Muḥammad ʿAbduh and Jamāl al-Dīn al-Afghānī, *al-ʿUrwa al-wuthqā* (Beirut: Dār al-Kitāb al-ʿArabī, 1980), no. 7, 89–98. The passage in question is included in this volume. Although Malcolm Kerr (*Islamic Reform*, 111) saw ʿAbduh's use of the term *kasb* as evidence of his Muʿtazilism, this is incorrect. In early Muʿtazilī usage *kasb* was closer in meaning to "moral desert" or even *karma* than it was to the theology of choice espoused by ʿAbduh. This theology is also somewhat comparable to the theology of will (*irāda*) espoused

by certain Andalusian mystics such as Ibn al-ʿArīf (d. 1141) and Ibn Sabʿīn (d. 1270). See Vincent J. Cornell, "The All-Comprehensive Circle (*al-Iḥāta*): Soul, Intellect, and the Oneness of Existence in the Doctrine of Ibn Sabʿīn," in *Sufism and Theology*, ed. Ayman Shihadeh (Edinburgh, UK: Edinburgh University Press, 2007), 41–42.

25. ʿAbduh, *Theology of Unity*, 158.

26. Sedgwick, *Muhammad Abduh*, 128.

Sayyid Abū l-Aʿlāʾ Mawdūdī (1903–79)

From *Our Message*

[Islam and secularism]

Three Fundamental Principles

Now I wish you further to understand clearly the principles of modern civilization which we desire to uproot and also the principles which we want to establish in their place.

Modern civilization on which revolves the whole present-day organisation of the world (intellectual, moral, cultural, political and economic) is, in reality, based on three fundamental principles which are:

1. Secularism, that is irreligiousness or worldliness;
2. Nationalism; and
3. Democracy.

Secularism

Of these the first principle "secularism" implies that the Divine guidance, the worship of God, and obedience to Him should be confined to the personal life of each individual and except for the small sphere of a person's private life, all the other affairs of this world should be settled purely from the worldly viewpoint according to our own wishes and expediency. In such matters it is out of question to think of what God may have commanded, what His guidance consists of and what the Divine books may lay down. This attitude owes its origin to the reaction that set in among Western peoples as a result of hatred of the man-made theology of Christian missionaries—a theology which had become a curse for them and which forged their shackles. Gradually, however, this attitude developed into an independent theory of life and then became the foundation-stone of modern civilization.

You must have quite often heard the utterance "Religion is a private affair between God and man." This brief sentence is in fact the creed of modern civilization. It implies that if a man's conscience bears witness to the fact that there is a God Who should be worshipped, he is welcome to do so in his individual and personal life. But God should have nothing to do with this world and its collective affairs. The system of life built upon the foundation of this creed seeks to free from the influence of God and religion all the relations between man and man and between man and this world. Culture, education, economics, law, parliament, politics, the administration of public affairs and international relations are all to be divested of this influence. Whatever is done in all these numerous aspects of life should be regulated by one's own whims and knowledge. It would be irrelevant, nay, wrong in principle and even a sign of the utmost ignorance, to say that God has prescribed certain principles and laid down some commandments for us for the regulation of such matters.[1]

Irreligiousness

Let us take first of all the irreligious or worldliness which is the first and foremost foundation-stone of this way of life. The theory that God and religion are concerned only with the individual life of a man is completely meaningless, having nothing to do with reason and argument. It is perfectly obvious that the relations of man and God cannot lie beyond either of two alternatives. Either God is the Creator of man and the world in which he lives, as well as being its Master and Sovereign, or He is not so. If He is neither the Creator nor the Master, nor again the Sovereign then it is entirely unnecessary to have even any private relations with Him. It is utterly absurd to worship a Being entirely unconcerned and having nothing to do with us. But if He is in reality our Creator, Master, and Sovereign, and so also of this universe, then it is equally meaningless that His jurisdiction should be limited to the private life of an individual and from the very point from which the contact of one person with another commences His jurisdiction should cease and come to an end.

If this limitation has been imposed by God Himself then there should be some authority for it; but if man assumed this independence himself and discarded God from his collective life, then this constitutes an open rebellion against his Creator, Master and Sovereign. And only a lunatic can claim to combine with this rebellious attitude the claim that he accepts God, His religion, guidance and directions in his individual life. There can be nothing more absurd than that each person should claim individually to be the servant and slave of God but when these separate individuals collectively form themselves into a society, they should cease to be servants of the Almighty God; that each component in a society should constitute God's servant but the composite whole of these parts should not be His servants. . . . So much for the intellectual side of this question. But when we look at it from the practical view-point the consequences are extremely serious. The fact of the matter is that whichever aspect of a man's life is divested of relationship with God, will be contacted by the Devil himself. Truly speaking, the private life of an individual is nothing but a mere name. Man is social being and his whole life is in fact collective and social. To start with, he is born as a result of the social contact of a mother and a father. On coming into this world he opens his eyes in a family and as soon as he comes of age he comes in contact with society, a brotherhood, a township, a nation, a cultural system, a social system, an economic system, and a political system. All these numerous contacts which bind him to others and the other people to him, on the rectitude of them all indeed depends the welfare and success of each individual and all the human beings as a whole. And it is God alone Who is capable of vouchsafing to a man stable, enduring, equitable, and correct principles, and to prescribe proper limits for the regulation of human contacts. Whenever a man acts independently of the Divine guidance, nothing is left of the permanent and firm principles of truth and justice. This is because after depriving himself of God's guidance no other source is left to seek guidance from, except man's own passions, imperfect knowledge, and experience. That is why in a society, based on the secular system, or irreligiousness, principles are made and unmade every now and then due to the shifting passions of the people. You can see how in every aspect of human relations have entered the evils of injustice, oppression, faithlessness, unbelief and lack of mutual confidence. Individual, class, tribal and racial selfishness has overshadowed all human affairs. . . . Hence irreligiousness or secularism implies nothing more than this: that whoever adopts it as his creed and attitude in life will reduce himself to an irresponsible and unbridled servant of his own self, be it an individual, a group, a country, a nation or a group of nations.[2]

Beware!

In so far as the Muslims are concerned I must say very clearly that modern secular national democracy is utterly against their faith and religion. If they bow to it and accept it they will be turning their backs on the Holy Quran. If they take part in its establishment and maintenance it will constitute an open rebellion against the Holy Prophet. And if they stand up to raise its standard they will only be raising the standard of revolt against their Lord God. The spirit of Islam, which you profess to believe and from which you derive the name Muslim, is in conflict with the spirit of this dirty and rotten system; its fundamental principles are at loggerheads with the fundamental principles of the other system; and every part of the one is opposed to every part of the other. Islam and this system cannot meet for compromise at any stage. Wherever system is on top or in vogue, Islam departs and is nowhere; and wherever Islam reigns supreme, this system can have no place. If you really believe in Islam, which is the message of the Holy Quran and the Holy Prophet, then it is your duty to oppose this national-secular-democracy. Wherever you may happen to be, you should struggle for the establishment in its place of Godworshipping caliphate of the masses.[3]

From *Human Rights in Islam*

Democracy in Islam

The above explanation of the term *khilāfa* also makes it abundantly clear that no individual or dynasty or class can be *khalīfa*, but that the authority of *khilāfa* is bestowed on the entire group of people, the community as a whole, which is ready to fulfill the conditions of representation after subscribing to the principles of *tawhīd* (Unity of God) and *risāla* (prophethood). Such a society carries the responsibility of the *khilāfa* as a whole and each one of its individuals shares the Divine *khilāfa*. This is the point where democracy begins in Islam. Every person in an Islamic society enjoys the rights and powers of the caliphate of God and in this respect all individuals are equal. No one takes precedence over another or can deprive anyone else of his rights and powers. The agency for running the affairs of the state will be formed with the will of these individuals, and the authority of the state will only be an extension of the powers of the individuals delegated to it. Their opinion will be decisive in the formation of the government which will be run with their advice and in accordance with their wishes.

Whoever gains their confidence will undertake the duty and obligations of the caliphate on their behalf: and when he loses this confidence he will have to step down. In this respect the political system of Islam is a perfect form of democracy—as perfect as a democracy can ever be. Of course what distinguishes Islamic democracy from Western democracy is that while the latter is based on the concept of popular sovereignty the former rests on the principle of popular *khilāfa*. In Western democracy, the people are sovereign, in Islam sovereignty is vested in God and the people are His caliphs or representatives. In the former the people make their own laws; in the latter they have to follow and obey the laws (*Sharīʿa*) given by God through His Prophet. In one the government undertakes to fulfill the will of the people; in the other the government and the people who form it have all to fulfill the purpose of God. In brief, Western democracy is a kind of absolute authority which exercises its powers in a free and uncontrolled manner whereas Islamic democracy is subservient to the

Divine law and exercises its authority in accordance with the injunctions of God and within the limits prescribed by him.[4]

Before I discuss the human rights in Islam I would like to explain a few points about two major approaches to the question of human rights: the Western and the Islamic. . . .

The Western Approach

The people in the west have the habit of attributing every good thing to themselves and try to prove that it is because of them that the world got this blessing, otherwise the world was steeped in ignorance and completely unaware of all these benefits. Now let us look at the question of human rights. It is very loudly and vociferously claimed that the world got the concept of basic human rights from the *Magna Carta* of Britain; though the *Magna Carta* itself came into existence six hundred years after the advent of Islam. But the truth of the matter is that until the seventeenth century no one even knew that the *Magna Carta* contained the principles of Trial by Jury, *Habeas Corpus*, and the Control of Parliament on the Right of Taxation. If the people who had drafted the *Magna Carta* were living today they would have been greatly surprised if they were told that their document also contained all these ideals and principles. They had no such intention, nor were they conscious of all these concepts which are now being attributed to them. As far as my knowledge goes the Westerners had no concept of human rights and civic rights before the seventeenth century. Even after the seventeenth century the philosophers and the thinkers on jurisprudence though presented these ideas [*sic*], the practical proof and demonstration of these concepts can only be found at the end of the eighteenth century in the proclamations and constitutions of America and France. After this there appeared a reference to the basic human rights in the constitutions of different countries. But more often the rights which were given on paper were not actually given to the people in real life. In the middle of the present century, the United Nations, which can now be more aptly and truly described as the Divided Nations, made a Declaration of Universal Human Rights, and passed a resolution against genocide and framed regulations to check it. But as you all know there is not a single resolution or regulation of the United Nations which can be enforced. They are just an expression of a pious hope.[5]

The Islamic Approach

The second point which I would like to clarify at the very outset is that when we speak of human rights in Islam we really mean that these rights have been granted by God; they have not been granted by any king or by any legislative assembly. The rights granted by the kings or the legislative assemblies can also be withdrawn in the same manner in which they are conferred. The same is the case with the rights accepted and recognised by the dictators. They can confer them when they please and withdraw them when they wish; and they can openly violate them when they like. But since in Islam human rights have been conferred by God, no legislative assembly in the world, or any government on earth has the right or authority to make any amendment or change in the rights conferred by God. No one has the right to abrogate them or withdraw them. Nor are they the basic human rights which are conferred on paper for the sake of show and exhibition and denied in actual life when the show is over. Nor are they like philosophical concepts which have no sanctions behind them.[6]

Freedom of Expression

Islam gives the right of freedom of thought and expression to all citizens of the Islamic State on the condition that it should be used for the propagation of virtue and truth and not for spreading evil and wickedness. This Islamic concept of freedom of expression is much superior to the concept prevalent in the West. Under no circumstances would Islam allow evil and wickedness to be propagated. It also does not give anybody the right to use abusive or offensive language in the name of criticism. The right to freedom of expression for the sake of propagating virtue and righteousness is not only a right in Islam but an obligation. One who tries to deny this right to his people is openly at war with God, the All-Powerful. And the same thing applies to the attempt to stop people from evil. Whether this evil is perpetrated by an individual or by a group of people or the government of one's own country, or the government of some other country; it is the right of a Muslim and it is also his obligation that he should warn and reprimand the evil-doer and try to stop him from doing it. Over and above, he should openly and publicly condemn it and show the course of righteousness which that individual, nation or government should adopt.[7]

From *Rights of Non Muslims in Islamic State*

Freedom of Expression

In an Islamic State, all non-Muslims will have the same freedom of conscience, of opinion, of expression (through words spoken and written) and of association as the one enjoyed by the Muslims themselves, subject to the same limitations as are imposed by law on the Muslims. Within those limitations they will be entitled to criticize the government and its officials, including the Head of the State.

They will also enjoy the same rights of criticizing Islam as the Muslims will have to criticize their religion.

They will likewise be fully entitled to propagate the good points of their religion, and if a non-Muslim is won over to another non-Islamic creed, there can be no objection to it. As regards Muslims, none of them will be allowed to change creed. In case any Muslim is inclined to do so, it will be he who will be taken to task for such a conduct, and not the non-Muslim individual or organization whose influence might have brought about this change of mind.

The *Zimmis* will never be compelled to adopt a belief contrary to their conscience, and it will be perfectly within their constitutional rights if they refuse to act against their conscience or creed, so long as they do not violate the law of the land.[8]

From *Towards Understanding the Qur'ān*

[Here Mawdūdī comments on Qur'ān 9:29, translated in the work cited as follows: "Those who do not believe in Allah and the Last Day—even though they were given the scriptures, and who do not hold as unlawful that which Allah and His Messenger have declared to be unlawful, and who do not follow the true religion—fight against them until they pay tribute out of their hand and are utterly subdued."]

The purpose for which the Muslims are required to fight is not as one might think to compel the unbelievers into embracing Islam. Rather, their purpose is to put an end to the sovereignty and supremacy of the unbelievers so that the latter are unable to rule over men. The authority to rule should only be vested in those who follow the true faith; unbelievers who do not follow this true faith should live in a state of subordination. Unbelievers are required to pay *jizyah* (poll tax) in lieu of the security provided to them as the *Dhimmis* ("Protected People") of an Islamic state. *Jizyah* symbolizes the submission of the unbelievers to the suzerainty of Islam. "To pay *jizyah* of their own hands humbled" refers to payment in a state of submission. "Humbled" also reinforces the idea that the believers, rather than the unbelievers, should be the rulers in performance of their duty as God's vicegerents. . . .

Some nineteenth-century Muslim writers and their followers in our own times never seem to tire of their apologies for *jizyah*. But God's religion does not require that apologetic explanations be made on its behalf. The simple fact is that according to Islam, non-Muslims have been granted the freedom to stay outside the Islamic fold and to cling to their false, man-made, ways if they so wish. They have, however, absolutely no right to seize the reins of power in any part of God's earth nor to direct the collective affairs of human beings according to their own misconceived doctrines. For if they are given such an opportunity, corruption and mischief will ensue. In such a situation the believers would be under an obligation to do their utmost to dislodge them from political power and to make them live in subservience to the Islamic way of life.[9]

From *Purdah and the Status of Woman in Islam*

When our so-called reformers saw with dazed eyes the European ladies in their full make-up moving freely and participating actively in social life, they could not help longing to see their own womenfolk also tread the same path of freedom and progress. They were also influenced by the modern concepts of the emancipation and education of women and the propaganda of the equality of the sexes that was incessantly being carried out by powerful logic and the printing machine. The literature thus produced was so attractive and powerful that it adversely affected their powers of thinking and discrimination. It forced them to believe in these concepts without question, and propagate them by all possible means. They were convinced that enforcing these concepts in the practical life was absolutely essential for one who liked to be called "enlightened and broad-minded" as against "rigid and old-fashioned." Therefore, when modestly dressed veiled women were dubbed "moving tents and shrouded funerals," these so-called reformers felt shamed into disgrace. Obviously, they could not put up with this disgrace and humiliation for a long time. They were, therefore, impelled to wash off this shameful blot from the face of their social life as soon as possible.

Such were the feelings and trends that gave birth to the movement for the emancipation of women among the Muslims towards the end of the 19th century.[10]

Now, any intelligent person can see how sadly mistaken are those people who, on the one hand, feel inclined to follow the Western civilization and, on the other, cite Islamic principles of social life in support of their trends. According to the Social System of Islam, a woman at the most can uncover her hands and face, if necessary, and can go out of her house for genuine needs. But these people take this last limit as their starting point. They set out from the point where Islam comes to halt, and transgress all limits of decency and modesty without hesitation. Not to speak of the hands and face, beautifully parted hair on the head, bare arms to the shoulders, and semi-covered breasts are also displayed. Rest of the bodily charms are so covered in gauzy attires as to satisfy the hungry sexual gaze of men. . . .

The limited and conditional freedom that women had been allowed by Islam in matters other than home science is being used as argument to encourage the Muslim women to abandon home life and its responsibilities like the European women and make their lives miserable by running after political, economic, social and other activities shoulder to shoulder with men. . . .

One wonders how people can seek justification for such a shameless way of life from the *Qur'an* and *Hadith*. If some people feel like adopting it, they should boldly do so and declare their desertion of Islam and its law unequivocally. This would indeed be the height of hypocrisy and dishonesty on their part if they openly adopted in the name of the Qur'an that system and way of life whose basic principles, objectives and practices have been condemned, one and all, as unlawful by the Qur'an. By citing the Qur'an at the outset they perhaps want to deceive the world into believing that they are following the Qur'an in their entire lives.[11]

Notes

1. Sayyid Abul Ala Maudoodi, *Our Message*, 4th ed. (Lahore: Islamic Publications, 1998), 16–18.
2. Ibid., 22–26.
3. Ibid., 39–40.
4. Abul Aʿla Mawdudi, *Human Rights in Islam*, 2nd ed. (Lahore: Islamic Publications, 1995), 6–7.
5. Ibid., 11–12.
6. Ibid., 12.
7. Ibid., 28.
8. Syed Abul ʿAla Maudoodi, *Rights of Non Muslims in Islamic State*, 7th ed. (Lahore: Islamic Publications, 1982), 29.
9. Sayyid Abul Aʿlā Mawdūdī, *Towards Understanding the Qur'ān*, Vol. III, *Surahs 7–9*, trans. and ed. Zafar Ishaq Ansari (Leicester: Islamic Foundation, 1990), 202.
10. Abul Aʿla Maududi, *Purdah and the Status of Woman in Islam* (Lahore: Islamic Publications, n.d.), 21–22.
11. Ibid., 23–24.

Mawdūdī and the Challenges of Modernity

ABDULLAH SAEED

ABŪ L-AʿLĀʾ MAWDŪDĪ (often referred to as Mawlānā Mawdūdī) was born in 1903 as the youngest of three sons. He lived with his family in Aurangabad, a well-known town in the former state of Hyderabad (Deccan, now known as Maharashtra), in India. His family was strongly religious and had a long tradition of spiritual leadership, with a number of Mawdūdī's ancestors serving as leaders of Sufi orders. Mawdūdī attended high school and began undergraduate studies, but these were interrupted by the death of his father. However he continued to educate himself with the help of various prominent scholars, and became—to a large extent—a self-taught man. As well as speaking Urdu (his native tongue), Mawdūdī became fluent in Arabic, Persian, and English.[1]

Mawdūdī's early career was in journalism: at age seventeen he became a correspondent, and then later editor, of the Urdu newspaper *Tāj* (in Jabalpur). He held a series of appointments in Muslim journals, publishing his views on Islam, the conflict between Islam and contemporary ideologies, and how Muslims should respond to modern challenges. Mawdūdī became involved in politics in the 1930s, responding to the political situation in India and the positions of its major parties, the Hindu-dominated Indian National Congress and the Muslim League, which sought to represent the views of the Muslim minority. He strongly criticized trends toward nationalism and believed that the solution to the problems faced by Indian Muslims was for each person to recognize Islam as providing their sole source of identity, and for the populace to become more devout Muslims. In 1941 Mawdūdī founded Jamāʿat-i Islāmī (the Islamic Society) so that he could train Muslims to become capable of establishing an "Islamic system" of government and society. The organization later became a major player in Pakistani national politics.

When the Indian subcontinent was partitioned in 1947, Mawdūdī moved with some of his followers to Pakistan, where he quickly took on an important political role as a principal advocate of an Islamic state. In this context he wrote extensively to explain different aspects of the Islamic way of life, especially the sociopolitical aspects. Mawdūdī is reported to have written more than 120 books, booklets, and pamphlets, and to have made more than 1,000 speeches and press statements (of which around 700 are publically available). He was a prolific writer and addressed many subjects and disciplines related to Islam, including *tafsīr* (Qur'ānic exegesis), ḥadīth, law, theology, and history. He discussed (and proposed what he considered to be Islamic solutions to) a wide variety of modern problems in the political, economic, social, and cultural spheres, and addressed numerous theological issues.

Mawdūdī died in September 1979 in Rochester, New York, while visiting his son and receiving medical treatment for a long-standing kidney ailment. He left behind an impressive legacy, including important scholarly contributions to *tafsīr*, Islamic ethics, social studies, and the problems facing Islamic revival. His multivolume commentary, *Towards Understanding the Qur'ān* (which is regarded as his greatest work) took thirty years to complete. It presents the meaning and message of the Qur'ān in a language and style that is accessible to men and women today and shows the relevance of the Qur'ān to their everyday problems. This work has had a far-reaching impact on contemporary Islamic thinking in the subcontinent, and (in translation) abroad. Mawdūdī is one of the most widely read Muslim thinkers of modern times and his books have been translated into many major languages of the world, including Arabic, Turkish, Persian, Hindi, Bengali, Tamil, Swahili, English, French, and German.

Some Muslims have directed criticism at Mawdūdī, highlighting that he was not formally trained in Islamic disciplines and was therefore not qualified to express many of the views on Islam which he published, and that he was wrong to emphasize the political dimension of Islam. He has also been widely blamed for the prevalence of anti-Western attitudes among Muslims.

Key Aspects of Mawdūdī's Thought as Reflected in the Selected Texts

Mawdūdī's worldview was based on the notion that God is Creator, Master, and Sovereign. He believed that God created humankind and that it is therefore the duty of human beings to live in accordance with God's guidance and decrees. To pursue independence from what God commanded or what the scriptures had laid down is, according to Mawdūdī, open rebellion against God. This fundamental idea influenced much of his thinking.

At a time of British colonial retreat, and with the rise of a national consciousness, Mawdūdī wrote to address the issues facing those in the minority Muslim community in India, who struggled to maintain their religious, political, and cultural identity. Mawdūdī saw the influence of Western colonialism as a serious threat to Muslim identity. He argued that Muslims should struggle to uproot the secularism, nationalism, and democracy promoted by the West because these ideas were, in his view, fundamentally opposed to Islam. Secularism, Mawdūdī believed, was nothing more than an attempt to free civilization from the influence of God because it implied that God should have nothing to do with this world and its collective affairs and instead should be confined to the personal life of individuals. Referring to those who argued that religion was a private affair between God and human beings, Mawdūdī countered that this "creed of modern civilization" was nothing short of open rebellion against God the Creator, Master, and Sovereign.[2]

In practical terms, Mawdūdī saw secularism as divesting people of their relationship with God, which ultimately, he predicted, would have devastating consequences for society at large. He argued that whenever a person acted independently of God's guidance, he or she set aside the divine principles of truth and justice, drawing instead upon personal "passions, imperfect knowledge and experience." For Mawdūdī, the end result of removing God from public and collective affairs and deferring to the "shifting passions of the people" would be "the evils of injustice, oppression, faithlessness, unbelief and lack of mutual confidence."[3]

Mawdūdī was also strongly critical of Western notions of democracy. As with secularism, he saw democracy as displacing God's authority in the world, placing sovereignty in the hands of the people, allowing them to make their own laws (as opposed to following God's laws), and allowing them to pursue their own purposes (as opposed to the purposes of God). For him, the danger in allowing the affairs of the state to be subject to the will of individuals was that this could result in the free and uncontrolled use of authority. In contrast to Western notions of democracy, Mawdūdī argued for what he believed to be the Islamic model of democracy based upon God's sovereignty and with authority vested in individuals as representatives of God (*khilāfa*). Mawdūdī argued that this Islamic model of democracy is far superior to the Western model because all members of society carry responsibility for the *khilāfa* as a whole and, as equals, enjoy the rights and powers of the *khilāfa*.[4]

Mawdūdī was also strongly critical of nationalism, describing it as "a dirty and rotten system" that is fundamentally in conflict with the spirit of Islam.[5] By accepting it, he asserted, Muslims were turning their back on the Holy Qur'ān, rebelling against the Prophet, and raising a standard of revolt against God; thus all genuine Muslims had the duty to oppose it.

Mawdūdī saw the "West" as a fundamental threat to Muslim influence and identity in India. His antagonism toward Western ideas and principles can be seen in his writings on human rights. Noting that "people in the West have the habit of attributing every good thing to themselves," he asserted that a framework for human rights was established by Islam long before Magna Carta in the thirteenth century, and certainly prior to the eighteenth century, when the concepts of human rights and civic rights were enshrined in some Western constitutions.[6] Moreover, he argued that although rights were affirmed in such instruments, they were not actually enjoyed by people at that time, or indeed subsequently, since, for example, the resolutions of the United Nations cannot be enforced. Islam, Mawdūdī argued, has set down a superior conception of human rights because these rights have been conferred by God and cannot be withdrawn, amended, or changed by any government or legislative assembly in the world.[7]

In his writings, Mawdūdī pursued the ideal of an Islamic state as one where God would be sovereign and Islamic identity preserved. In the Islamic state, citizenship would be based on membership of Islam. Non-Muslims within the Islamic state would live in a state of subordination to Muslim authority, as symbolized by the payment of a poll tax (*jizya*). They would not be allowed to exercise power in any way or to rule within the state in order to protect the Muslim community from the "corruption and mischief" that would ensue.[8] Non-Muslims would, however, be guaranteed certain rights within the state, including freedom of conscience, opinion, expression, and association, on a par with Muslims. They would be afforded the same rights to criticize Islam as Muslims would have to criticize their religion, and would be fully entitled to propagate the "good points of their religion." They would also be guaranteed freedom of religion: they would be free to convert to Islam if they should so choose but would not be compelled to convert contrary to their conscience. Muslims, on the other hand, were not to be allowed to change religion.[9]

Mawdūdī's writings on women also sought to protect Islamic identity from the influence of the West. He was strongly critical of Muslim reformers who had joined the movement for the emancipation of Muslim women toward the end of the nineteenth century. For Mawdūdī, Muslims who advocated equality between the sexes had been dazzled by Western women to the extent that their powers of thinking had been affected. In his eyes, those who followed such aspects of Western civilization and justified this by citing Islamic principles were "sadly mistaken" and had deserted Islam and its law. Mawdūdī elaborated that Islamic principles of social life allowed women limited and conditional freedom: for example, a woman should uncover—at most—her hands and face only if necessary, and should leave her house only for genuine needs. To extend such limits further was to "transgress all limits of decency and modesty without hesitation."[10]

Mawdūdī between Tradition and Modernity

In some senses, Mawdūdī was very traditionalist, as can be seen in many areas of his thinking. For example, he supported the strict segregation of the sexes, with women being restricted to an inferior role.[11] He also believed that cinema, the theater, and fine arts should be forbidden: "Islam does not approve of such pastimes, entertainments and recreations as they tend to stimulate sensual passions and vitiate the canons of morality."[12] Like the traditionalists, Mawdūdī emphasized the validity of traditional Islamic law for all times. On the subject of jihād he also wrote extensively, again from a purely traditionalist point of view.[13]

On the other hand, the traditionalist *ʿulamāʾ* often saw what they considered to be Mawdūdī's "modernism" as a source of contention. Many of the *ʿulamāʾ* who criticized Mawdūdī believed he was stripping Islam of its spirituality.[14] For example, thinkers such as Sufi Nazir Kashmiri identified Mawdūdī as having an affinity with the "atheist philosophers" of the present age and declared that accepting his teachings was "no less than apostasy."[15] However, Mawdūdī's own view was that he was using modern arguments to support Islamic conclusions in order to present Islam as a rational religion that was not outdated.[16]

According to Mawdūdī, Islam needed to be "rediscovered." He criticized the approach of the traditionalists, who blindly rejected all that was Western or invented by the West. For him, Islam was society in motion, and he argued that any attempts to arrest the process of motion would be damaging to the cause of Islam. He observed that there was a pressing need to rethink Islam in a modern context, and to make Islam relevant to the specific needs of the day.[17] Through his writings, Mawdūdī explained how this reformation could be brought about in various fields.[18]

Mawdūdī differed from the traditionalist *ʿulamāʾ* in that he acknowledged certain shortcomings of traditional Islamic law (*fiqh*) in meeting modern challenges: in particular, he highlighted its perceived inability to deal with the constitutional, international, and criminal legal spheres as separate disciplines. These, he suggested, could be modernized (to a certain extent) by the study and selective appreciation of the modern sciences of economics and finance, for example, and by the evolution of an Islamic law of evidence, penal code, and civil and criminal codes of procedure.[19]

Mawdūdī also diverged from the traditional perspective to a significant degree in his teachings on *dīn* and the Islamic state, and in his understanding of faith, the meaning of spirituality, and the nature of the relations between Islam and society. Underlying these differences with traditionalism was the fact that much in Mawdūdī's project to revitalize Islam came from his engagement with modern Western thought, and that many of his perspectives on religion and politics were formed in debate with Western sources.[20] "To debate effectively with 'modernity,' Mawdudi had to accept many modernist assumptions, especially those involving scientific truths, which he saw as value neutral."[21] In contrast to other revivalists, he sought to appropriate modern scientific thought and "Islamize" it rather than to accept it as the basis for interpreting Islam. To free Islam from its anachronistic existence he also advocated the adoption of modern social thought and organization. Mawdūdī's approach to modernization extended beyond adopting its technologies to encompassing its values, ideas, and institutions; the modern world thus provided "the path on which Muslims would be able to repeat the glories of the past."[22]

In attempting to rebut the "secular naturalists," Mawdūdī took on the structure of their arguments and their thinking.[23] For example, in *Towards Understanding Islam* (1940), Mawdūdī made an eloquent, logical, and persuasive case for Islamic orthodoxy, using modern skepticism and speculative detachment as his outlook and frame of reference. Mawdūdī argues here that even if Islamic truth were not available in the form of a revealed text, it would exist as a rational—even scientific—explanation for the mysteries of life.[24]

Politically, Mawdūdī and his followers went to great lengths to reassure their audience of the democratic nature of their concept of the Islamic state (a result of Mawdūdī's debate with Western political thought and involvement of the Jamāʿat in electoral politics in Pakistan) and to define the concept of the Islamic state as compatible with Western conceptions (in terms of liberalism in particular). His writings describe the prophetic model of the state in Western terms, eventually adopting terms such as "democratic caliphate" and "theodemocracy."[25]

The influence of Western modernity on Mawdūdī was also manifest in the new meanings he gave to words and practices, including: *dīn* (religion), *qawm* (nation), *ʿibādat* (worship), and *jamāʿat* (party). His idea of Islamic history bore the imprint of Hegelian and Marxist idioms, and his notions of an Islamic vanguard and party were both apparently modeled on Leninist principles.[26] He incorporated into his view of the Islamic state Western ideas of due process (and an apparatus to oversee it) and the codification and centralization of law.[27]

Thus, in the words of Seyyed Vali Reza Nasr, "Mawdudi's ideal Islamic order was far more tolerant of Western values, ideals, and institutions than his rejectionist rhetoric has suggested. This is an important aspect of Mawdudi's contribution to contemporary Islamic thought, because it sets him apart from those who wish simply to 'reform' Islam, and it sets the Jamaʿat apart from those forms of Islamic revivalism that pit Islam against modernization."[28] The synthesis between Islam and modernity present in Mawdūdī's thought on the Islamic state has helped to open up the structure of traditional Islamic thought and to initiate a debate with Western ideas.[29]

For Further Reflection

1. Mawdūdī stated that modern secular national democracy is utterly against the faith and religion of Muslims. Do you agree? Can democracy, secularism, and nationalism be compatible with Islam?
2. What are "human rights" according to Mawdūdī? Where do they stem from? According to Mawdūdī, how is the Islamic account of human rights superior to the accounts assumed by the various human rights instruments we have today?
3. What rights do non-Muslims have within an Islamic state as proposed by Mawdūdī? Can a non-Muslim be a full citizen of this "Islamic state"?
4. How did Mawdūdī view the liberties that he observed Western women had embraced? What was his understanding of a Muslim woman's role today?
5. What is the role of sociohistorical context in Mawdūdī's approach to the interpretation of the Qur'ān today?
6. To what extent was Mawdūdī influenced by the modernity that he appears to be consciously rejecting?

Notes

1. For more information on Mawdūdī's life and for discussion of his thought, see (among many other sources): Khurshid Ahmad and Zafar Ishaq Ansari, eds., *Islamic Perspectives: Studies in Honour of Mawlānā Sayyid Abul Aʿlā Mawdūdī* (Leicester: Islamic Foundation, 1979); Seyyed Vali Reza Nasr, *Mawdudi and the Making of Islamic Revivalism* (Oxford: Oxford University Press, 1996); Roy Jackson, *Mawlana Mawdudi and Political Islam: Authority and the Islamic State* (Abingdon, UK: Routledge, 2011); and Abdul Rashid Moten, "Islamic Thought in Contemporary Pakistan: The Legacy of ʿAllāma Mawdūdī," in *The Blackwell Companion to Contemporary Islamic Thought*, ed. Ibrahim M. Abu-Rabiʿ (Oxford: Blackwell, 2006), 175–94.

2. Sayyid Abul Ala Maudoodi, *Our Message*, 4th ed. (Lahore: Islamic Publications, 1998), 17.

3. Ibid., 25.

4. Abul Aʿla Mawdudi, *Human Rights in Islam*, 2nd ed. (Lahore: Islamic Publications, 1995), 6–7.

5. Maudoodi, *Our Message*, 39.

6. Mawdudi, *Human Rights in Islam*, 11.

7. Ibid., 12.

8. Sayyid Abul Aʿlā Mawdūdī, *Towards Understanding the Qurʾān*, Vol. III, *Surahs 7–9* (Leicester: Islamic Foundation, 1990), 202.

9. Syed Abul ʿAla Maudoodi, *Rights of Non-Muslims in Islamic State*, 7th ed. (Lahore: Islamic Publications, 1982), 29.

10. Syed Abul ʿAla Mawdudi, *Purdah and the Status of Woman in Islam* (Lahore: Islamic Publications, n.d.), 23.

11. Aziz Ahmad, "Mawdudi and Orthodox Fundamentalism in Pakistan," in *Middle East Journal*, 21 (1967): 373; and Mawdudi, *Towards Understanding Islam*, trans. K. Ahmad (Lahore: 1960), 182–3.

12. Ahmad, "Mawdudi and Orthodox Fundamentalism in Pakistan," 373.

13. Ibid., 372.

14. Humeira Iqtidar, *Secularizing Islamists? Jamaʿat-e-Islami and Jamaʿat-ud-Daʿwa in Urban Pakistan* (Chicago: University of Chicago Press, 2011), 53.

15. Irfan Ahmad, *Islamism and Democracy in India: The Transformation of Jamaat-e-Islami* (Princeton: Princeton University Press, 2009), 217.

16. Iqtidar, *Secularizing Islamists?*, 53.

17. Thameem Ushama and Noor Mohammad Osmani, "Sayyid Mawdudi's Contribution towards Islamic Revivalism," *IIUC Studies*, 3 (December 2006), 97; www.banglajol.info/index.php/IIUCS/article/viewFile/2668/2264, citing Masudul Hassan, *Sayyid Abul Aʿala Maududi and His Thought*, 1st ed. (Lahore: Islamic Publications Ltd., 1984), 2:500–502.

18. Ushama and Osmani, "Sayyid Mawdudi's Contribution towards Islamic Revivalism," 97.

19. Ahmad, "Mawdudi and Orthodox Fundamentalism in Pakistan," 377.

20. Nasr, *Mawdudi and the Making of Islamic Revivalism*, 33, 108.

21. Ibid., 50, citing Peter van der Veer, *Religious Nationalism: Hindus and Muslims in India* (Berkeley: 1994), 133–34.

22. Nasr, *Mawdudi and the Making of Islamic Revivalism*, 50–51.

23. Iqtidar, *Secularizing Islamists?* 53.

24. Jonah Blank, "Modernity and Islamic Fundamentalism," in *Mullahs on the Mainframe* (Chicago: University of Chicago Press, 2001). Excerpt available at www.press.uchicago.edu/Misc/Chicago/056767.html.

25. Nasr, *Mawdudi and the Making of Islamic Revivalism*, 84, 88.

26. Ahmad, *Islamism and Democracy in India*, 218.

27. Nasr, *Mawdudi and the Making of Islamic Revivalism*, 102.

28. Ibid., 52.

29. Ibid., 102.

Lesslie Newbigin (1909–98)

Tradition and History

THE CHRISTIAN MISSION is the clue to world history, not in the sense that it is the "winning side" in the battle with the other forces of human history, but in the sense that it is the point at which the meaning of history is understood and at which men are required to make the final decisions about that meaning. It is, so to say, not the motor but the blade, not the driving force but the cutting edge. Christians do not go through the battles of history as the master race. They go through them as the servant people, looking up to the Father who is alone the Lord of history, accepting his disposition of events as the context of their obedience, relying on his Spirit as their guide.[1]

The Bible speaks of acts of God in history. It is, in its main outline, a continuous record of such acts. In the Old Testament the central act is the deliverance of Israel from slavery to the tyranny of Egypt at the crossing of the Red Sea; in the New Testament the central act is the raising of Jesus from the dead. But these are the climactic acts in a story in which God's mighty power is seen at work throughout the whole history of the chosen people.

This way of speaking has always been totally unacceptable to the main tradition of pagan philosophy. Stories told to illustrate timeless truths about the nature of the world and the duty of man have always been acceptable. But the idea of a God who somehow reaches out his hand to intervene here or there in the affairs of the world has been held by the majority of philosophers to be an impossible anthropomorphism. The famous word of Pascal, found sewed up in his jacket after his death, tersely expresses the contrast I am making: "Fire! Not the god of the philosophers! The God of Abraham, the God of Isaac, the God of Jacob." No one who reads the Bible as a whole with any attention can doubt that this is the fire which burns at its heart: the belief in a God who acts and who is therefore related in a special way to certain names and certain events. And no one can read what is being written in our time to interpret the Gospel to modern secularized man without noting that at this point the writers are generally on the side of the philosophers rather than of Pascal.[2]

The concept of *missio Dei* has sometimes been interpreted so as to suggest that action for justice and peace as the possibilities are discerned within a given historical situation *is* the fulfillment of God's mission, and that the questions of baptism and church membership are marginal or irrelevant. That way leads very quickly to disillusion and often to cynical despair. No human project however splendid is free from the corrupting power of sin. To invest one's ultimate commitment in such proximate goals is to end in despair. The history of the Church furnishes plenty of illustrations of the point I am making. At various times and places loyalty to the Church has been identified as invoking the defense of feudalism against capitalism, the defense of aristocracy against democracy, the defense of the free market against Marxism, and the support of movements of liberation based on a Marxist analysis of the human situation. . . . It does not require much knowledge of history to recognize that, with all its grievous sins of compromise, cowardice, and apostasy, the Church outlasts all these movements in which so much passionate faith has been invested. In their time each of these movements seems to provide a sense of direction, a credible goal for the human project. The slogans of these movements become sacred words which glow with ultimate authority. But they do not endure. None of them in fact embodies the true end, the real goal of history.[3]

Religious Authority and the Challenge of Modernity

If the reality that we seek to explore, and of which we are a part, is the work of a personal Creator, then authority resides in this one who is the Author. If, on the other hand, this reality is the result of processes within itself—if, for example, it is the outcome of a struggle for existence in which the strongest survives the rest—then authority is simply one way of describing superior strength. Power and authority are one and the same. The Christian tradition maintains, of course, that the former is the case, that authority resides in the One who is the Author of all being. And because personal being can be known only insofar as the person chooses to reveal herself or himself, and cannot be known by the methods that are appropriate to the investigation of impersonal matters and processes, then authority, in this view, must rest on divine revelation. Modernity has declined to accept this authority.[4]

Modernity is distrustful of authority. It was born in a movement of emancipation from what were seen as external authorities, and its appeal was to the freedom and responsibility of the individual reason and conscience to judge between rival claims to truth. In the famous words of Kant, the slogan has been "Dare to know." And there are many situations in which this is the most important thing to say. Authority that is merely imposed from outside is not true authority. We are so made that we need to see for ourselves that something is true or right. Yet, if this demand for individual freedom of judgment is taken as our sole guide to reality, we are in trouble.[5]

All our knowing comes to us through our apprenticeship in a tradition of knowing that has been formed through the effort of previous generations. This tradition is the source of the mental faculties through which we begin to make sense of the world. In this sense the tradition has authority, but it is not a purely external authority. We are responsible for internalizing the tradition by our struggle to understand the world with the help of the tools it furnishes, and in this process the tradition itself develops and is changed. This calls for a combination of reverence for the tradition with courage to bring our own judgment to bear upon its application to new circumstances. The idea that we could construct an entire edifice of knowledge without reliance on the tradition by the exercise of our own powers of observation and reasoning (an idea that was certainly present in the formative process of modernity) is surely illusion. We are not in a position where we could lay down in advance the terms on which we will accept any claim to truth.[6]

It is of crucial importance in any discussion of authority to consider the significance of the fact that Jesus did not write a book. The only example recorded of Jesus' writing is when he wrote in the dust. He did not bequeath a book to his followers. He devoted his ministry, as far as we know, to the formation of a community that would represent him to those who would come after. He taught them in ways that would be remembered and passed on to others, but he did not provide a written text. It is, surely, very important that almost all the words of Jesus have come to us in versions that are not identical. To wish that it were otherwise would evidently go against the intention of Jesus. The fact that we have four Gospels rather than one is cited by Muslims as evidence that the real gospel (Injil) has been lost. But the Church refused to substitute one harmonized version for the four disparate ones. . . .

The story the Bible tells is tied to particular times, places, languages and cultures. If it were not, it would be no part of human history. It is told as the clue to the entire story—human and cosmic,—from creation to the end of time. It cannot function as the clue to the whole story if it is simply repeated in the same words. It has to be translated, and translation is (fallible) interpretation. The many-layered material of the Old Testament is witness to the repeated retelling of the fundamental story in new terms for new occasions. Jesus expressly tells his disciples, in the Johannine interpretation, that although they have received a true and full revelation of the Father, they have yet much to learn that they cannot learn until later. They are promised that the Holy Spirit will guide them "into all the truth." . . . The church is not tied to a text in such a way that nothing will ever be done for the first time. In new situations, those who "indwell" the story of which Jesus is the center will have to make new and risky decisions about what faithfulness to the Author of the story requires. There can be no drawing of a straight line from a text of Scripture to a contemporary ethical decision; there will always be the requirement of a fresh decision in responsibility to the one whose story it is.[7]

Truth, Modernity, and Freedom

The centuries since Newton have seen the project of enlightenment carried to the furthest parts of the earth, offering a vision for the whole human race of emancipation, justice, material development and human rights. It was, and is, a noble project. Yet it has failed disastrously to deliver what was promised. Forces of darkness, irrationality, and violence are perhaps more devastating throughout the world today than they have ever been. And in Europe itself, the birthplace of the Enlightenment and long regarded as the bastion of its values, there is disintegration. Those who fought to overthrow the dark forces of fascism and national socialism in the Second World War and believed that Europe would never sink again into such barbarism have lived to see these same forces once more taking the stage. Even where such violent forms of irrationality are only on the margins of society, the great visions for the future that inspired the social legislation of the nineteenth and twentieth centuries are now widely rejected. Rational planning for human welfare is widely abandoned in favor of leaving everything to the irrational forces of the market.

It would seem that the splendid ideals of the Enlightenment—freedom, justice, human rights—are not "self-evident truths," as the eighteenth century supposed. They seemed self-evident to a society that had been shaped for more than a thousand years by the biblical account of the human story. When that story fades from corporate memory and is replaced by another story—for example, the story of the struggle for survival in a world whose fundamental law is violence—they cease to be "self-evident." Human reason and conscience, it would seem, do not operate in a vacuum. Their claim to autonomy is unsustainable. They are shaped by factors that are in operation prior to the thinking and experience of the individual. They are shaped most fundamentally by the story that a society tells about itself, the story that shapes the way every individual reason and conscience works.[8]

Although the ideas of modernity still have a strong residual hold at the level of unacknowledged assumptions, for an increasing number of people there is no longer any confidence in the alleged "eternal truths of reason" of which Lessing spoke. Eternal and ultimate truths are unknowable, and any claim to know them is simply an assertion of the will to power. In respect of such claims one does not ask, "Is it true?" but, "In whose interest is the claim being made? What support does it have? Who is hoping to profit by it?"

In this situation it is a very great mistake for Christians to seek to commend the authority of the gospel by asserting what is said to be eternal and indubitable truths. The knowledge of God given to us through the gospel is a matter of faith, not indubitable certainty. This statement is challenged by some Christians who fear that it opens the door to relativism and subjectivism. But this challenge has to be resisted. It comes from captivity to the typical modernist illusion that there is available to us a kind of objective knowledge wholly sanitized from contamination by any "subjective" elements. There are some conservative Christians who believe that it is only by asserting the *objective* truth of the gospel that one can affirm its authority. The most damaging effect of this is that it severs the knowledge of God from the grace of God. As I have already argued, the knowledge of God can be only by grace through faith. The attempt to eliminate this deeply personal element in the knowledge of God, out of fear of subjectivism, can lead only to a kind of hard rationalism that is remote from the gospel. Certainly we must insist on the objectivity of what we affirm in preaching the gospel if that means that we are speaking of realities "beyond ourselves" and not just of our own feelings. But God is not an object for our investigation by scientific methods in the style of Descartes. God is the supreme Subject who calls us by grace to put our faith in Him. One may thus speak of two kinds of certainty. There is the kind of certainty for which Descartes sought and that modernity has constantly sought, a certainty that rests on my own possession of indubitable truth. And there is the kind of certainty that is expressed in the apostolic word: "I know whom I have believed, and I am sure that he is able to guard until that Day what has been entrusted to me" (2 Tim. 1:12).[9]

Surely the greatest gift the Enlightenment has left us is the recognition of the right of all people to freedom of thought and conscience. It is a gift we can never surrender. And we have penitently to acknowledge that it was won in the teeth of determined opposition from the churches. We have to confess also, if we are honest, that the same churches that demanded freedom of conscience when they were in a minority have, when they became majorities, denied to others the freedom they claimed for themselves. How, if we are to think of a Christian society, can we ensure that the same sins are not repeated when and if Christians are in a position to impose their views on others? If we insist, as I have done, that the state has an obligation to recognize truth, how can the state offer protection to something it recognizes as error? If there were a Christian state, would it not necessarily be intolerant? These are real questions to be faced.[10]

To affirm the Gospel as public truth does not mean . . . that belief in the truth of the Gospel is to be ensured by the use of political power. It has been made clear from the beginning, though often forgotten in subsequent centuries, that the form of the affirmation is given once and for all in the witness which Jesus bore in his dying. The fact that the cross is at the heart of the Gospel, and that it was the powers of state, Church and popular opinion which sought to silence the divine word, must forever forbid the Church to seek an identification of the Gospel with political power.[11]

In a society where agnostic pluralism reigns, freedom is understood to be the liberty to do what you want provided it does not interfere with the freedom of other people. Freedom is the absence of limits. In that case, the ideal model of freedom would be an astronaut, floating weightless in space and out of contact with the spacecraft. Obviously such a man would not be free at all, for freedom means the possibility of choosing between options in the real world, and the more we learn about the real world the less scope there is for fantasy. A society in which any kind of nonsense is acceptable is not a free society. An agnostic pluralism has no defense against nonsense. So while a committed pluralism values freedom as necessary (though not sufficient) condition for grasping the truth about the real world, the fundamental relation between truth and freedom is that enunciated by Jesus when he said, "The truth shall make you free." That saying, we remember, provoked the furious anger of the hearers, who affirmed that they were free already and did not need anyone to set them free. Jesus tells them that they are not free until the truth makes them free, and they respond by threatening to stone him. When we affirm that freedom is not the natural endowment of every human being but is something to be won by acknowledgment of the truth, and that in the end the truth is something given in the sheer grace of God to be received in faith, there is bound to be anger. There is bound to be the feeling that the free society is once again threatened by dogma. I think the Church cannot evade the sharpness of this encounter.[12]

The ideology which we have to recognize, unmask, and reject is an ideology of freedom, a false and idolatrous conception of freedom which equates it with the freedom of each individual to do as he or she pleases. We have to set against it the Trinitarian faith which sees all reality in terms of relatedness. In explicit rejection of an individualism which puts the autonomous self at the center and sees other selves as limitations on our freedom, we have to set the basic dogma entrusted to us, namely that freedom is to be found by being taken into that community of love given and received which is the eternal reality from which and for which all things exist.[13]

Notes

1. Lesslie Newbigin, *The Relevance of Trinitarian Doctrine for Today's Mission* (London: Edinburgh House, 1963), 37.
2. Lesslie Newbigin, *Honest Religion for Secular Man* (London: SCM Press, 1966), 47.
3. Lesslie Newbigin, *The Gospel in a Pluralist Society* (London: SPCK, 1989), 138.
4. Lesslie Newbigin, *Truth and Authority in Modernity* (Leominster: Gracewing, 1996), 1–2
5. Ibid., 11.
6. Ibid., 12–13.
7. Ibid., 43–45.
8. Ibid., 73–74.
9. Ibid., 77–78.
10. Lesslie Newbigin, *Foolishness to the Greeks: The Gospel and Western Culture* (London: SPCK, 1986), 137.
11. Lesslie Newbigin, "The Gospel as Public Truth," *The Gospel and Our Culture*, January 1992, 1.
12. Lesslie Newbigin, *Truth to Tell: The Gospel as Public Truth* (Grand Rapids, MI: Eerdmans, 1991), 60–61.
13. Ibid., 75.

Newbigin and the Critique of Modernity

PAUL WESTON

Life in Brief

FOLLOWING LESSLIE NEWBIGIN'S death in 1998, the obituary in *The Times* described him as "one of the foremost missionary statesmen of his generation," and "one of the outstanding figures on the world Christian stage in the second half of the century."[1] Born in 1909 to Quaker parents, he studied at Cambridge University and went to India in 1936 as an ordained missionary with the Church of Scotland. He spent the best part of thirty-eight years there until retirement in 1974. During his early years there, he was involved in the discussions that led to the formation of the ecumenical Church of South India in 1947. He became one of its founding bishops, serving the new diocese of Madurai and Ramnad. He was soon drawn into the work of the World Council of Churches (WCC) and in 1961 became the first director of the new WCC division of World Mission and Evangelism and editor of the *International Review of Missions*. In 1965 he returned to India on his election as Bishop of Madras, and, alongside his diocesan responsibilities, continued to travel extensively both to speak and to lecture, and to take part in various consultations in connection with the WCC. During his working life, he also wrote extensively, with significant publications on the nature of the church, on ecumenism, and on trinitarian approaches to mission.[2]

Newbigin "retired" to the United Kingdom in 1974 and was appointed to the staff of Selly Oak Colleges in Birmingham to teach students training for missionary work. He became a minister in the United Reformed Church (becoming its national moderator in 1978–79), and in 1981—at the age of seventy-two—took on the leadership of a small inner-city congregation in Winson Green, Birmingham, which he led for the next seven years.

It was during this time that Newbigin's engagement with the questions facing the church in the West began to take a coherent shape. He had written a short pamphlet arising out of a working party convened by the British Council of Churches, which was published in 1983 under the title *The Other Side of 1984: Questions for the Churches.*[3] It soon became a bestseller and was the first in a series of publications by Newbigin that concentrated on the missionary challenges raised by the dominance of an increasingly secularized culture in the West. He was genuinely surprised at how rapidly the questions it raised were taken up by churches both in the United Kingdom and abroad. What became "The Gospel and Our Culture" program soon gathered pace and led to two regional conferences in 1990 and 1991 and to an international conference of four hundred delegates held in July 1992 at Swanwick in Derbyshire.

In tandem with these public discussions, Newbigin's writings began to focus increasingly on the issues that were being raised by the missionary challenge of the West. A further 14 books and 160 articles and smaller pieces followed the publication of *The Other Side of 1984*, the most well-known of these being *Foolishness to the Greeks*, *The Gospel in a Pluralist Society*, and *Proper Confidence.*[4] Lesslie Newbigin died in 1998 at the age of eighty-eight.

Introductory Comments on Newbigin and Modernity

At the heart of Newbigin's later writings is a critique of, and response to, the Western church's captivity to the culture of "modernity." His diagnosis is predominantly philosophical and more especially epistemological, tracing the origins of the crisis of modernity to the thought of philosophers such as René Descartes and John Locke in the seventeenth century. It was these thinkers, he argues, who effectively laid the philosophical foundations upon which post-Enlightenment assumptions in the West about knowledge and truth are based, and they have undergirded the culture of modernity in the West ever since.

Newbigin argues that at the center of the Enlightenment "project" was a decisive move away from the kind of "fiduciary" approach to knowledge that was characteristic of earlier thinkers such as Augustine who saw the knowledge of God as the predicate upon which all other knowing is based.[5] Descartes effectively replaced this with a more circumscribed view of the process of knowing predicated on the only thing we could know to be certain: the existence of the thinking individual as an autonomous knower (summed up by his dictum: *cogito ergo sum*—"I think, therefore I am").

It is the perceived epistemological reductionism at the heart of the Enlightenment's approach to knowledge that comes under the fiercest criticism from

Newbigin's pen. Not only does it truncate the fuller conception of knowing by its dubious search for objective certainties that cannot be doubted but, in requiring scientific criteria for the establishing of truth-claims, it marginalizes both aesthetic and interpersonal forms of truth and decisively negates the possibility of religious knowing. Much of Newbigin's later writing therefore attempts to bring back together the subjective and objective poles of knowing that the Enlightenment had effectively put asunder.

His great ally in this quest is the scientist-turned-social philosopher Michael Polanyi, whose 1958 book *Personal Knowledge* provides in many ways the hermeneutical key to Newbigin's later thinking about epistemology. Polanyi sought to show "that complete objectivity as usually attributed to the exact sciences is a delusion and is in fact a false ideal."[6] Even within the scientific community, he argues, the kind of knowledge that is usually understood as objective (on the basis of a Cartesian process of experiment and accumulation of evidence) is in fact also deeply personal, incorporating and reintegrating the subjective side of the knower. Polanyi argues that even in science, discovery about reality nearly always begins with some kind of unproven (and unprovable) faith-commitment: a personal intuition about the nature of reality that forms the starting point from which new discoveries and coherences are possible.

Polanyi's thinking enables Newbigin both to critique Enlightenment presuppositions on the one hand and to open up theological (and missiological) possibilities on the other. In his critique of modernity, Newbigin sets out to demonstrate two things: on the one hand that "scientific knowledge" (so-called) is not as objective as its proponents make out, and on the other that "religious knowledge" is not as subjective as its Enlightenment opponents may claim. And because personal trust can be shown to be integral to the process of any kind of knowing, it is supremely the case, Newbigin argues, in the sphere of religious knowing. After all, it is only as God makes himself vulnerable in the act of self-revelation that we can come to know him at all. As he puts it in *Honest Religion for Secular Man*, "We know God as he reveals himself to us. There is no other way to the knowledge of persons";[7] or, as in an extract from *Truth and Authority in Modernity* included in this volume, "God is the supreme Subject who calls us by grace to put our faith in him."[8] The knowledge of God, the Author of creation—the truest and deepest knowledge of all—is therefore a gift of grace without which all other knowing is partial and limited.

Newbigin's epistemological critique offers not only a radically different narrative to that of the Enlightenment but also opens up creative approaches to the themes of "tradition and history," "authority and modernity," and "truth and freedom," which the extracts from his works included in this volume illustrate.

Tradition and History

For Newbigin—as for Polanyi—knowing is always anchored in the context of living communities.[9] It is a community, for example, that "apprentices" the knower by teaching and passing on the framework of language and the principles of recognition and analysis. But communities also provide the discipline of a "context," with its rules and mores, expectations, and visions. Another way of putting this is to say that a community creates and sustains a "tradition" of knowing that enables the development of thinking and provides a catalyst for fresh discoveries.

As a result, Newbigin welcomes the notion of "tradition," seeing it not as some heavy or burdensome weight or obstacle that might somehow impede the possibility of progress but as the inescapable and foundational context in which all true knowing and learning takes place. As he puts it in one of the extracts included in this volume, "The idea that we could construct an entire edifice of knowledge without reliance on the tradition . . . is surely illusion."[10]

This is the context in which Newbigin discusses the concept of the church as the community of believers in which God by his grace has made himself known, and in which such knowledge is nurtured and fed. The church carries and responds to this divine disclosure in the context of an historical but evolving tradition. The scriptures are the unfolding story of the interplay of divine revelation and human response, demonstrating both the possibilities of a deepening understanding of God and of what faithful response to him in changing situations and contexts might look like. Thus the concept of "tradition" for Newbigin is both an epistemological necessity and a place of learning and opportunity that opens up new and revitalizing hermeneutical possibilities. So he writes: "We are responsible for internalizing the tradition by our struggle to understand the world with the help of the tools it furnishes, and in this process the tradition itself develops and is changed. This calls for a combination of reverence for the tradition with courage to bring our own judgment to bear upon its application to new circumstances."[11]

Newbigin's understanding of "tradition" as something uniquely connected to the self-revelation of God in human history is deeply "unmodern" (if not antimodern). As he puts it in another of the extracts: "the idea of a God who somehow reaches out his hand to intervene . . . in the affairs of the world has been held by the majority of philosophers to be an impossible anthropomorphism."[12] Yet this, he argues, is the sine qua non of Christian truth.

There are at least two reasons why Newbigin's approach is inherently unmodern. First, although the knowledge of God is personally mediated in the course of human history, it is not something that can be owned as if it were a possession.[13] It is not an object of discovery, or a conclusion reached by deduction, but rather a calling to obedience, or a stewardship of trust. As he puts it in another extract: "Christians do not go through the battles of history as the master race. They go through them as the servant people, looking up to the Father who is alone the Lord of history, accepting his disposition of events as the context of their obedience, relying on his Spirit as their guide."[14]

Secondly, Newbigin's approach opens up the human story both to past significance and to future possibility and final resolution. History is going somewhere because its nature and purpose has been revealed by its Author. In this context Newbigin is fond of referring to Christ as the "clue" to history, or—as in the extract from *The Gospel in a Pluralist Society*—as the "true end, the real goal of history."[15] This conception of history opens it out into a space of possibility and invitation: and all within the framework of an eschatological goal to which history is heading, a time when all things will be made new. The revelation of Christ in history is the "clue" to this meaning, interpreting and enfolding all that has been, and all that is yet to come. The "otherness" of this story is in sharp contrast to the worldview of modernity, as the remainder of the extract from *The Gospel in a Pluralist Society* makes clear. For modernity's departure from the narrative of God in history effectively forecloses the scope of the future and tends to exchange its eschatological goals for earthly substitutes and human projects. As Newbigin puts it, "To invest one's ultimate commitment in such proximate goals is to end in despair."[16]

Religious Authority and the Challenge of Modernity

"Modernity is distrustful of authority," says Newbigin, with due reason. Indeed, he interprets the whole Enlightenment "movement" as one of emancipation from external authorities. Its appeal, he argues, was "to the freedom and responsibility of the individual reason and conscience to judge between rival claims to truth."[17] Here, as elsewhere, Newbigin quotes Kant's slogan *sapere aude* ("dare to know") as supporting evidence, emphasizing the loosening of modernity's attachments to more traditional sources of authority.[18] Descartes's emphasis on the individual autonomy of the knower leads inevitably both to a rejection of the notion of divine authority, and to its relocation as an aspect of human agency. Indeed, the exclusion of the possibility of revelation must be interpreted as an act of the will, the inevitable consequence of modernity's insistence that truth-claims must now justify themselves in the light of human reason.

In epistemological terms, this is a trajectory that moves toward Nietzsche's conception of knowledge as the "will to power" as the logical—if not inevitable—consequence of the Enlightenment. For if authority "is the outcome of a struggle for existence in which the strongest survives the rest," then it is "simply one way of describing superior strength."[19] The cultural counterpart of this epistemological shift has also tended to privilege instrumental forms of rationality over styles of reasoning that are more connected with human emotional discourse and interpersonal relationships. As a result, one of modernity's less attractive cultural characteristics is that individuals come to be valued for their technical usefulness in achieving technical goals rather than for their intrinsic worth.

Newbigin's response to modernity's relocation of authority within the processes of human activity is to raise once more the question of origins. Drawing on Polanyi's foundational observation that we come to know another person only as and when they choose to reveal something of themselves, Newbigin applies this argument to the nature of the created order itself and locates the answer in the self-revelation of God in Jesus Christ. The nub of this argument is that "if the reality that we seek to explore, and of which we are a part, is the work of a personal Creator, then authority resides in this one who is the Author." As a result, authority must "rest on divine revelation," which modernity "has declined to accept."[20]

But, as we have seen, the form of authority that his argument entails is hardly static. It does not reside in a deposit of fixed dogmas from which direct lines of application can be drawn to the particularities of contemporary living. Rather, Newbigin develops the conception of what we might describe as a process of "creative hermeneutical reappraisal." "The church is not tied to a text in such a way that nothing will ever be done for the first time." On the contrary, those who " 'indwell' the story of which Jesus is the center will have to make new and risky decisions about what faithfulness to the Author of the story requires."[21]

Truth, Modernity, and Freedom

The final selection of extracts deals with the issue of freedom. The idea of freedom is, of course, a central feature of the project of modernity enshrined, as it were, in its very foundation deeds. But one of Newbigin's central arguments about modernity is that "the splendid ideals of the Enlightenment—freedom, justice, human rights—are not 'self-evident truths.' "[22] These ideals have become detached from the biblical narrative in whose context alone they can properly be interpreted and that—for more than a thousand years—effectively shaped their meaning. Once dislocated, and then relocated within different narratives, these "truths" take on other, and sometimes more dangerous, meanings. In particular, the unanchored expression of personal freedom (a modern theme if ever there was one) can become an aggressive force, leading to the curtailment of the freedom of others.[23]

How, then, is freedom to be safeguarded in contemporary societies? This had been a central question for Newbigin since his earliest writings.[24] His discussions frequently begin with the sober recognition that the history of Christianity has often been marked by force and oppression when Christians have occupied places of power. In one extract he therefore raises the question of whether a Christian society can truly safeguard the interests of those with whom it disagrees. "If there were a Christian state, would it not necessarily be intolerant? These are real questions to be faced."[25]

In connection with this question, Newbigin's work in addressing the secularism of the 1980s and '90s came to be associated with his call to recognize the gospel as "public truth," and one of the extracts comes from the *Gospel and Our Culture Newsletter* (1992) in which this vision was launched. Newbigin was often accused of wanting to a return to some form of "Constantinianism," which effectively identified Christianity with political power. He consistently refuted this charge, arguing (as here) that "the fact that the cross is at the heart of the Gospel, and that it was the powers of state, Church and popular opinion which sought to silence the divine word, must forever forbid the Church to seek an identification of the Gospel with political power."[26]

Moreover, true freedom has always to do with real contextual choices rather than freedom without limits. What he calls "agnostic pluralism" formalizes this latter idea by removing the constraints within which true freedom can operate. This he refers to as an "ideology of freedom, a false and idolatrous conception . . . which equates it with the freedom of each individual to do as he or she pleases."[27] By contrast, Newbigin affirms that true freedom is not a "natural" right, but a gift of grace, anchored in, and recognized by, the community which has come to embrace it. This he calls a "committed pluralism."[28]

In this context a truly Christian society preserves the freedom of others both to explore and to disagree. For God, who has acted to reveal himself through both the cross and the resurrection of Jesus, has also provided a "space and a time during which faith is possible because unbelief is also possible."[29] For until the final consummation of all things, God continues to reveal himself in love and mercy, providing that "space" in which, by freedom of choice, men and women may respond to his call.

For Further Reflection

1. Newbigin criticizes a more "conservative" Christian approach to the commendation of the gospel in the modern world. Is it clear what approach he commends between "liberal" and "conservative" approaches?

2. How are authority and freedom related for Newbigin? Does his affirmation of the Enlightenment's "gift" to us of freedom of thought sit comfortably with his wider thought?
3. Is it coherent or realistic to aspire after a "Christian society" while rejecting the ideal of a "Christian state"?
4. Newbigin criticizes the attempts of some (more "liberal") theologians to relate Christianity to modernity as involving a loss of something central to the faith. Is the intra-Christian dispute here broadly similar to what we find in Mawdūdī's criticism of Muslims who seem to him to reinterpret their faith too far in the direction of Western modernity? Would Newbigin share aspects of Mawdūdī's criticism of Western modernity?

Notes

1. *The Times*, January 31, 1998.

2. Up to 1974 he published 32 books and pamphlets and 118 articles or book chapters. See especially *The Household of God: Lectures on the Nature of the Church* (London: SCM Press, 1953); and *The Open Secret: Sketches for a Missionary Theology* (Grand Rapids, MI: Eerdmans, 1978). All works cited in this essay are by Lesslie Newbigin unless stated otherwise.

3. Geneva: World Council of Churches, 1983.

4. *Foolishness to the Greeks: The Gospel and Western Culture* (London: SPCK, 1986); *The Gospel in a Pluralist Society* (London: SPCK, 1989); and *Proper Confidence:* (London: SPCK, 1995).

5. The dictum that came to be associated with this approach was *credo ut intelligam* ("I believe in order that I might understand"), which though not specifically present in Augustine's writings is certainly characteristic of his approach. The actual phrase is used by Anselm in his *Proslogion*, ch. 1.

6. Michael Polanyi, *Personal Knowledge: Towards a Post-Critical Philosophy* (Chicago: University of Chicago Press, 1958), 18.

7. Lesslie Newbigin, *Honest Religion for Secular Man* (London: SCM Press, 1966), 94.

8. Lesslie Newbigin, *Truth and Authority in Modernity* (Leominster: Gracewing, 1996), 78.

9. See, for example, Newbigin's first discussion of this theme in *Honest Religion for Secular Man*, 77–99; also Newbigin, *Proper Confidence*, 44–64.

10. Newbigin, *Truth and Authority*, 13.

11. Ibid., 12–13.

12. Newbigin, *Honest Religion*, 47.

13. Although the church has often fallen into this kind of trap in the course of its history.

14. Lesslie Newbigin, *The Relevance of Trinitarian Doctrine for Today's Mission* (London: Edinburgh House, 1963), 37. This is the context in which Newbigin understands the biblical idea of "election." It is a calling for the sake of others. See, for example, Newbigin, *Gospel in a Pluralist Society*, 80–88.

15. See, for example, Lesslie Newbigin, *The Finality of Christ* (London: SCM Press, 1969), 65–87; and Newbigin, *Gospel in a Pluralist Society*, 103–15, 138.

16. Newbigin, *Gospel in a Pluralist Society*, 138.

17. Newbigin *Truth and Authority*, 11.

18. Immanuel Kant, "An Answer to the Question: What Is Enlightenment?," in *Perpetual Peace and Other Essays*, trans. T. Humphrey (Indianapolis: Hackett, 1983), 41–48. The quotation from Kant is framed as follows: "Enlightenment is man's exodus from his self-incurred tutelage. Tutelage is the inability to use one's understanding without the guidance of another person . . . 'Dare to know' (*sapere aude*)! Have the courage to use your own understanding; this is the motto of the Enlightenment." The passage is quoted in full in *The Other Side of 1984*, 15.

19. Newbigin, *Truth and Authority*, 1

20. Ibid., 1–2.

21. Ibid., 45.

22. Ibid., 73.

23. Note again the connection with Nietzsche's "will to power."

24. His first published book was titled *Christian Freedom in the Modern World* (London: SCM Press, 1937).

25. Newbigin, *Foolishness to the Greeks*, 137.

26. Lesslie Newbigin, "The Gospel as Public Truth," newsletter of The Gospel and Our Culture, January 1992, 1.

27. Lesslie Newbigin, *Truth to Tell: The Gospel as Public Truth* (Grand Rapids, MI: Eerdmans, 1991), 75.

28. Ibid., 60–61.

29. Lesslie Newbigin, "A Light to the Nations: Theology in Politics," in *Faith and Power: Christianity and Islam in 'Secular' Britain*, ed. Lesslie Newbigin, Lamin Sanneh, and Jenny Taylor, 135–65 (London: SPCK, 1998), 162.

Alasdair MacIntyre (1929–)

From *After Virtue*

[Excerpted from a chapter titled "The Virtues, the Unity of a Human Life and the Concept of a Tradition"]

It is now possible to return to the question from which this enquiry into the nature of human action and identity started: In what does the unity of an individual life consist? The answer is that its unity is the unity of a narrative embodied in a single life. To ask "What is the good for me?" is to ask how best I might live out that unity and bring it to completion. To ask "What is the good for man?" is to ask what all answers to the former question must have in common. But now it is important to emphasise that it is the systematic asking of these two questions and the attempt to answer them in deed as well as in word which provide the moral life with its unity. The unity of a human life is the unity of a narrative quest. Quests sometimes fail, are frustrated, abandoned or dissipated into distractions; and human lives may in all these ways also fail. But the only criteria for success or failure in a human life as a whole are the criteria of success or failure in a narrated or to-be-narrated quest. A quest for what?

Two key features of the medieval conception of a quest need to be recalled. The first is that without some at least partly determinate conception of the final *telos* there could not be any beginning to a quest. Some conception of the good for man is required. Whence is such a conception to be drawn? Precisely from those questions which led us to attempt to transcend that limited conception of the virtues which is available in and through practices. It is in looking for a conception of *the* good which will enable us to order other goods, for a conception of *the* good which will enable us to extend our understanding of the purpose and content of the virtues, for a conception of *the* good which will enable us to understand the place of integrity and constancy in life, that we initially define the kind of life which is a quest for the good. But secondly it is clear the medieval conception of a quest is not at all that of a search for something already adequately characterized, as miners search for gold or geologists for oil. It is in the course of the quest and only through encountering and coping with the various particular harms, dangers, temptations and distractions which provide any quest with its episodes and incidents that the goal of the quest is finally to be understood. A quest is always an education both as to the character of that which is sought and in self-knowledge.

The virtues therefore are to be understood as those dispositions which will not only sustain practices and enable us to achieve the goods internal to practices, but which will also sustain us in the relevant kind of quest for the good, by enabling us to overcome the harms, dangers, temptations and distractions which we encounter, and which will furnish us with increasing self-knowledge and increasing knowledge of the good. The catalogue of the virtues will therefore include the virtues required to sustain the kind of households and the kind of political communities in which men and women can seek for the good together and the virtues necessary for philosophical enquiry about the character of the good. We have then arrived at a provisional conclusion about the good life for man: the good life for man is the life spent in seeking for the good life for man, and the virtues necessary for the seeking are those which will enable us to understand what more and what else the good life for man is. We have also completed the second stage in our account of the virtues, by situating them in relation to the good life for man and not only in relation to practices. But our enquiry requires a third stage.

For I am never able to seek for the good or exercise the virtues only *qua* individual. This is partly because what it is to live the good life concretely varies from circumstance to circumstance even when it is one and the same conception of the good life and one and the same set of virtues which are being embodied in a human life. What the good life is for a fifth-century Athenian general will not be the same as what it was for a medieval nun or a seventeenth-century farmer. But it is not just that different individuals live in different social circumstances; it is also that we all approach our own circumstances as bearers of a particular social identity. I am someone's son or daughter, someone else's cousin or uncle; I am a citizen of this or that city, a member of this or that guild or profession; I belong to this clan, that tribe, this nation. Hence what is good for me has to be the good for one who inhabits these roles. As such, I inherit from the past of my family, my city, my tribe, my nation, a variety of debts, inheritances, rightful expectations and obligations. These constitute the given of my life, my moral starting point. This is in part what gives my life its own moral particularity.

This thought is likely to appear alien and even surprising from the standpoint of modern individualism. From the standpoint of individualism I am what I myself choose to be. I can always, if I wish to, put in question what are taken to be the merely contingent social features of my existence. I may biologically be my father's son; but I cannot be held responsible for what he did unless I choose implicitly or explicitly to assume such responsibility. I may legally be a citizen of a certain country; but I cannot be held responsible for what my country does or has done unless I choose implicitly or explicitly to assume such responsibility. Such individualism is expressed by those modern Americans who deny any responsibility for the effects of slavery upon black Americans, saying "I never owned any slaves." It is more subtly the standpoint of those other modern Americans who accept a nicely calculated responsibility for such effects measured precisely by the benefits they themselves as individuals have indirectly received from slavery. In both cases "being an American" is not in itself taken to be part of the moral identity of the individual. And of course there is nothing peculiar to modern Americans in this attitude: the Englishman who says, "*I* never did any wrong to Ireland; why bring up that old history as though it had something to do with *me*?" or the young German who believes that being born after 1945 means that what Nazis did to Jews has no moral relevance to his relationship to his Jewish contemporaries, exhibit the same attitude, that according to which the self is detachable from its social and historical roles and statuses. And the self so detached is of course a self very much at home in either Sartre's or Goffman's perspective, a self that can have no history. The contrast with the narrative view of the self is clear. For the story of my life is always embedded in the story of those communities from which I derive my identity. I am born with a past; and to try to cut myself off from that past, in the individualist mode, is to deform my present relationships. The possession of an historical identity and the possession of a social identity coincide. Notice that rebellion against my identity is always one possible mode of expressing it.

Notice also that the fact that the self has to find its moral identity in and through its membership in communities such as those of the family, the neighbourhood, the city and the tribe does not entail that the self has to accept the moral *limitations* of the particularity of those forms of community. Without those moral particularities to begin from there would never be anywhere to begin; but it is in moving forward from such particularity that the search for the good, for the universal, consists. Yet particularity can never be simply left behind or obliterated. The notion of escaping from it into a realm of entirely universal maxims which belong to man as such, whether in its eighteenth-century Kantian form or in the presentation of some modern analytical moral philosophies, is an illusion and an illusion with painful consequences. When men and women identify what are in fact their partial and particular causes too easily and too completely with the cause of some universal principle, they usually behave worse than they would otherwise do.

What I am, therefore, is in key part what I inherit, a specific past that is present to some degree in my present. I find myself part of a history and that is generally to say, whether I like it or not, whether I recognise it or not, one of the bearers of a tradition. It was important when I characterized the concept of a practice to notice that practices always have histories and that at any given moment what a practice is depends on a mode of understanding it which has been transmitted often through many generations. And thus, insofar as the virtues sustain the relationships required for practices, they have to sustain relationships to the past—and to the future—as well as in the present. But the traditions through which particular practices are transmitted and reshaped never exist in isolation for larger social traditions. What constitutes such traditions?

We are apt to be misled here by the ideological uses to which the concept of a tradition has been put by conservative political theorists. Characteristically such theorists have followed Burke in contrasting tradition with reason and the stability of tradition with conflict. Both contrasts obfuscate. For all reasoning takes place within the context of some traditional mode of thought, transcending through criticism and invention the limitations of what had hitherto been reasoned in that tradition; this is as true of modern physics as of medieval logic. Moreover when a tradition is in good order it is always partially constituted by an argument about the goods the pursuit of which gives to that tradition its particular point and purpose.

So when an institution—a university, say, or a farm, or a hospital—is the bearer of a tradition of practice or practices, its common life will be partly, but in a centrally important way, constituted by a continuous argument as to what a university is and ought to be or what good farming is or what good medicine is. Traditions, when vital, embody continuities of conflict. Indeed when a tradition becomes Burkean, it is always dying or deaf.

The individualism of modernity could of course find no use for the notion of tradition within its own conceptual scheme except as an adversary notion; it therefore all too willingly abandoned it to the Burkeans, who, faithful to Burke's own allegiance, tried to combine adherence in politics to a conception of tradition which would vindicate the oligarchical revolution of property of 1688 and adherence in economics to the doctrine and institutions of the free market. The theoretical incoherence of this mismatch did not deprive it of market. The theoretical incoherence of this mismatch did not deprive it of ideological usefulness. But the outcome has been that modern conservatives are for the most part engaged in conserving only older rather than later versions of liberal individualism. Their own core doctrine is as liberal and as individualist as that of self-avowed liberals.

A living tradition then is an historically extended, socially embodied argument, and an argument precisely in part about the goods which constitute that tradition. Within a tradition the pursuit of goods extends through generations, sometimes through many generations. Hence the individual's search for his or her good is generally and characteristically conducted within a context defined by those traditions of which the individual's life is a part, and this is true both of those goods which are internal to practices and of the goods of a single life. Once again the narrative phenomenon of embedding is crucial: the history of a practice in our time is generally and characteristically embedded in and made intelligible in terms of the larger and longer history of the tradition through which the practice in its present form was conveyed to us; the history of each of our own lives is generally and characteristically embedded in and made intelligible in terms of the larger and longer histories of a number of traditions. I have to say "generally and characteristically" rather than "always," for traditions decay, disintegrate and disappear. What then sustains and strengthens traditions? What weakens and destroys them?

The answer in key part is: the exercise or lack of exercise of the relevant virtues. The virtues find their point and purpose not only in sustaining those relationships necessary if the variety of goods internal to practices are to be achieved and not only in sustaining the form of an individual life in which that individual may seek out his or her good as the good of his or her whole life, but also in sustaining those traditions which provide both practices and individual lives with their necessary historical context. Lack of justice, lack of truthfulness, lack of courage, lack of relevant intellectual virtues—these corrupt traditions, just as do those institutions and practices which derive their life from the traditions of which they are the contemporary embodiments. To recognise this is of course also to recognise the existence of an additional virtue, one whose importance is perhaps most obvious when it is least present, the virtue of having an adequate sense of the traditions to which one belongs or which confront one. This virtue is not to be confused with any form of conservative antiquarianism; I am not praising those who choose the conventional conservative role of *laudator temporis acti*. It is rather the case that an adequate sense of tradition manifests itself in a grasp of those future possibilities which the past has made available to the present. Living traditions, just because they continue a not-yet-completed narrative, confront a future whose determinate and determinable character, so far as it possesses any, derives from the past.[1]

Note

1. Alasdair MacIntyre, *After Virtue: A Study in Moral Theory* (London: Duckworth, 1981), 203–7.

MacIntyre on Tradition

JOHN MILBANK

IS THE NOTION OF TRADITION applicable to all cultural phenomena, both secular and religious? Or is it to be associated especially with religious phenomena? We speak very easily of both cultural and religious traditions, and in general we tend to contrast a "traditioned" mode of life with a "modern" mode of life that is seen as having emanated from the West. "Tradition" as a category then appears to be at once global, ecumenical, and nostalgic. It is seen in contrast to the "modern," which—though contemporary and now global—is also regarded as parochial because of its specifically European lineage.

Yet precisely in the most seemingly innocent generic category, the danger of a concealed specificity can often lurk. One of the things which this colloquium needs to ask is whether this is true of the category "tradition." It is, after all a Roman word: is it specifically marked in a significant way by this Latin legacy, or are equivalent terms in other languages—for example, Arabic—strictly speaking equivalents? To this question I do not know the answer, but it is certainly true that the word "tradition" in Romance and semi-Romance tongues (such as English) carries a specific semantic freight. And that freight is reflexively to do with the notion of "carrying" itself. Or more exactly with "handing over": the handing over of a gift, as the etymological components of "*traditio*" in Latin are "*trans*" and "*dare.*" The semantic echoes here are very complex and include the proximity of the idea of "handing over" to that of a journey, just as the English word "passage" has such a double sense. Thus the English word "trade" lies close to the word "tradition." Although it now primarily indicates a process of exchange, it more originally meant a course, way, or path; the track of a beast; or the route of a wind. And this more self-contained and unilateral sense survives in the transference of "trade" as a practice to "trade" as a profession, as the chosen course of an individual life.

Similar points can be made about the equivalent Greek term "*paradosis,*" which also implies, at root, the handing on of a gift. Cognates of this term are used in several places in the New Testament (e.g., Luke 1:2) to indicate the passing on of the word of God, or of Christ. In fact, the enhanced importance of the notion of "tradition" in later Western culture stems precisely from this source.

In later usage "tradition" especially had to do with both the public passing on of oral words, ritual usages, and written texts besides elements of more esoteric tradition. Indeed, while *paradosis* was an important term in connection to "secret teachings" in originally proto-orthodox early Christian circles, it was then far more developed as a notion of central importance by Christian Gnosticism.[1] Only with Irenaeus and then Origen was the term reappropriated by Catholic Christianity. Here it once more refers to the exoteric and yet continues also to refer to the esoteric. Thus, Irenaeus contrasted the public and simple character of the *traditio* (in both substance and category) of Christian baptism, compared with the convoluted and hidden character of Gnostic rites, while both he and still more Origen insisted on the necessarily originally "secret" character (to guard truth from those lacking in insight) of Old Testament traditions hidden symbolically beneath historical events and literal-seeming texts.[2]

So for both the Latin and the Greek terms one can validly say that to be within a tradition means both to pass something on and to pursue one's way along a path. But although a path always leads into the future, its difference from a trackless waste in which one might wander is that it has been marked-out by previous walkers. To walk a path, therefore, is also to receive a gift, and in further tracing the path through one's own footsteps, it is to hand over this very same gift to future walkers.

One can therefore conclude that the unilateral, self-contained, and temporal dimension of tradition is more primarily interpersonal, and that for just this reason the root meaning of "handing over a gift," which can be spatial as well as temporal, retains its primacy. To act in a traditioned fashion is to pass on a gift that one has already received according to a particular laid-down manner, along the lines of a particular path. It is to give according to some sort of prescribed notion of measure and order. Not surprisingly then, *traditio* is above all a legal term, which referred to the transfer of the ownership of a slave by simple handing over within the *ius gentium*, or law of the nations, as opposed to the *ius civile* or the *ius naturale.*

Now it might well be plausible to argue that this structure of traditioning is proper to all human culture as such. However, it is also possible to argue that the Roman legacy is peculiarly obsessed with the traditional insofar as it tends paradoxically to balance an extreme sense of indebtedness, on the one hand, with an extreme pride in its own mission to "transmit to others," on the other hand. Thus Rémi Brague has argued that the peculiar mark of Western European culture that has come to dominate the world is its "eccentricity."[3] Its imperialistic impulses are not the consequence of an extreme self-centeredness; indeed, he argues that it is only in its postcolonial phase that the latter has set in. To the contrary, they are to do precisely with its sense of being caught in the middle of a process of *traditio*. Thus ancient Rome thought of itself, to an extreme degree beyond that of ancient Greek religiosity, as being in sacrificial debt to its gods and founders and bound to maintain and extend both inherited cultic rites and legal norms. But this sense of vertical indebtedness was also applied on the horizontal plane: thus Rome came to see itself as a transmitter of Greek culture to which it always felt inferior. Later, after Christianization, Rome in effect came to see itself also as a transmitter of Jewish culture. For, as Brague points out, there is a remarkable homology between the Roman sense of secondariness with respect to Greece and the Christian sense of secondariness with respect to Israel. For even though the Incarnation and the gospel are held by Christians to be a *novum*, they can only be recognized and interpreted by a ceaseless return to the Old Testament, which therefore retains a kind of primacy, just as God the Son only reveals God the Father and does not displace him, as for some Gnostic variants.

In the later post-Roman history of Europe, these two experiences of "belatedness" merge and are combined with a third that sees the entire classical world, including Rome, as in certain ways superior to what comes later. Thus, Europe as a whole sees itself as carrier of what precedes it and remains external to it. Yet this is no simple inferiority complex: the tradition of incarnational fulfillment in particular always suggests that a renaissance of antiquity can also be a surpassing and a new fulfillment. Nevertheless, the very hubris of imperial conquest continues strangely to be driven by a certain humility: the duty to give further onward what precedes and measures one, namely, the path which one has received wherein to walk.

Christianity, therefore, and perhaps Latin Christianity most especially, is not simply one religious tradition among many. Rather, one might suggest it is peculiarly dominated by the notion of tradition, which Christianity itself has most decisively promoted. At least up until 1300 and often beyond, it understood its self-authentication in terms of a constant handing over of a received gift, a constantly repeated elaboration that yet sustained a certain measure, a certain rhythmic pattern. Authority derived from a process of interpersonal temporal transmission and reinterpretation of natural and scriptural signs and not from a spatial center, either ecclesial or textual. Even the canonical scripture was internally constituted by a new handing over of an earlier body of scripture by a later, and this entire double body was itself understood to indicate the prior authority of the incarnate "bridegroom," God, and his "bride," the inspired church.

So in a peculiar sense, for authentic, Catholic Christianity, authority, or tradition, or the passage of a gift are entirely at one. Whether this is true for other religious traditions and to what degree, I do not pretend to know. Clearly, in the case of Islam, for example, something like tradition plays an enormous role and a greater one within some traditions of Islam than in others. Nevertheless, one could validly ask whether the idea that the Qurʾān is itself the original revelation of Allah does not mean that the notion of tradition is less fundamental here than for Christianity.

One might think that the opposite applied because Islam is far more concerned than Christianity with demonstrating the exact provenance of a ḥadīth, a record of a saying or deed of Muḥammad, by tracing it back through a series of named links in a chain to the prophet himself. But this process, called *tawatur*, in its zealous concern to demonstrate a purity of lineage reveals itself to be, arguably, precisely the opposite of a notion of tradition. How so? Because the concern here is to show that something survives unbroken and unchanged since its origin, whereas the idea of tradition privileges and encourages a continuous variation of the same, such that alteration need not betoken distortion. In addition, the very nontraceability of routes through time can serve to validate the authenticity of Christian tradition because it retained its "Gnostic" mark (throughout orthodoxy in both East and West) of a hidden, oral current guaranteed by the succession of the wise and saintly. So if one were looking for something more approximating to Christian and European tradition in the case of Islamic culture, one should surely consider primarily those Shīʿī traditions initially marked by a Gnostic legacy.

One needs also to realize here that the idea of a fundamental handing over is inherently paradoxical, for it posits nothing isolated to "being with" and so no real "original." Therefore, it is possible that to be traditioned through and through is one facet of that extreme paradoxicality of Christianity with which other religious traditions sometimes feel themselves to be slightly ill at ease. And while of course we think of Judaism as saturated by a sense and practice of tradition, Franz Rosenzweig's characterization of Judaism in *The Star of Redemption* could be taken as implying that traditionedness is actually not as constitutive of Judaism as it is of Christianity. Judaism always seeks a Sabbath return to the moment of Sinai, to the giving of the law. It is not, according to Rosenzweig, as obsessed by a sense of positioning within a historical chain as is the Christian faith.[4]

What I am trying to do here is to point up possible concealed differences between various cultural traditions around the very notion of tradition itself. Of course the extreme traditioned character of Christianity is not necessarily a good thing. I have already pointed out its constitutive link with a drive to a certain kind of imperial expansion—something that might very well be viewed askance by outsiders.

When we approach the views of Alasdair MacIntyre on tradition, it is well to bear all this in mind. He purports to write mainly as a philosopher, yet his own approach to the topic of tradition would surely allow that his very views on tradition are strongly marked by his insertion of himself within a Latin Christian tradition.

Most striking of all here is the way in which he makes (at least in *After Virtue*) the notion of narrative the way into the notion of tradition.[5] For the kind of radical traditionedness that I am ascribing to Christianity implies, as we have already seen, not simply that one hands on as a gift what was once not a gift, nor that one hands on what was once simply just given in the sense of inertly "there" like a stone by the wayside, but rather that one hands on what has always been there only as handed on, or in other words always as a gift. Christianity is tradition *en abyme*, and this means that it is not simply the historical story of the handing over of something that was not in the first place a story but rather that it is a repeated telling of what was always a story. For a *traditio*, the handing over of gifts, can only ever be told and cannot merely be asserted, like a proposition. Here it would seem that there is a clear contrast between the Christian gospels, for which the revelation is contained within certain narratives, and the Qurʾān, for which revelation is contained in certain authoritative utterances. The case of Judaism is perhaps by comparison a mixed one.

In this light one has to ask whether MacIntyre's favoring of narrative rather than law or norm or conditional criterion as the primary category for ethics is not a highly Christian one. Nevertheless, there are features of his discussions of narrativity that would seem to have a less controversially universal bearing. With persuasiveness he argues that narrative is equally split between fiction and history because history only occurs in the first place in a narrative mode. This is because we are inherently symbolic creatures: specifically human as opposed to natural action (the case of animals may be intermediate here) always involves a detour through meaningful descriptions that invoke categories which are, with respect to given nature simply gratuitous. A volcanic eruption of ash is a manifestation of mere natural power; a military victory is that indeed, but it is also an event that has only occurred at all because it is in a sense fictional: Thermopylae is taken to be lost by the Greeks and won by the Persians because symbolic conventions define some people as Greeks, others as Persians, and give a certain valuation to a certain sort of physical struggle conducted, despite its seeming chaos, according to certain conventional rules.

So even though human history has no very tidy beginnings and endings, it could not be history at all without ceaseless beginnings and endings and all sorts of emplotments in between. And after all, no dramatist could have perfected the pictured pathos of the departure of Gordon Brown's family from the steps of Number 10 Downing Street in May 2010, nor the way in which the easier psychic chemistry between David Cameron and Nick Clegg in part led to a new realignment within British politics that is likely to have fatal consequences for good or ill.

If, for MacIntyre, human history therefore contains characters who are literally characters within stories, then his further claim is that we only have characters or subjective identities as characters within stories. This is a more debatable claim, which many philosophers (for example, Galen Strawson) would dispute. But it seems to me defensible in the simple terms that we only come to understand ourselves at all through being first named, first spoken to, and first acted upon. Only gradually do we reflectively appropriate a cultural legacy within which we are situated by others. Nevertheless, it is important to note here that this situating involves something more like the giving of gifts than the mere according of status, and for this reason we can come to appropriate those gifts in our own way and start to take a hand in shaping our own selfhood. Cultures that try to eradicate gift in terms of status might well be considered pathological and can never be entirely successful. And the way in which we receive our identity as gift, and yet for this reason can help to mold it, reinforces the view that our identity is that of characters in a story. For in a good novel the novelist must, as it were, fantasize a shaping culture or ethos and yet make it appear that within that environment distinctive characters have a life of their own and even a will of their own—as Rowan Williams has pointed out with respect to Dostoyevsky.[6]

MacIntyre does not actually make it entirely clear just how tradition relates to narrative. But he seems to proceed in *After Virtue* from the latter to the former. This implies that tradition is something like a story of stories, a metanarrative, rather like a novel sequence. Just because we do not entirely shape our own characters but are born into cultural roles and biological legacies, we remain part of a longer story without any traceable beginning. One could also say that this metanarrative is "meta" not just in the sense of being a "story of stories" but also "meta" in the sense of providing the half-formulated norms, the literary theory within which all stories valid for a particular cultural legacy are to be played out. For MacIntyre in *After Virtue*, tradition therefore seems to be the endless embedding of stories within yet further stories according to a fairly coherent normative pattern.

More controversial still is MacIntyre's claim that the norms of both theoretical and practical reason are ultimately embedded in narrative. But he argues with cogency that, just as we cannot will anything at all without first being granted an identity by being addressed, so also we cannot think at all without first taking something for granted, something that we will never be able entirely to call into critical question, because it is the very basis upon which we are able to reason or to act. Hence our rational assumptions always remain akin to the first events in a story that have to be narrated rather than proved.

This can sound like a license for dogmatism. But here it is important to remember once again that what has been handed over by the tradition is a gift and not a fixed position. The gift has to be interpreted, and this applies most of all to that supreme gift which is our sociohistorical role. We must ask: What is this *for*? This is why MacIntyre appeals to the example of the medieval quest and rightly says that its point was not merely reaching a goal but trying to work out just what that goal might be. In a parallel fashion MacIntyre points out that while Plato, Aristotle, Augustine, and Aquinas all thought that there was an objectively good way to be human, they also thought that that good has to be continuously rediscerned. Hence, for Aristotle, one aspect of the good city that pursues the good life is that it creates a space for a constant debate about the nature of that good life.

MacIntyre raises two further pertinent questions. First, how do traditions radically change; and second, is it possible for a culture to live outside the notion of tradition altogether? In the first case he suggests (especially in works later than *After Virtue*)[7] that traditions change when other rival traditions turn out to have better answers to issues that have become problematic within their own trajectory. No doubt this is true for some instances if one takes "better" to mean more formally coherent and avoiding of contradiction. However, it is notable that MacIntyre more and more comes to speak of tradition without mentioning narrative, despite the fact that, as we have seen, the latter seems to be his paradigm for the former. This could be taken as symptomatic of the fact that MacIntyre does not sufficiently ask whether shifts in a tradition are not often more seemingly arbitrary matters of new twists in the plot that break with latent metanarrative norms, or else the adoption of someone else's story because it seems more attractive and compelling. Given the narrative assumptions of all cultures, it will surely often not be clear in merely rational terms whether a new narrative development is preferable or not.

Yet this is not to say that the seemingly arbitrary switches in focus are really just that. For MacIntyre himself insists that a crucial aspect of belonging to a tradition is knowing how to go on in a tacit sense for which there are no prescribed rules. This knowledge can only be that of an insider, just as only the trained musician can successfully improvise, even though improvisations might appear to be possible even for a beginner. Yet the latter's efforts are always likely to be awkward. Something ineffable but real would appear to be at work here, and we recognize this also in the ruleless tact that is exhibited within the social sphere by truly good people as opposed to annoying prigs.

In relation to the second issue regarding seeming rejection of the notion of tradition, MacIntyre takes modern Western liberalism as his example. For this political theory, the past can have no normative validity. Any justifiable order is rather set up by entirely freely choosing and isolated individuals on the basis of no preceding assumptions. They mutually agree to do certain things on condition that other people do certain things in a perfectly closed spatial circle of market contract and formal law. So no unconditional gifts are here passed down as both authorizations for the present and possibilities for the future. Therefore tradition is no longer supposed to govern our social and political behavior.

But MacIntyre thinks that traditionedness is inescapable. He admires ethical theories that recognize this reality, such as those of Aristotle and Hume (whom he rightly does not take to be a liberal, though he dislikes his elevation of feelings above reason). Theories that do not recognize this reality (Utilitarianism, Deontology) are for MacIntyre self-deluding; partly on this account they are neither really ethical theories at all, nor convincing accounts of human behavior. So just for this reason MacIntyre seems to think (though he is not perhaps entirely clear about this) that they institute quasi-traditions that they cannot themselves fully recognize on pain of self-dissolution.

MacIntyre's paradigm for this is Burke, who extolled not tradition-as-reasoning but tradition justified in utilitarian terms as providing social and political stability. By this maneuver he was able to recognize, beyond contractual Lockean liberalism, that English absolute property ownership was merely a historical event. In effect Burke, rooted in agrarian capitalism, recommends a sentimental attachment to this event, which is justifiable in terms of the social upshot—since he at least recognizes in pragmatic terms how human beings live in time as well as space.[8]

The conversion of liberalism into a tradition seems then, for MacIntyre, to be to do with a shift of liberalism from contract theory toward utilitarianism. Yet, as Alain Caillé points out, the latter still preserves the conditionalism of the former: for example, I agree to forego present pleasures for the guaranteed return of more stable and less threatened ones in the long term. The risk of handing over and receiving a gift that is the very essence of a tradition is here refused. Yet one can note here that the modern explorations of the "prisoner's dilemma," as Caillé has explained, are fatal for all modes of liberal conditionalism.[9] This is because isolated individuals could never, logically speaking, take the risk of trusting each other. Human society is only there at all because of an initial, arbitrary, "aristocratic," magnanimous offer that is relatively unconditional in the sense of seeking for an equal "abandonment" in return. Because tradition means "to hand over a gift" one can see how the primacy of handing down in time also implies an open spiral movement in space rather than the closed circular one of liberalism. Here we recognize that the primary social bond is not one of exactly kept laws and precisely fulfilled contracts but rather of a paradoxical sense of continued mutual and positive indebtedness in which each party always feels that she owes more to the other rather than the other way around.

It is therefore a consequence of MacIntyre's treatment of liberalism as a tradition that all modes of thought that seek to occlude the necessity of justification by tradition are doomed not only to erect a pseudotradition but also to tell mythical stories about human origins like that of the social contract, the perfect equilibrium of markets or the basic sway of purely utilitarian motives. They fail to see the primacy of the human search, as Hegel noted, for mutual recognition or mutual honoring, of which our honoring of wealth or fame for fame's sake are but particular (and one could argue debased) modes. This primacy of recognition is a simple consequence of our nature as a symbol-using animal that ensures the detour through gratuity that one could define as an unnecessary display.[10]

It follows from this that the tradition-denying theories of liberalism have to erect either the political or the economic, either the whole or the individual, as more primary than the social, and that in the course of so doing they are bound to obfuscate human history. And one can add that all secular thought will have this tendency because it will search for immanent modes of the justification of social order in terms of the naturally given. Here the likeliest candidates are always either an assumed organic whole or else allegedly isolated atomic individuals. But the only historically plausible understanding of the human social essence is a traditioned one where what is primary is human relationship, which can only be constituted by the play of relative unconditionality—the play of give and take in space and of inheriting and handing over through time. All human associations are constituted in this manner and any purportedly contractual polity or market in reality conceals the tacit bonds of custom and trust that are crucial for holding it together, as the later Burke realized.

Yet, given this primacy of the association over conditional groupings, one can see the secondariness of (merely) political and (merely) economic groupings compared to the association as such, which, as Augustine suggested, can be any formation of persons united by the object of its desire. In our present circumstances this can suggest a mode of counterpolemic for all the world religions. Far from it being the case that they are aberrant formations compared to the state or the market, just the opposite is true. For religions, just because they claim supernatural foundations, do not need to lie about their origins in time. They, and not secular bodies, can be critically honest about their own genealogy. This is because they can admit the unconditional character of their origins in gift, when a founder or founders offered something as a new foundation that had neither been voted for nor agreed upon, even though it awaited the "democratic" assent of the people in order to attest its authenticity. It is just this classical mixed constitution of every maturely reflexive world religion that ensures its critical rigor. It is able to understand its own traditioned process in ways that a purely secular body must necessarily obfuscate. This is mainly because telling the truth about unconditional origins would appear from a secular humanist point of view to reveal the role of the sheerly arbitrary. And at this point only secularity turned into a cult of power à la Nietzsche can tell something like the truth, yet only at the price of reducing all of the symbolic to the ruses of all nature and therefore exiting the human altogether. Therefore it is only a religious humanism that can be both honest and coherent. For the symbolic order that is passed on as gift—as the combination of sign and thing, having by definition no rational foundation—can only be justified if it is taken to participate in or to reveal a transcendent divine or heavenly order. In this context I would reject MacIntyre's implied suggestion that an immanent dialectical development of a tradition works in some respects as a justification in terms of natural law: for this leaves unaffected the problem of its seemingly arbitrary commencement.

These comments may throw some light on the way in which current global politics, especially British politics, seems to be tilting away from a left versus right axis toward one that pits secular believers in individual choice, and so in the primacy of state and market, against religious or ethical believers in the primacy of association and of human relatedness. For despite the antitraditional stridency of secular thinkers, the social illogic of the former position is beginning to be demonstrated in practice. An associative void has opened up, which new forms of association-making are rushing to fill.

At the end of this essay I have suggested a kind of pan-religious logic of tradition. But I began it by wondering how far an extreme insistence on the primacy of tradition was in fact an explicitly Christian stress. That is a matter for discussion, though I do not think that the two suggestions are entirely incompatible with each other.

For my own part (though I know that this would not command general assent) I would venture that Christianity is exactly that religion that reaches the clearest insights about a primacy of tradition that one can take as a sociological and metahistorical truth and is accordingly able to be the most critically honest about its origins—since if these were already a "handing over" they were necessarily both murky and complex and necessarily at once entirely symbolic and entirely real. It is further able to rest its faith upon "tradition alone" (tradition being also the ever-generative scripture and the historicity of reason) because "handing over" is taken to be exhaustively an interchange of love that has refused all competition save in the degree of self-abandonment. The revelatory and participatory justification of the Christian order is moreover in terms of a divine order that is internally a mediating and a handing over. It is in this respect no accident that the New Testament names the third person of the Trinity "gift" and insists that the Holy Spirit's specific mode of personal action that conveys the action of the entire Godhead is to give gifts to us in every sense. The Triune God is an eternally established and yet forever reignited *traditio.*

One could then further suggest that the crisis of Christian tradition involves a sudden doubt about whether after all it is love that is handed over, and in consequence a highly novel attempt (as compared with other cultures) to abandon the ground of tradition altogether. The later alternative to this initial response to crisis, is, as we have seen, a nihilistic construal of tradition that naturalizes it and so abolishes it once more. In various modes, though (of which Mauss's discovery of gift-exchange is one and the explorations of the Polanyi brothers another), modern secular Western thinkers have rediscovered the primacy of tradition in a way that covertly rejoins both their Latin and Christian legacy and yet may be of universal import.

For Further Reflection

1. Is "tradition" really a peculiarly Christian and Western notion?
2. Does Islam have its own, but somewhat different, notion of the transmission of truths through time?
3. Are MacIntyre's ideas about the traditionedness of reason compatible with the objectivity of truth?
4. Are MacIntyre's ideas on tradition useful for interreligious dialogue?

Notes

1. See Dom Bruno Reynders, "Paradosis: Le progrès de l'idée de la tradition jusqu'à Saint Irénée," *Recherches de théologie ancienne et médiévale* 5 (1933): 155–91.

2. See Jean Daniélou, *Gospel Tradition and Hellenistic Culture*, trans. John A. Baker (London: Westminster Press, 1973); and Henri de Lubac, *History and Spirit: The Understanding of Scripture According to Origen*, trans. Anne Englund Nash (San Francisco: Ignatius, 2007), 173.

3. Rémi Brague, *Eccentric Culture: A Theory of European Civilisation,* trans. Samuel Lester (South Bend, IN: St Augustine's Press, 2002).

4. Franz Rosenzweig, *The Star of Redemption*, trans. Barbara E. Galli (Madison: University of Wisconsin Press, 2005).

5. Alasdair MacIntyre, *After Virtue: A Study in Moral Theory*, 3rd ed. (1981; repr. Notre Dame, IN: Notre Dame University Press, 2007).

6. Rowan Williams, *Dostoevsky: Language, Faith and Fiction* (London: Continuum, 2008).

7. Alasdair MacIntyre, *Whose Justice? Which Rationality?* (Notre Dame, IN: Notre Dame University Press, 1988); and Alasdair MacIntyre, *Three Rival Versions of Moral Enquiry* (Notre Dame, IN: Notre Dame University Press, 1990).

8. MacIntyre fails to mention the later Romantic Burke who surpassed this earlier perspective and, partly in a Humean trajectory, adumbrated in *Reflections on the Revolution in France* a very theological virtue ethic on the basis of feeling and imagination—an approach to which MacIntyre remains problematically averse.

9. Alain Caillé, *Anthropologie du Don* (Paris: La Découverte, 2007).

10. One can note here, however, that an important tradition in modern biology argues that all biological organisms exist only in order to display themselves, functional survival being secondary to this and wholly impotent to explain the variety of species that are all equally well "adapted."

Seyyed Hossein Nasr (1933–)

From *Islam and the Plight of Modern Man*

[The tension between the traditional Muslim outlook and that of modern Western civilization]

THE CONTEMPORARY MUSLIM who lives in the far corners of the Islamic world and has remained isolated and secluded from the influence of modernism may be said to live still within a homogeneous world in which the tensions of life are those of normal human existence. But the Muslim who lives in the centres of the Islamic world touched in one degree or another by modernism lives within a polarized field of tension created by two contending world views and systems of values. This tension is often reflected within his mind and soul, and he usually becomes a house divided against itself, in profound need of re-integration. If he is of an intellectual bent he sees on one side the rich, intellectual heritage of Islam as a still-living reality, a heritage which is precisely a message from the Centre and a guide for man in his journey from the rim to the Centre. It is a world view based on the supremacy of the blinding reality of God before whom all creatures are literally nothing, and then on the hierarchic Universe issuing from His Command (*Amr*) and comprising the multiple levels of being from the archangelic world to the level of material existence. It is a *Weltanschauung* based on viewing man as the "image of God" . . . as God's vicegerent (*khalīfah*) on earth but also as His perfect servant (*ʿabd*) obeying His every command. It is based on the idea that all phenomena in the world of nature are symbols reflecting divine realities and that all things move according to His Will and their spiritual nature (*malakūt*), which is in His Hands. It is based on the conception that only the law of God, the *Sharīʿah*, has ultimate claim upon the allegiance and respect of men and that it alone can provide for their felicity in its true sense.

On the other side and in contrast to this world view, the contemporary Muslim sees the basic assumptions of modern Western civilization, nearly all of which are the very antithesis of the Islamic principles he cherishes. He sees philosophies based either on man considered as a creature in rebellion against Heaven or on the human collectivity seen as an ant-heap in which man has no dignity worthy of his real nature. He sees the Universe reduced to a single level of reality—the spatio-temporal complex of matter and energy—and all the higher levels of reality relegated to the category of old wives' tales or—at best—images drawn from the collective unconscious. He sees the power of man as ruler upon the earth emphasized at the expense of his servanthood so that he is considered to be not the *khalīfatallāh*, the vicegerent of God, but *khalīfah* of his own ego or of some worldly power or collectivity. He sees the theomorphic nature of man either mutilated or openly negated. He reads the arguments of Western philosophers and scientists against the symbolic concept of nature, a concept which is usually debased by being called "totemistic" or "animistic" or some other term of that *genre*, usually loaded with pejorative connotations. He is, in fact, made to believe that the transformation from seeing the phenomena of nature as the portents or signs (*āyāt*) of God to viewing these phenomena as brute facts is a major act of progress which, however, only prepares nature for that ferocious rape and plunder for which modern man is now beginning to pay so dearly. Finally, the contemporary Muslim is taught to believe that the law is nothing but a convenient agreement within a human collectivity and therefore relative and ever-changing, with the implication that there is no such thing as a Divine Law which serves as the immutable norm of human action and which provides the measures against which man can judge his own ethical standards objectively.[1]

[Freedom]

As an example of the contrasts created within these fields and the dilemmas brought into being for the present-day Muslim who is aware of the world about him may be mentioned the concept of freedom. In the traditional Islamic view, absolute freedom belongs to God alone and man can gain freedom only to the extent that he becomes God-like. All the restrictions imposed upon his life by the *Sharīʿah* or upon his art by the traditional canons are seen not as restrictions upon his freedom but as the indispensable aids which alone make the attainment of real freedom possible. The concept of *hurriyyah* (the word into which "freedom" is usually translated today in modern Arabic) is taken from the post-Renaissance idea of individual freedom, which means ultimately imprisonment within the narrow confines of one's own individual nature. This totally Western idea is so alien to traditional Islam that this word cannot be found in any traditional text with the same meaning it has now gained in modern Arabic. In the Islamic world-view, freedom to do evil or to become severed from the source of all existence is only an illusory freedom. The only real freedom is that which enables man to attain that perfection which allows him to approach and ultimately become unified with the One Who is at once absolute necessity and absolute freedom. How far removed is this concept from the current Western notion of freedom, and what confusions are created within the mind of a man who is attracted by the pull of both ideas! These confusions affect nearly all of his daily decisions and his relations with nearly all the institutions of society from the family to the state. And they reflect upon art as well as morality, influencing individual patterns of behaviour in matters as far apart as sex and literary style.[2]

[The traditional **ʿulamāʾ** *and the modernists]*

There are today essentially two main classes of people in the Islamic world concerned with religious, intellectual and philosophical questions: the *ʿulamāʾ* and other religious and traditional authorities in general (including the Sufis), and the modernists still interested in religion. Only now is a third group gradually coming into being which is traditional like the *ʿulamāʾ* but also knows the modern world. As far as the *ʿulamāʾ* and other traditional spiritual authorities are concerned, it has already been shown that they usually do not possess a profound knowledge of the modern world and its problems and complexities. But they are the custodians of the Islamic tradition and its protectors, without whom the very continuity of the tradition would be endangered. They are usually criticized by the modernists for not knowing European philosophy and science or the intricacies of modern economics and the like. . . .

As for the second class whose attitudes have been analyzed in previous chapters, they are the product of either Western universities or universities in the Islamic world which more or less ape the West. Now, universities in the Islamic world are themselves in a state of crisis which stems from the question of identity, for an educational system is organically related to the culture within whose matrix it functions. A jet plane can be made to land in the airport of no matter which country in Asia or Africa and be identified as part of that country. But an educational system cannot be simply imported; the fact that modern universities are facing a crisis in the Islamic world of a different nature from that which is found in the West is itself proof of this assertion. The crisis could not but exist because the indigenous Islamic culture is still alive. Moreover, this crisis affects deeply those who are educated in these universities and who are usually called the "intelligentsia." This term, like that of "intellectual," is a most unfortunate one, in that often those so characterized are the farthest removed from the domain of the intellect in its true sense. But, by whatever name they are called, most of those who are products of Western-oriented universities have one feature in common: a predilection for all things Western and a sense of inferiority relative to things Islamic. This sense of inferiority *vis-à-vis* the West . . . is the greatest malady facing the Islamic world, and afflicts most deeply the very group which one would expect to face the challenge of the West. The encounter of Islam with the West cannot therefore be discussed without taking into consideration that mentality which is in most cases the product of a modern university education, a mentality which, during the past century, has been responsible for most of the apologetic Islamic works concerned with the encounter of Islam and the West.[3]

[Western and Islamic literature]

Truly Islamic literature is very different from the kind of subjective literature we find in the writings of Franz Kafka or at best in Dostoevsky. These and similar writers are, of course, among the most important in modern Western literature, but they, along with most other modern Western literary figures, nevertheless present a point of view which is very different from, and usually totally opposed to, that of Islam. Among older Western literary figures who are close to the Islamic perspective, one might mention first of all Dante and Goethe who, although profoundly Christian, are in many ways like Muslim writers. In modern times, one could mention, on of course another level, T. S. Eliot, who, unlike most modern writers, was a devout Christian and possessed, for this very reason, a vision of the world not completely removed from that of Islam.

In contrast to the works of such men, however, the psychological novel, through its very form and its attempt to penetrate into the psyche of men without possessing any criterion with which to discern Truth as an objective reality is an element that is foreign to Islam. Marcel Proust was, without doubt, a master of the French language and his *In Search of Time Past* is of much interest for those devoted to modern French literature, but this type of writing cannot under any conditions become the model for a genuinely Muslim literature. Yet it is this very type of psychological literature that is now beginning to serve as a "source of inspiration" for a number of writers in Arabic and Persian. It is of interest to note that the most famous modern literary figure of Persia, Sadeq Hedayat, who was deeply influenced by Kafka, committed suicide because of psychological despair and that, although certainly a person of great literary talent, he was divorced from the Islamic current of life.[4]

From *Traditional Islam in the Modern World*

[Traditional and "fundamentalist" Islam]

Nowhere, however, does the veneer of Islamicity that covers so many movements claiming a revival of Islam wear more thinly than in the field of politics.

Here, while calls are made to return to the origin of Islam, to the pure message of the Quran and to the teachings of the Prophet, and to reject all that is modern and Western, one ends up by adopting all the most extreme political ideas that have arisen in Europe since the French Revolution, but always portraying them as Islamic ideas of the purest and most unadulterated kind. One therefore defends revolution, republicanism, ideology and even class struggle in the name of a supposedly pure Islam prior to its early adulteration by the Umayyads, but rarely bothers to inquire whether the Quran or *Hadith* ever used those terms or even why a movement which claims Islamicity is so direly in need of them, or indeed why the attack against traditional Muslim political institutions coincides so "accidentally" with those of the left in the modern world?

The case of ideology is very telling as far as the adaptation of modern notions in the name of religion is concerned. Nearly every Muslim language now uses this term and many in fact insist that Islam is an ideology. If this be so, then why was there no word to express it in Arabic, Persian and other languages of the Islamic peoples? Is *ʿaqīdah* or *usūl al-ʿaqāʾid*, by which it is sometimes translated, at all related to ideology? If Islam is a complete way of life, then why does it have to adopt a 19th century European concept to express its nature, not only to the West but even to its own adherents? The truth of the matter is in fact that traditional Islam refuses ever to accept Islam as an ideology and it is only when the traditional order succumbs to the modern world that the understanding of religion as ideology comes to the fore, with momentous consequences for religion itself, not to speak of the society which is ruled in the name of religion ideology rather than according to the *dicta* of the *Sharīʿah*, as traditionally understood. To fail to distinguish between these two modes is to fail to grasp the most manifest distinction between traditional Islam and the "fundamentalist"; in fact, it marks the failure to comprehend the nature of the forces at play in the Islamic world today.[5]

[Man and woman in Islam]

No tradition can pass over in silence the central question of the relationship between man and woman in religious as well as in social life. Islam is no exception to this rule. On the contrary, traditional Islam, basing itself on the explicit teachings of the Quran and the guiding principles of the life of the Prophet, has developed the doctrine of the relationship between the male and the female and formulated the norms according to which the two sexes should live and cooperate in the social order. At a time when innovations of every sort have destroyed for most contemporary people, including many Muslims, the perennial teachings of Islam concerning the male and female relationship, from its metaphysical and spiritual to its most outward aspects, it is particularly necessary to reinstate the traditional Islamic point of view, beginning with the metaphysical principles which govern human nature and the complementary relationship between the male and the female on the highest level.[6]

Furthermore, the difference between the two sexes cannot be only biological and physical because, in the traditional perspective, the corporeal level of existence has its principle in the subtle state, the subtle in the spiritual and the spiritual in the Divine Being Itself. The difference between the sexes cannot be reduced to anatomy and biological function. There are also differences of psychology and temperament, of spiritual types and even principles within the Divine Nature which are the sources *in divinis* of the duality represented on the microcosmic level as male and female. God is both Absolute and Infinite. Absoluteness—and Majesty, which is inseparable from it—are manifested most directly in the masculine state; Infinity and Beauty in the feminine state. The male body itself reflects majesty, power, absoluteness; and the female body reflects beauty, beatitude, and infinity.[7]

Moreover, each sex symbolizes in a positive manner a Divine aspect. Therefore, not only is sexual deviation and perversion a further step away from spiritual perfection, and a great obstacle to it, but also the loss of masculinity and femininity, and movement both psychologically and emotionally toward a neuter common type and ground implies, from the Islamic perspective, an irreparable loss and further fall from the perfection of the primordial *insān*—who was both male and female. The "neuter" person is in fact a parody of the primordial human being, who was both Adam and Eve. Islamic teachings have emphasized this point very clearly. There are in fact *hadīths* of the Prophet which allude to men dressing and acting like women and vice-versa as being signs of the world coming to an end. In Islam, both the male and the female are seen as two creatures of God, each manifesting certain aspects of His Names and Qualities, and in their complementary union achieving the equilibrium and perfection that God has ordained for them and made the goal of human existence.

The tenets of Islam based upon sexual purity, separation of the sexes in many aspects of external life, the hiding of the beauty of women from strangers, division of social and family duties and the like all derive from the principles stated above. Their specific applications have depended on the different cultural and social milieus in which Islam has grown and have been very diverse. For example, the manner in which a Malay woman hides her female beauty is very different from the way of a Syrian, a Pakistani or a Senegalese; and even within a single country, what is called the veil (*hijāb*) has never been the same among nomads, villagers and city dwellers. Nor has the complementary role of the two sexes in all walks of life prevented Muslim women from participating in nearly all aspects of life, from ruling countries to owning major businesses in bazaars or even running butcher shops. Nor has the Islamic world been without eminent female religious and intellectual figures.[8]

The revolt of the sexes against that equilibrium which results from their complementarity and union is both the result and a concomitant of the revolt of modern man against Heaven. Man cannot reach that peace and harmony which is the foretaste of the paradise human beings carry at the center of their being, except by bringing to full actualization and realization the possibilities innate in the human state, both male and female. To reject the distinct and distinguishing features of the two sexes and the Sacred Legislation based on this objective cosmic reality is to live below the human level; to be, in fact, only accidentally human. It is to sacrifice and compromise the eternal life of man and woman for an apparent earthly justice based on a uniformity which fails, ultimately even on the purely earthly level, since it does not take into consideration the reality of that which constitutes the human state in both its male and female aspects.[9]

Notes

1. Seyyed Hossein Nasr, *Islam and the Plight of Modern Man* (London: Longman, 1975), 18–19.
2. Ibid., 21.
3. Ibid., 132–33.
4. Ibid., 141–42.
5. Seyyed Hossein Nasr, *Traditional Islam in the Modern World* (London: Kegan Paul International, 1987), 20–21.
6. Ibid., 47.
7. Ibid., 48–49.
8. Ibid., 53–54.
9. Ibid., 56.

Seyyed Hossein Nasr on Tradition and Modernity

JOSEPH E. B. LUMBARD

BORN IN TEHRAN in 1933, Seyyed Hossein Nasr has been at the forefront of discussions of the relation between Islam and modernity for more than four decades. He has published more than five hundred articles and more than fifty books that have been translated into some twenty languages. Nasr is one of only three intellectuals who have delivered the Gifford Lectures in Natural Theology (1980–81) and also been included in the Library of Living Philosophers (2000), the others being John Dewey (Gifford 1928–29, Library 1939) and Alfred North Whitehead (Gifford 1927–28, Library 1941). *Knowledge and the Sacred*, which resulted from his Gifford Lectures, has been referred to by Huston Smith as "one of the most important books of the twentieth century."[1]

Nasr's unique blend of philosophical, religious, and scientific expertise led him to write such groundbreaking works as *The Encounter of Man and Nature: The Spiritual Crisis in Modern Man* (1968) and *Religion and the Order of Nature* (1996), which present the environmental crisis as an outer reflection of modern man's spiritual crisis. In the 1960s and '70s, his was one of the first philosophical voices to warn of the environmental crisis. He was also among the first scholars to introduce Western audiences to the Islamic scientific tradition in works such as *An Introduction to Islamic Cosmological Doctrines* (1964), *Science and Civilization in Islam* (1968), and *Islamic Science: An Illustrated Study* (1976). Moreover, his extensive work on Islamic philosophy has inspired an entire generation of scholars to engage Islamic philosophy in its own right rather than treating it as a mere footnote to the Western philosophical tradition. Nasr has also been among the most influential scholars in the field of Sufism for the last fifty years. After writing several books and essays about Sufism, Nasr penned *The Garden of Truth: The Vision and Promise of Sufism, Islam's Mystical Tradition* (2008), which presents Sufi teachings from within while remaining accessible to a diverse modern audience.

Nasr's contributions in any one of these fields—philosophy, Sufism, environmental studies, or comparative religion—would constitute a major contribution to intercivilizational and interreligious dialogue. But when his significant impact in each of these fields is considered together, he is arguably one of the most influential thinkers of the past fifty years. This influence has been evident in his crucial contributions to the initiative known as A Common Word. As the main Muslim speaker, opposite the pope, at the first Catholic–Muslim forum held at the Vatican in November 2008, Nasr called upon all participants to bring the message of understanding and reconciliation to their communities: "Those who are guides and trailblazers in religious matters must come forward and seek to bring about understanding to those in their own communities who hearken to their call. They should bring about further knowledge about the other whom they should present as friend, not enemy, to be loved and not vilified."[2]

Currently university professor of Islamic studies at the George Washington University, Seyyed Hossein Nasr has had an illustrious teaching career. In 1958 he became professor of the history of science and philosophy at Tehran University, and in 1972 became chancellor of Aryamehr University in Iran where he instituted educational reforms that are still in effect today. Nasr was also the founding president of the Imperial Iranian Academy of Philosophy, whose purpose was to revive the intellectual traditions of Persia and to bring them into greater dialogue with other philosophical traditions with the goal of applying the fruits of this dialogue to the exigencies of contemporary man.

Tradition and Modernity

The conflict between tradition and modernity, regarding both humanity in general and Islam in particular, is central to many of Nasr's writings, foremost among them, *Knowledge and the Sacred*, *Traditional Islam in the Modern World* (1987), and *Islam and the Plight of Modern Man* (1976). To understand Nasr's position regarding this relationship, one must first understand how he defines these terms.

As employed by Nasr and other "traditionists," such as René Guénon, Frithjof Schuon, Titus Burckhardt, and Martin Lings, "tradition" is not meant to indicate custom, habit, or inherited patterns of life and thought; rather "tradition is of sacred and divine origin and includes the continuity and transmission of that sacred message over time."[3] When used in this manner, "tradition" indicates revelation and all forms of thought, art, and culture that are fashioned by it, extending the reverberations of revelation on earth, and thus serving to remind human beings of the "Divine Center" and "Ultimate Origin" to which all must return. In delineating his own use of the term "tradition" Nasr writes: "As used by the 'traditionists,' the term implies both the Sacred as revealed to man through revelation and the unfolding and development of the sacred message in the history of the particular humanity for which it was destined in a manner that implies both horizontal continuity with the Origin and a vertical nexus which relates each moment of the life of the tradition in question to the meta-historical Transcendental Reality."[4]

Although Nasr and other "traditionists" maintain that the term "tradition" conveys a reality that has existed as long as man has existed, Nasr also notes: "The usage of the term and recourse to the concept of tradition as found in the contemporary world are themselves, in a sense, an anomaly made necessary by the anomaly which constitutes the modern world as such."[5] The aim of using the term is thus "to bring about awareness of the fundamental distinction between that reality described by this particular usage of the term 'tradition' and all that lacks a divine origin but issues from the merely human and sometimes the subhuman."[6]

If "traditional" indicates that which remains tied to its Transcendent Origin and can also lead back to it, "modern" is for Nasr synonymous with "secular" and indicates "that which is cut off from the Transcendent, from the immutable principles which in reality govern all things."[7] Modernism and modernity are thus the opposite of tradition and imply "all that is merely human and now ever more increasingly subhuman, and all that is divorced and cut off from the Divine Source."[8]

The sharp and uncompromising distinction that Nasr makes between tradition and modernity also entails a sharp contrast between modern man and traditional man, or what he refers to as pontifical man, who functions as a bridge between heaven and earth, and promethean man, who has rebelled against heaven. Regarding the former he writes: "Pontifical man, who, in the sense used here, is none other than traditional man, lives in a world which has both an Origin and a Center. He lives in full awareness of the Origin which contains his own perfection and whose primordial purity and wholeness he seeks to emulate, recapture, and transmit."[9] He further clarifies, "Promethean man, on the contrary, is a creature of this world. He feels at home on earth, earth not considered as virgin nature which is itself an echo of paradise, but as the artificial world created by Promethean man himself in order to make it possible for him to forget God and his own inner reality. . . . Having lost the sense of the sacred, he is drowned in transience and impermanence and becomes a slave to his own lower nature, surrender to which he considers to be freedom."[10]

From Nasr's perspective, the human being "is created to seek perfection and final spiritual beatitude through intellectual and spiritual growth," hence "man is only man when he seeks perfection and attempts to go beyond himself."[11] The traditional world is then a world that allows for the realization of these higher possibilities by reminding men and women that their true nature is not only of this world. This is not a romanticized or utopian view of tradition, for it is not mere nostalgia for the past, as some think when misreading Nasr's use of the word "tradition."[12] Nasr fully recognizes that the abode of heaven cannot but be beyond the earthly abode.[13] Nonetheless, the value of a civilization lies not in its technological capabilities but in the spiritual capabilities of the members of that civilization, and the quality of human life derives not from one's standard of living but from one's spiritual orientation. From this perspective, the age of modernity, which makes of man an earthly creature responsible to none but himself and thus detached from his Center and ignorant of his Origin, is the lowest kind of civilization: "if the nature of man is to seek and reach the sacred, then we are *now* living in the dark ages based upon metaphysical ignorance, no matter how much we illuminate our cities at night with electricity."[14]

Tradition, Modernity, and Islam

Regarding the relationship between tradition and modernity in Islam and among Muslims, Nasr decries the inability of many contemporary Muslims to discern the true nature of modernity and the challenges its secular and promethean worldview poses to any traditional religious worldview: "The lack of clarity, precision and sharpness of both mental and artistic contours, which characterizes the modern world itself, seems to plague the contemporary Muslim's understanding of modernism, whether he wishes to adopt its tenets or even to react against it. The influence of modernism seems in fact to have diminished that lucidity and blurred that crystalline transparency which distinguishes traditional Islam in both its intellectual and artistic manifestations."[15]

Any attempt to reconcile Islamic philosophy and theology with modern philosophy is thus a nonstarter for Nasr, since at the level of principles and starting points, they are utterly divergent. In this vein, he decries attempts to arrive at compromise, which lead only toward theological modernism:[16] "I have always opposed the intellectual inferiority complex of Muslim modernists who can hardly think independently vis-à-vis whatever current or fashion of thought happens to issue from the West."[17] From this perspective, Islamic philosophy, like other religious philosophies, is a traditional philosophy founded upon eternal principles while modern philosophy is founded upon the very rejection of those principles.

Given this fundamental contrast between modern philosophy and traditional philosophy, the confrontation of Islam with modern thought cannot take place on a serious level if the primacy of the sacred in the perspective of Islam and its rejection by modern thought is not first taken into consideration. If Muslim intellectuals are to discourse with the modern West on the basis of Islamic teachings, they must acknowledge that the two are operating within different paradigms. Rather than operating within the secular Western paradigm while using a thin veneer of Islamic terminology, as is so often done, Muslims must instead evaluate the secular paradigm on the basis of the traditional Islamic paradigm and critique it accordingly. Only then can any true dialogue occur. Failing to take this initial step, modernist Muslims too often cede the ground to the modern secular humanistic worldview by allowing it to define the terms of the debate and then attempting to redefine Islam in order to better compete on those grounds.[18] Regarding such tendencies Nasr writes: "one cannot accept the attack against the body of Islamic tradition on the pretext of carrying out *ijtihād* by a person whose mind is cluttered by concepts of a secularist nature drawn from another civilization. Such an activity could not but bring about the destruction of the religion itself, not to speak of its philosophy and theology."[19]

In arguing against incorporating modern philosophical tendencies into the body of Islamic thought, Nasr does not advocate a static orthodoxy. Rather he maintains that the only way for contemporary Islam to adequately address the issues that confront Muslims in the modern world is by affecting a renewal (*tajdıd*) of traditional Islamic philosophy.[20] This he contrasts to "the modernist so-called reforms (*iṣlāḥ*) which usually lead to deformation rather than reformation and have moreover produced for the most part intellectually pitiful results in the present-day Islamic world."[21] No matter the circumstances, Nasr insists that true renewal can only be achieved by adhering to orthodoxy understood in its most universal sense, and by allowing orthodoxy to be manifest in all its theological, philosophical, and metaphysical depth in both the exoteric and esoteric domains.

Religion and Science

Perhaps the most controversial aspect of Nasr's critique of modernity is his unrelenting assault upon modern scientism. As a trained scientist with a bachelor's degree in mathematics and physics from MIT, a master's degree in geology and geophysics from Harvard, and a doctorate in the history of science from Harvard, Nasr is well situated to assess the relation between religion and science in the modern world. From his perspective, science in and of itself is neutral, and the information that scientific discovery provides is true on its own plane, but science falls into error when it crosses from the realm of scientific investigation into that of scientistic ideology, generalizing and absolutizing a particular vision of the physical domain of the universe that science is able to study and then judging other disciplines in accord with that narrow vision. In this vein, what Nasr writes of Frithjof Schuon could be equally applied to himself: "[his] criticism is not of what science has discovered but of what is claimed as scientific knowledge while being only hypothesis and conjecture and of what is left aside by modern science."[22] To be properly situated, the relative information provided by the physical sciences must be viewed in relation to the whole of which it is a part, for the relative cannot be fully understood only on its own terms. To bring about such an understanding, Nasr calls for a reintegration of modern science into metaphysics and the traditional cosmological sciences in which knowledge of the level of reality that each discipline is equipped to analyze is perceived through the light of higher forms of knowledge, "at the apex of which stands the knowledge of the One before which all is reduced to nothingness."[23] In this way, discoveries pertaining to the lower levels of reality, those that pertain to the physical world, will become more intelligible because they are then understood not as brute facts but as manifestations of higher realities and all forms can be seen in relation to their ontological and causal principle. Such an adjustment would completely alter the contemporary understanding of the relation between religion and science.

Conclusion

In the final analysis, Nasr's uncompromising critique of modernity derives not from disdain or hate but from his love for truth itself, for, as he maintains, "One cannot love God without rejecting that which would deny Him."[24] He seeks to expose the fallacies upon which modernism is founded in order to save contemporary man from a world that denies his pontifical nature, reducing him to his rational and animal aspects and leaving him to wander in a desacralized wasteland, oblivious to his Origin and estranged from his true self, living on the periphery with no orientation towards the Center. From Nasr's perspective, "Only tradition can provide the weapon necessary to carry out that vital battle for the preservation of the things of the spirit in a world which would completely devour man as a spiritual being if it could."[25] His critique is not against any particular civilization but against that which undermines what he believes is best in all civilizations. Having been raised in the Islamic tradition, he focuses extensively upon it, but ultimately the wisdom that he seeks is "neither of the east nor of the west" (Qur'ān 24:35). It is knowledge of the infinite and eternal sacred that Nasr believes to be present in all traditional religions, and that liberates man from the fetters of his earthly limitations. For he maintains that only through such knowledge can contemporary man escape the current of errors that is modernity, reawaken his immortal pontifical self, and reverse the spiritual and physical destruction that its promethean shadow has wrought.

For Further Reflection

1. Is it inevitable that traditional Muslims will come to the negative view expressed by Nasr in the selection of texts of the modern concept of "freedom"? To what extent are traditional Christians likely to share his view?
2. How would representatives of the Islamic modernism criticized by Nasr respond to his description of their "inferiority complex" in relation to the modern West?
3. How convincing is Nasr's critique of the ideologization of Islam by "fundamentalists"?

Notes

1. Huston Smith, "Foreword" to *The Essential Seyyed Hossein Nasr*, ed. William C. Chittick (Bloomington, IN: World Wisdom, 2007), xii.

2. Seyyed Hossein Nasr, "We and You—Let Us Meet in God's Love," exp. ver. *Sophia: The Journal of Traditional Studies* 14, no. 2 (Winter 2009).

3. While these thinkers are also known as "perennialists" or as representatives of the "perennial philosophy," this essay will focus on the term "tradition" because it is the subject of the volume and to avoid confusion with many other definitions of "perennial" and "perennial philosophy." See Seyyed Hossein Nasr, *Knowledge and the Sacred* (Albany, NY: SUNY Press, 1989), 67; and Seyyed Hossein Nasr, "Reply to Shu-Hsien Liu," in *The Library of Living Philosophers*, vol. 27, *The Philosophy of Seyyed Hossein Nasr*, ed. Lewis Edwin Hahn, Randall E. Auxier, and Lucian W. Stone Jr. (Peru, IL: Open Court Press, 2000), 270.

4. Seyyed Hossein Nasr, *Traditional Islam in the Modern World* (London: Routledge and Kegan Paul, 1987), 13.

5. Nasr, *Knowledge and the Sacred*, 66.

6. Nasr, "Reply to Shu-Hsien Liu," 270.

7. Nasr, *Traditional Islam in the Modern World*, 98.

8. Ibid.

9. Nasr, *Knowledge and the Sacred*, 160.

10. Ibid., 161.

11. Nasr, *Traditional Islam in the Modern World*, 105.

12. In addressing this common misunderstanding, Nasr writes, "The last thing I have ever spoken of is romantic nostalgia for the past. My nostalgia has always been for that spiritual reality at the center of man's being, that eternal home from which we have become exiled. If I defend premodern periods of culture, or what we call traditional cultures, it is because they still reflected the light of that Center to which we must all ultimately return. Far from being

based on romantic nostalgia, this perspective is rooted in the most rigorous form of realism" ("Reply to Shu-Hsien Liu," 274).

13. For Nasr, "utopianism" is in fact a modern phenomenon whose manifestations within the Islamic world have led to fundamentalism and deformation; see *Traditional Islam in the Modern World*, 106–8.

14. Nasr, "Reply to Shu-Hsien Liu," 273.

15. Nasr, *Traditional Islam in the Modern World*, 98.

16. For Nasr's critique of "Theological Modernism," see "Reflections on the Theological Modernism of Hans Küng" in *The Need for a Sacred Science* (Albany: SUNY Press, 1993), 159–69.

17. Nasr, "Reply to Marietta Stepaniants," in *The Library of Living Philosophers*, vol. 27, *The Philosophy of Seyyed Hossein Nasr*, ed. Lewis Edwin Hahn, Randall E. Auxier, and Lucian W. Stone Jr. (Peru, IL: Open Court Press, 2000), 810.

18. From the perspective of the traditional school, the most obvious example of this tendency toward sycophantic capitulation in modern theology would be the work of Teilhard de Chardin, regarding whom Nasr writes, "From the traditional point of view Teilhard represents an idolatry which marks the final phase of the desacralization of knowledge and being." *Knowledge and the Sacred*, 241.

19. Nasr, "Reply to Marietta Stepaniants," 810–11.

20. Ibid., 810.

21. Ibid.

22. Nasr, "Introduction" to *The Essential Writings of Frithjof Schuon*, ed. Seyyed Hossein Nasr (Rockport, MA: Element, 1986), 47.

23. Nasr, "Response to Ibrahim Kalin," in *The Library of Living Philosophers*, vol. 27, *The Philosophy of Seyyed Hossein Nasr*, ed. Lewis Edwin Hahn, Randall E. Auxier, and Lucian W. Stone Jr. (Peru, IL: Open Court Press, 2000), 465.

24. Nasr, *Essential Writings of Frithjof Schuon*, 46.

25. Ibid., 50.

Elisabeth Schüssler Fiorenza (1938–)

From *In Memory of Her*

[The ekklēsia *of women]*

In the Greek Old Testament *ekklēsia* means the "assembly of the people of Israel before God." In the New Testament *ekklēsia* comes through the agency of the Spirit to visible, tangible expression in and through the gathering of God's people around the table, eating together a meal, breaking the bread, and sharing the cup in memory of Christ's passion and resurrection. *Christian* spirituality means eating together, sharing together, drinking together, talking with each other, receiving each other, experiencing God's presence through each other, and, in doing so, proclaiming the gospel as God's alternative vision for everyone, especially for those who are poor, outcast, and battered. As long as women Christians are excluded from breaking the bread and deciding their own spiritual welfare and commitment, *ekklēsia* as the discipleship of equals is not realized and the power of the gospel is greatly diminished. The true spiritual person is according to Paul the one who *walks* in the Spirit, she who brings about this new world and family of God over and against the resistance and pull of all oppressive powers of this world's enslaving patriarchal structures.

A feminist Christian spirituality, therefore, calls us to gather together the *ekklēsia of women* who, in the angry power of the Spirit, are sent forth to feed, heal, and liberate our own people who are women. It unmasks and sets us free from the structural sin and alienation of sexism and propels us to become children and spokeswomen of God. It rejects the idolatrous worship of maleness and articulates the divine image in female human existence and language. It sets us free from the internalization of false altruism and self-sacrifice that is concerned with the welfare and work of men first to the detriment of our own and other women's welfare and calling. It enables us to live "for one another" and to experience the presence of God in the *ekklēsia* as the gathering of women. Those of us who have heard this calling respond by committing ourselves to the liberation struggle of women and all peoples, by being accountable to women and their future, and by nurturing solidarity within the *ekklēsia* of women. Commitment, accountability, and solidarity in community are the hallmarks of our calling and struggle.

Two major objections are usually raised at this point. The first is that the church of women does not share in the fullness of church. This is correct, but neither do exclusive male hierarchical assemblies. Women's religious communities have always existed within the Catholic tradition. They were generated as soon as the local structures became patriarchal and hierarchical and therefore had to relegate women to subordinate roles or to eliminate them from church office altogether. The male hierarchical church in turn has always sought to control these communities by colonizing them through male theology, liturgy, law, and spirituality, but was never quite able to do so. By abolishing these religious communities of women the Protestant Reformation has strengthened patriarchal church structures and intensified male clerical control of Roman Catholic women's communities in modern times. In the past centuries, however, women founders and leaders of their people have arisen again and again who sought to gather communities of women free from clerical and monastic control. A Christian feminist spirituality claims these communities of women and their history as our heritage and history and seeks to transform them into the *ekklēsia* of women by claiming our own spiritual powers and gifts, by deciding our own welfare, by standing accountable for our decisions, in short, by rejecting the patriarchal structures of laywomen and nun-women, of laywomen and clergywomen, which deeply divide us along patriarchal lines.

The second objection made is the charge of "reverse sexism" and the appeal to "mutuality with men" whenever we gather together as the *ekklēsia* of women in Her name. However, such an objection does not face sufficiently the issues of patriarchal oppression and power. It looks too quickly for easy grace, having paid lip service to the structural sin of sexism. Do we call it "reverse imperialism" if the poor of South and Central America gather together as a people? Or do we call it "reverse colonialism" whenever Africans or Asians gather together as a people? We do not do so because we know too well that the coming together of those exploited does not spell the oppression of the rich or that the oppressed are gaining power over white men and Western nations, but that it means the political bonding of oppressed people in their struggle for economic and cultural survival. Why then do men feel threatened by the bonding of women in our struggle for liberation? Why then can churchmen not understand and accept that Christian women gather together for the sake of our spiritual survival as Christians and women persons? It is not over and against men that we gather together but in order to become *ekklēsia* before God, deciding matters affecting our own spiritual welfare and struggle. Because the spiritual colonialization of women by men has entailed our internalization of the male as divine, men have to relinquish their spiritual and religious control over women as well as over the church as the people of God, if mutuality should become a real possibility.

Women in turn have to reclaim their spiritual powers and to exorcise their possession by male idolatry before mutuality is possible. True, "the dream of a common language" belongs to God's alternative world of cohumanity in the power of the Spirit. Yet it can only become reality among the people of God, when male idolatry and its demonic structures are rejected in the confession of the structural and personal sin of sexism and when the fullness of *ekklēsia* becomes a possibility in a genuine conversion of individual persons and ecclesiastical structures. Not women, but churchmen exclude women from "breaking the bread and sharing the cup" in eucharistic table community.

Images have a great power in our lives. For almost two hundred years two biblical images have dominated the American women's movement in and outside of organized religion. The image of Eden-home determines today the arguments and appeals of the so-called Moral Majority, while that of the Exodus has inspired radical feminism, calling us to abandon the oppressive confines of home and church. The "cult of true womanhood" proclaims that the vocation of women is "homemaker." The fulfillment of her true nature and happiness consists in creating the home as a peaceful island in the sea of alienated society, as Eden-Paradise to which men can retreat from the exploitations and temptations of the work-world. Women must provide in the home a climate of peace and happiness, of self-sacrificing love and self-effacing gentility in order to "save the family." Therefore, feminine spiritual calling is superior to that of men. This praise of femininity conveniently overlooks that poor and unmarried women cannot afford to stay "at home"; it overlooks the violence done to women and children in the home, and it totally mistakes patriarchal dependency for Christian family.

The Exodus image on the other hand compels women to leave everything behind they treasure: loving community with men, shelter and happiness, children, nurturance and religion because all this has contributed to their oppression and exploitation in patriarchal family and church. Women have to move away from "the fleshpots" of patriarchal slavery and institution and live "in a new space and time." The image of the Exodus calls women to move out from the sanctity of the home, to leave the servitude of the patriarchal family, and to abandon the certitudes of patriarchal religion. The spirituality of Exodus, however, overlooks not only that the patriarchal oppression of "Egypt" is everywhere but also that God is present not just on the boundaries but also in the center, if God is "in the midst of us" wherever and whenever we struggle for liberation. These two biblical images—that of Eden and that of Exodus—place us before the alternatives: either to become Martha serving Jesus in the home or to become Miriam, the sister of Moses, leading her people into the desert. These images, however, do not lead us into the center of patriarchal society and church bringing about God's vision of cohumanity in our struggle and solidarity with each other.

The Roman Catholic variation of these alternative biblical images is the image of Martha, as laywoman, serving Jesus and the family in the home, and that of Mary, as nun-woman, leaving the world of family and sexuality and serving Jesus in "religious life" and patriarchally defined ecclesiastical orders. The dichotomy evoked by the images of Exodus and Eden becomes structurally expressed in a dichotomy of lifestyles: virgin-mother, religious-lay, spiritual-biological. Women's sexual or spiritual relationship with men or the lack of it becomes constitutive for their Christian vocation. The calendar of saints therefore marks women, but not men, as "virgins" when extolling their sanctity.

Rather than defining women's relationship to God by their sexual relationship to men and through the patriarchal structures of family and church, a feminist Christian spirituality defines women's relationship to God in and through the experience of being called into the discipleship of equals, the assembly of free citizens who decide their own spiritual welfare. The image of the *ekklēsia of women*, the gathering of women as a free and decision-making assembly of God's people, replaces the other biblical images mentioned: that of Eden-home, Exodus-world, and virgin-mother by integrating them with each other. It can however only do so if the structural-patriarchal dualisms in which these alternative images have their spiritual roots are overcome. The *ekklēsia of women* as the new model of church can only be sustained if we overcome the structural-patriarchal dualisms between Jewish and Christian women, laywomen and nun-women, homemakers and career women, between active and contemplative, between Protestant and Roman Catholic women, between married and single women, between physical and spiritual mothers, between heterosexual and lesbian women, between the church and the world, the sacral and the secular. However, we will overcome these dualisms only through and in solidarity with all women and in a catholic sisterhood that transcends all patriarchal ecclesiastical divisions. These patriarchal divisions and competitions among women must be transformed into a movement of women as the people of God. Feminist biblical spirituality must be incarnated in a historical movement of women struggling for liberation. It must be lived in prophetic commitment, compassionate solidarity, consistent resistance, affirmative celebration, and in grassroots organizations of the *ekklēsia of women.*

Such a movement of women as the people of God is truly ecumenical insofar not only as it has in common the experience of patriarchal ecclesiastical sexism but also as it has as its central integrative image the biblical image of God's people that is common to Jewish as well as to Christian religion. Moreover, it is distinctive but not separated from the so-called secular women's movements.

Any struggle against the structural sin of sexism won for Episcopal, Jewish, or Mormon women benefits the liberation struggle of all women and vice versa. Solidarity in the struggle with poor women, third-world women, lesbian women, welfare mothers, or older and disabled women spells out our primary spiritual commitment and accountability.[1]

From *Discipleship of Equals*

Christian Identity

A second liberating experience that the Catholic tradition provided for me as a woman is the teaching that everyone is called to *sainthood.* Even the vocation to the priesthood is superseded by the call to become a saint. Any Catholic girl who grows up reading the "lives of the saints" has probably internalized all kinds of sexual hang-ups, but she could not believe that her only vocation and her genuine Christian calling consist in getting married and having children. Granted, from a theological and hagiographical point of view the life-choices of the women saints were often limited and conformed to male stereotypes. Nevertheless they still contradicted the middle-class cultural message that woman's true vocation is the sacrifice of her life for the career of her husband and the total devotion of her time to diapering babies or decorating her living room. The biographies of the saints are indeed different from the image of the "total woman" propagated by the cultural-religious feminine mystique.

The "lives of the saints" provide a variety of role-models for Christian women. More importantly they teach that women, like men, have to follow their vocation from God, even if this means that they have to go up against the ingrained cultural mores and images of woman. Women, as well as men, are not defined by their biology and reproductive capabilities but by the call to discipleship and sainthood. The early Christians considered themselves as those who were called and elected by God, as the saints of God, This call broke through all limitations of religion, class, race, and gender. The gospels affirm in various ways that Jesus' call to discipleship has precedence over all other obligations, religious duties, and family ties. Jesus did not respect the patriarchal family and its claims, but replaced it with the new community of disciples. When his mother and brothers asked for him, he replied, according to Mark:

> Who is my mother? Who are my brothers? And looking round at those who were sitting in the circle about him he said: "Here are my mother and my brothers. Whoever does the will of God is my brother, my Sister, my mother." (Mark 3:31–35)

This theological self-understanding of the Christian community is best expressed in the baptismal formula of Galatians 3:27–29. In reciting this confession, the newly initiated Christians proclaimed their vision of discipleship and inclusive community. Over and against the cultural-religious patterns shared by Hellenists and Jews alike, the Christians affirmed at their baptism that the Christian calling eliminates all status distinctions of religion, race, class, and caste and leads into a truly universal and catholic community of disciples. Early Christian self-identity is defined by the call to become disciples of Jesus and members of the Christian community. Unfortunately, this early Christian self-understanding did not continue to determine the definitions of Christian self-identity and Christian community proposed by later theology. Instead, theology often derived the understanding of Christian identity from cultural anthropology and patterned the structures of the Christian community after the patriarchal societal orders. Instead of formulating a new Christian anthropology in accordance with the call to discipleship and sainthood, it spelled out Christian vocation and discipleship in terms of a cultural anthropology embedded in patriarchy.[2]

The Pilgrim Church

To affirm that Christian faith and theology are not inherently patriarchal and sexist and to maintain, at the same time, that Christian theology and the Christian churches are guilty of the sin of sexism is the task of a Catholic Christian feminist theology. Christian feminists respond to the ideology and praxis of sexism in the church basically in two different ways. We do not differ so much in our analyses and critique of the cultural and theological establishment as in our spirituality and strategies. Those who advocate an exodus from all the institutions of Christianity for the sake of the gospel and the genuine experience of transcendence point to the history of Christianity and to their own personal histories as justification for this exodus. They argue that the submission of women is absolutely essential to the churches' functioning. Women can never be more than marginal beings in the present Christian structures and theologies.

Christian feminists who hope for the repentance and radical change of the Christian churches and biblical religion affirm on the other hand our own prophetic roles and critical mission within organized Christianity. We attempt to bring our feminist analysis and critique to bear upon theology and the Christian church in order to set free the traditions of emancipation, equality, and genuine human community that we have experienced in our Christian heritage. We do not overlook or cover up the oppression and sin that we have suffered at the hands of Christian institutions and traditions, but we point them out in order to change them.

Catholic feminists who identify with the Christian tradition and remain within the institutional structures of the church can do so because we take seriously the Roman Catholic Church's self-understanding expressed in Vatican II. The Constitution on Divine Revelation, for instance, asserts that only those statements of the Bible are the revealed Word of God that pertain to "our salvation." Cultural and anthropological frameworks are not the content of divine revelation, just as scientific and cosmological statements are only expressions of the human perception and knowledge of the sacred authors. The council takes seriously the principle of incarnation when it asserts that divine revelation is only given in human, cultural, and societally conditioned language. This principle of incarnation is also employed by various other council documents that describe the reality of the church.

> Until there is a new heaven and a new earth where justice dwells (2 Peter 3:13), the Pilgrim Church in her sacraments and institutions which pertain to this present time takes on the appearance of this passing world. (*Lumen Gentium* 48)

This incarnational principle demands a feminist hermeneutic understanding that is directed not simply toward the actualizing continuation and perceptive understanding of Christian tradition and church, but rather toward a critique of Bible, tradition, and church to the extent that they contribute to the oppression and domination of women in a patriarchal and sexist culture and religion. Feminist spirituality must grow out of feminist theology understood as a critical theology of liberation. Such a spirituality has the task to uncover Christian theological traditions and myths that perpetuate sexist ideologies, violence, and alienation. A Christian feminist spirituality thus is based on the theological presupposition that Christian women as well as the Christian community are in constant need for renewal and conversion. Christian life, church, and theology are caught in the middle of history and, therefore, are in constant need of prophetic critique.

A positive formulation of a feminist Christian spirituality and identity can, in my opinion, never prescind from theological and cultural critique. It must not demand of women that they forget their own anger and hurt and overlook the violence done to their sisters. In Christian terms: no cheap grace is possible. At the beginning of Christian life and discipleship stands *metanoia*, a new orientation in the life-power of the Spirit. Christian theology and the Christian community will only be able to speak in an authentic way to the quest for feminist spirituality and for the religious identity of women when the whole church, as well as its individual members, has renounced all forms of sexist ideology and oppressive praxis that are manifested in church structures, theologies, and liturgies. The Roman Catholic Church must publicly and officially confess that it has wronged women. As it has officially rejected national and racial exploitation and publicly repented of its tradition of anti-Semitic theology, so the Catholic Church is still called to abandon all forms of sexism.

An analysis of Catholic Christian traditions and history, however, indicates that church and theology will transcend their own sexist ideologies only when women are granted full spiritual, theological, and ecclesial equality. The Christian churches will overcome their oppressive patriarchal traditions and their present sexist theologies and practices only if the very basis of these theologies and practices is changed. If women were admitted to full leadership in church and theology, the need would no longer exist to affirm theologically the maleness of God and Christ and to suppress the Spirit who moves women to full participation in the Catholic Church and its ministry. Church leaders and theologians who do not respect the Spirit of liberty and responsibility among Catholic Christian women deny full catholicity to church theology. Only if we, women and men, are able to live in nonsexist Catholic communities, celebrate nonsexist Christian liturgies, think in nonsexist theological terms, and call on God with many names and images will we be able to formulate a genuine Christian feminist spirituality.[3]

Notes

1. Elisabeth Schüssler Fiorenza, *In Memory of Her: A Feminist Theological Reconstruction of Christian Origins* (London: SCM, 1983), 345–49.
2. Elisabeth Schüssler Fiorenza, *Discipleship of Equals: A Critical Feminist Ekklesia-logy of Liberation* (New York: Crossroad, 1993), 95–97.
3. Ibid., 101–3.

Elisabeth Schüssler Fiorenza

A Christian Feminist Responds to Betrayals of the Tradition

LUCY GARDNER

THE THEME OF TRADITION, the handing on of something to be both treasured and handed on again, harbors within it the apparently counter theme of betrayal. All traditions are vulnerable to betrayal for, in the very process of handing on, the original gift may be distorted or even lost. Different traditions no doubt develop different strategies for minimizing the element of betrayal, often centering on the authority to interpret, but these strategies themselves bear witness to the impossibility of reducing the risk of betrayal to zero. Yet the theme of betrayal remains itself ambiguous, for while the guardians or recipients of a tradition may turn out to have betrayed it, the tradition itself, in a very different sense, may persist in "betraying" (i.e., displaying) its true identity.

In Christianity this theme is particularly complex since certain key aspects at its heart can be read in terms of this ambiguity of "handing over": at the Incarnation God is handed over into the created world as a human being; at the crucifixion Jesus is betrayed by Judas, and even Peter, and allows himself to be handed over into and between various human powers and then his body is handed over for burial; in the Eucharist Christ's body is again handed over to the recipients. From the earliest texts we have, it is clear that Christ's followers believed that their message should be translated and even in some sense adapted, often on the basis of their understanding of the Incarnation, thus magnifying the potential for its betrayal.

This difficult and intriguing theme of betrayal is tackled in particular ways by feminist theologians, who detect significant betrayals of the tradition within the tradition as they have received it and set to work responding to them, often in very different ways. Elisabeth Schüssler Fiorenza, a Roman Catholic, is one of those feminist theologians; she has been the Krister Stendahl Professor at the Harvard Divinity School since 1988. Born in Romania in 1938, she grew up and was educated in Germany. She was the first woman to complete the theology course at the University of Würzburg, alongside men training to be priests. She understands feminist theology as a liberationist movement and has devoted her energies, in a way that often cuts across traditional academic theological disciplines, to exposing unjust religio-political structures (past and present), particularly "patriarchy," and critiquing their relationships (both in terms of origin and in terms of legacy) to the rhetorics in and about Christian texts, cultures, and orthodoxy.

Schüssler Fiorenza's theological activity has a double focus. The first is the reconstruction of Christian history (largely early Christian history, particularly in the New Testament era) in a rereading of the tradition that seeks to bring to the fore the cultural, social, and religious situations of women (both positive and negative) and the ways that these are both products of and defenses for (or against) certain readings of the tradition (some "orthodox," others not) in particular contexts. But her interest is not merely historical; she seeks to liberate women from being forgotten or misrepresented in "official" or "orthodox" accounts of history not merely for their sake or for the sake of a "better" account of history but precisely in order to understand the true legacy of those early years and thus turn to expose contemporary "official" or "orthodox" accounts that exclude people today and so betray the central themes of Christianity. Thus, her second focus is to reread present-day expressions of this tradition, analyzing and critiquing contemporary claims to and uses of religious authority, and considering their relationships to the readings of the tradition upon which they depend and which they are inclined to perpetuate. In particular she seeks to expose continuing patriarchal structures and assumptions, and to kindle a lively hope and trust in other possibilities contained within the Gospel message.

Unlike some other feminist scholars such as Daphne Hampson, then, Schüssler Fiorenza does not understand these unjust, patriarchal structures as legitimately inevitable components of the Christian religion, although she is fully aware of their apparent inevitability in the face of certain political power struggles and theological pressures.[1] On the contrary, fundamental to her project is the belief that, in an important and utterly irreducible, inalienable sense, women and men are "equals," and that the Gospel should bring liberation to all. This is a belief that might appear to some to be a "modern" or "secular" ideal, but for Schüssler Fiorenza it is entirely proper to and rooted in the biblical revelation and the revolutionary Gospel of Jesus Christ in particular, a theological point which her attention to religio-sociological study of early Christian texts, beliefs, and practices seeks to establish.

The "reconstruction" of Christian origins with which *In Memory of Her* is concerned recognizes the problems of looking for the truth about women (their oppression *and* their roles in social transformation) in androcentric texts that were produced by middle-class men, heavily influenced and affected by patriarchy (themselves often disadvantaged by its class structures), reflecting assumptions and rhetoric that tend to marginalize women and stress their differences from men.[2] For this reason, careful attention is paid to surrounding cultures, including similarities and differences to them, and to small variations within and between the texts under discussion. The resulting method might somewhat inelegantly be termed a feminist theological-sociological-historical-excavatory hermeneutic that seeks to grant women the dignity of being subjects (and not just objects) of Christian history.[3]

Schüssler Fiorenza's work unearths a complex variety of roles for and views of women in the New Testament texts. Roughly speaking, these can be divided into two groups. One (earlier) group represents a revolt against the dominant Roman socio-religious system of the time. The texts of the Gospels that bear the names of Mark and John, in particular, preserve this sense of Christianity as an alternative movement with an emancipatory culture, with active, authoritative, religious roles for women to play, and an alternative, egalitarian sense of "family" defined by relationship to Christ replacing blood ties or the carefully ordered Roman class system defended by the paterfamilias. The other (later) group adopts a more limiting approach to women's religious roles, more accommodating of the dominant surrounding social views, probably in an attempt to appear attractive and "respectable." In this the later group appears to be trying to avoid the persecutions that the earlier writers regard as inevitable.

The history of these two different visions is far from straightforward. While it can be argued that

> in historical retrospective the New Testament's sociological and theological stress on submission and patriarchal superordination has won out over its sociological and theological stress on altruistic love and ministerial service . . . [,] the writers of Mark and John have made it impossible for the Christian church to forget the invitation of Jesus to follow him on the way to the cross. Therefore, wherever the gospel is preached and heard . . . what the women have done is not totally forgotten because the Gospel story remembers that the discipleship and apostolic leadership of women are integral parts of Jesus' 'alternative' praxis of *agape* and service.[4]

Importantly for Schüssler Fiorenza and her work, then, this is not the end of the story; the patriarchal view has not entirely "won out" over and conquered the vision of a new heaven and a new earth. Her approach, she warns at the end of part 1 of *In Memory of Her*, is *not* one in search "of true pristine, orthodox beginnings, which have been corrupted either by early Catholicism or by 'heresy,'" nor is it an argument for the necessary patriarchalization of Christianity for its historical survival.[5] Either of these would be to take a much too simplistic understanding of "tradition." Her reading sets forth an account of a struggle that has been present from the beginning and that continues today (and that is far more nuanced than present space allows to present). On this type of account, the challenge for Christian feminists, it seems, lies in learning how to respond to and take responsibility for a tradition which brings instruments of oppression along with its promises of and realizations of liberation and equality. The tradition is always at once an invitation and a challenge (on this and many other points), whenever the "modernity" of the reader is to be found.

The texts included in this volume present examples of how Schüssler Fiorenza responds to and takes responsibility for this tradition as a feminist. In the epilogue to *In Memory of Her* ("Toward a Feminist Biblical Spirituality: The *Ekklēsia* of Women"), she turns to reflect on the spiritual implications of the reading she has presented (and I have just briefly summarized), and how it can enable scripture to be used as a resource in the liberation struggle of women and other subordinated people. To attempt to use scripture (and the tradition that preserved it and that flows from it) without a sensitivity to its internal conflicts is, by implication, in danger of confusing oppression with liberation, and therefore ultimately of refusing the challenging invitation offered.[6]

Here we see Schüssler Fiorenza struggling with the tradition not just in terms of scriptural exegesis and early church history but also in terms of how to take up the struggle to which it is a summons today. For her, this includes being bold enough to gather together an *ekklēsia* of women, to refuse false dichotomies of virgin versus mother, "lay" versus "religious," contemplative versus activist, spiritual versus biological, and to refuse all definitions of female spirituality conducted by means of descriptions of the presence or absence of sexual relationships. And this is in the face of those (male and female) voices who claim to speak for and from the same "tradition," who wish to condemn women taking up religious leadership roles (gathering people, breaking the bread, and sharing the cup), who condemn the apparent separatism of gathering as women, and who hold up alternative visions of "true"—submissive—femininity and feminine spirituality.

Furthermore, in place of the false dichotomies offered by other "traditional" interpretations of biblical revelation and its understanding of the meaning of sexual differences and also by some of the radical responses to them, in place of the equally impossible and stunting symbolic ideals of "Eden-Paradise" (domestic femininity) versus campaigning "Exodus" (radical feminism seeking God in an elusive "elsewhere"), or of religious, contemplative Mary versus lay, servile Martha, Schüssler Fiorenza argues for a more holistic vision that brings together what is good and true from both sides of each sets of imagery.[7] Women should not have to choose between equally oppressive cozy domesticity and harsh, rootless exile. Working toward this vision (toward holding it in the first place but also toward making it a reality) creates for her an exciting "ecumenicity" (we might even say "catholicity"), in bringing together people—women, but ultimately not only women—who have shared experiences of oppression and so who do not need to "create" false structures of union but who can discover their commonality in joining in a shared struggle against the structural sin of sexism and other forms of oppression.

The passage from *In Memory of Her* included in this volume ends with a passionate attempt to find an expression of God's will for women and humanity that moves beyond patriarchy and simple reactions to it, through responding to the mixed nature of the Christian inheritance of its sacred texts and interpretations of them; the passage on "Christian Identity" from *Discipleship of Equals* speaks much more directly from the experience of liberation as a woman that Schüssler Fiorenza herself found within the tradition, in relation to the "lives of the saints."[8] She recognizes that these are something of a "mixed blessing"; the descriptions of women saints often conform to patriarchal views and the dichotomies we have seen challenged earlier. And yet at the same time their very existence undercut the idea that woman's "true" goal must be domesticity and awoke Schüssler Fiorenza to the sense that everyone has a vocation and encouraged her to believe that vocation can require one to oppose surrounding social and cultural assumptions.[9] Despite the ways in which she saw the tradition betraying women (and thus itself), she also saw that same tradition betraying a different image of women (and thus displaying its true colors). In the lives of women (and men) saints, she found an expression of Jesus' call to join a new family, a new community, that eliminates status distinctions on whatever basis, be that blood, class, religion, race, caste, or gender.[10]

The ways in which the academic endeavor of *In Memory of Her* (which I have briefly outlined), the personal experiences and sense of vocation represented by the passage on "Christian Identity," and the ecclesial program outlined in the passage from the end of *In Memory of Her* come together are described in the final excerpt titled "Pilgrim Church." Here Schüssler Fiorenza provides an account of the choice she believes the two-veined tradition poses Christian feminists: to leave the organized church and churches (for the sake of the Gospel—to do so for any other reason would be to cease to be a *Christian* feminist) or to stay within the organized church and attempt to transform it (again, for the sake of the Gospel).[11] That she can cite the texts of Vatican II (texts produced by and legitimated by a male-dominated hierarchy) as part of her defense for staying shows again the complex admixture delivered by the Christian tradition.[12]

The Christian religious scene, then, cannot simply be drawn as one inhabited by "goodies" and "baddies." Oppressive structures can still pronounce liberating truth; the oppressed themselves are also in constant need of renewal and conversion. She argues, citing the council, that the Incarnation means that divine revelation is given only in culturally conditioned forms; some of that cultural conditioning, she suggests, works against (betrays) the truth that is being delivered.[13] Interpreters of the tradition, therefore, need to work at discerning challenging, liberative, revealed truth—the Word of God—from elements that derive from and perpetuate elements that "contribute to the oppression and domination of women [and presumably, on the basis of arguments made elsewhere, men] in a patriarchal and sexist culture and religion."[14] This is not simply an academic endeavor but a matter of ecclesial engagement and of the ordering of one's own personal life (including attention to prayer—"spirituality"); doctrine, discipleship, and the relation to God and self belong together. Schüssler Fiorenza appears to believe that, insofar as the Church institutionally refuses to engage in the conversations and conversions needed, and refuses to allow women to take up leadership roles, it is rejecting (at least part of) the divine revelation given in Christ and thereby in a sense denying its own identity; it is in fact "not yet church."

For some "modern" and "postmodern" writers, the academic discipline of history itself has become a problem for religion. For some commentators, "history" always seems to speak against "tradition" and often seems to ignore or debunk "true religion." For Schüssler Fiorenza, Christian history (in terms of its actual events) is indeed problematic; it has encompassed and defended the abuse and oppression of women. On the other hand, it is the study of history, the academic discipline of history, that provides something of a key to handling and living with this tradition and its "history," unlocking its potential, freeing what is liberative from what is oppressive, and thus envisioning and creating a very different future.

Despite the rigor of her engagement, and for all that she warns against it, Schüssler Fiorenza sometimes appears to present an image of some kind of "original perfection" which tradition (and not least theological and political expediency) have betrayed and distorted, although perhaps this in fact only really (and properly) resides in God, and therefore also in Christ himself, the Incarnate One who *is* divine revelation and does not merely witness to it. At times she seems to present the tradition in terms of an imperfect vessel carrying within it a good, liberative revelation; sometimes the vessel contradicts its contents. My questions to this view are something like: What if the apparently "bad" and "contrary" aspects of the tradition are part of the revelation? What if the revelation in fact only comes to view not against the backdrop of badness and lies but in the very act of trying to discern, judge, and name right *and* wrong, revelation *and* delusion? What if the revelation is not of truth and goodness but of truth *and* lies, of goodness *and* wickedness, or even of how to tell, hear, see, and speak the truth well and live according to it?

For Further Reflection

1. Is the "tradition"—including scripture—(for Schüssler Fiorenza or for us) a "mixed blessing" (i.e., part blessing and part curse, freedom always arriving with new forms of enslavement?) of "good" and "bad" elements? Or is it an admixture of good and bad elements, and is that precisely the nature of its blessing (providing a genuine opportunity to move out of slavery)?
2. Is Schüssler Fiorenza overly optimistic or overly simplistic to imagine that we can stand for what is good in the tradition and against what is bad in it without repeating the curses and oppression it brings (i.e., without repeating the "sins of the fathers" and visiting them on our own children)? Or, to put this another way, can we "externalize" what we have wrongly "internalized" from the tradition (i.e., exorcise its demons) without damaging and demonizing others? If we can, how do we do so?
3. Is Schüssler Fiorenza right to argue that the liberation of women necessarily requires women's inclusion in church leadership?[15] That is, could there—does there—need to be liberation without or before women's inclusion? To what extent might women's inclusion in what are themselves often oppressive, patriarchal structures be merely a political expediency (rather than a theological necessity or moral imperative) as a means to liberation?
4. If there are (as Schüssler Fiorenza suggests) significant differences between Christian and religious feminist activity and secular women's movements, what are they? To what extent do the different groups work with different visions of "freedom"?
5. What meaningful distinctions can be drawn (if any) between the terms "tradition" and "history"? How might these affect our sense of how God reveals, is revealed, or can be known?
6. How are imperfections (or even delusions and sins) in "orthodoxy" to be exposed and responded to? Or how might "official-but-wrong" be distinguished from "orthodox-and-right"? How do we properly distinguish between "accepted" interpretations and practices within the tradition from "acceptable" ones?

7. How does Schüssler Fiorenza help us to understand how claims for (and the exercise of) "religious authority" actually work in practice, and on what bases they can be made, contested, or judged?

Notes

1. For Hampson, the apparent "favoritism" shown by God in the Bible, to the people of Israel in the Old Testament and then to men by Incarnation in only one, male human person in the New Testament, and the resultant human "sexism" is unavoidable in biblical religions; furthermore, the incarnation itself results in the privileging of male symbolism for God. This, however, she believes to be unworthy of a truly enlightened view of God as benevolent, just, fair, creative, life-giving and never-death-dealing Spirit. See, for example, the arguments set out in her *Theology and Feminism* (Oxford: Blackwell, 1990).

2. Elisabeth Schüssler Fiorenza, *In Memory of Her: A Feminist Theological Reconstruction of Christian Origins* (London: SCM, 1983).

3. For Schüssler Fiorenza's own account, see "The Problem of Women's History," in ibid., 84–93.

4. Ibid., 334.

5. Ibid., 92.

6. See, for example, ibid.: "A feminist biblical spirituality must remain a critical and communal spirituality. . . . The history of patriarchal oppression must not be allowed to cancel out the history of the life, struggles, and leadership of women in biblical religion."

7. These distinctions are set up and discussed in ibid., 347–49.

8. Elisabeth Schüssler Fiorenza, *Discipleship of Equals: A Critical Feminist Ekklesia-logy of Liberation* (New York: Crossroad, 1993), 95–97.

9. See, for example, ibid., 95: "Any Catholic girl who grows up reading the 'lives of the saints' has probably internalized all kinds of sexual hang-ups, but she could not believe that her only vocation and her genuine Christian calling consist in getting married and having children."

10. Again, see ibid., 96: "Over and against the cultural-religious patterns shared by Hellenists and Jews alike, the Christians affirmed at their baptism that the Christian calling eliminates all status distinctions of religion, race, class and caste and leads into a truly universal and catholic community of disciples."

11. Ibid., 101.

12. Ibid., 101–2.

13. Ibid.

14. Ibid., 102.

15. See ibid., 103: "An analysis of Catholic Christian traditions and history, however, indicates that church and theology will transcend their own sexist ideologies only when women are granted full spiritual, theological, and ecclesial equality. . . . If women were admitted to full leadership in church and theology, the need would no longer exist to affirm theologically the maleness of God and Christ and to suppress the Spirit who moves women to full participation in the Catholic Church and its ministry."

Tariq Ramadan (1962–)

From *Western Muslims and the Future of Islam*

[Distinguishing between the unchanging and the changing]

THE WORK OF CATEGORIZATION left by scholars through the ages is phenomenal. Specialists in the foundations of law and jurisprudence (*usul al-fiqh*), who labored at this exercise of extrapolating and categorizing rules on the basis of a reading that was both careful to be faithful to the norm and profoundly rational, have bequeathed to us an unparalleled heritage. A careful reading of these works reveals that very precise modes of grasping the sources were set down very early. Consideration of the language was supported by a double process of distinguishing on the one hand between the unequivocal and the equivocal and on the other between the presence (explicit or implicit) or absence of a causal link (*illa*) in the pronouncement of rules. The other essential side of this work was the elaboration of methodologies differentiated according to the area being studied. Thus, in the area of religious practice (*al-ibadat*), it was determined that it was the texts that were the only ultimate reference because the revealed rites are fixed and not subject to human reason: here one can do only what is based on a text, and the margin for interpretation is virtually nil. In the wider area of human and social affairs, the established methodology is the exact opposite: bearing in mind the positive and trusting attitude of the Qur'anic message, as we have seen, toward the universe and human beings, everything is permitted except that which is explicitly forbidden by a text (or recognized as such by the specialists). Thus, the scope for the exercise of reason and creativity is huge, in contrast with the situation in matters to do with religious practice, and people have complete discretion to experiment, progress, and reform as long as they avoid what is forbidden. So the fact that the fundamental principles of Islam, and its prohibitions, are stated can never allow Muslims to dispense with a study of the context and the societies in which they live. This is the price they must pay for their faithfulness.

It is on the basis of these same logical categorizations that it has been possible to differentiate, through reading the scriptural sources, between the universal principles to which the Muslim consciousness must seek to be faithful through the ages and the practice of those principles, which is necessarily relative, at a given moment in human history. We are here confronting the fundamental distinction that should be established between timeless principles and contingent models, a distinction that is a direct consequence of a normative reading of the sources and, as such, is in itself fundamental. So, a distinction should be made, in the case of the society of Medina, for example, between the fundamental principles on which it was established (e.g., the rule of law, equality, freedom of conscience and worship) and the form in which that society historically appeared. Faithfulness to principles cannot involve faithfulness to the historical model because times change, societies and political and economic systems become more complex, and in every age it is in fact necessary to think of a model appropriate to each social and cultural reality.

For example, one could investigate further the areas of custom and culture, because these concern Western Muslims very directly. The methodological distinction between religious practice and social affairs, like the difference in nature, as far as the basis of reference is concerned, between universal principles and historical temporal models, brings out another demarcation—that which distinguishes between the religious judgment and its cultural garb. *Al-urf*, custom, has been considered one of the sources of law in the sense that all that is recognized as "established for the good" (*maruf*) in a given culture (and that is not in contradiction with any prohibition) is, in practice, integrated into the local Islamic sphere of reference. In fact, as we have seen, even if the forms of religious practice do not change with changes in time and space, some religious commands related to the affairs of the world naturally take on the color of the culture of various countries: the principles remain the same, but the ways of being faithful to them are diverse. So the concern should not be to dress as the Prophet dressed but to dress according to the principles (of decency, cleanliness, simplicity, aesthetics, and modesty) that underlay his choice of clothes.[1]

From *Radical Reform*

[Between isolationism and assimilation]

Indeed, something "radical" does exist about the reform I call for. The very idea of returning to the dimension of "transformation" instead of just "adaptation" to the requirements of the modern world demonstrates an intellectual and ethical posture that is both clear and demanding. Many in the West, Muslims or non-Muslims alike, expect Muslims to adapt to the modern world, to modernity, to modernism, to postmodernism, to progress, to democracy, and to the sciences. Besides the fact that those general and generous appeals mix up spheres of totally different natures (ideology, science, and political models), it often appears that what is expected of the Muslim world in general, and of Muslims in particular, is that they should adapt, catch up with advanced societies, and integrate their achievements. In effect, this means developing enough awareness and critical debates about themselves (their relation to scriptural sources, their interpretations, etc.) to enable them to attain modernity through self-criticism (or more precisely, to attain a criticism-free modernity). While the first part of the statement is laudable (nurturing critical awareness and self-criticism), the second is far less so in its assumptions and consequences. Islam and Muslims are expected to adapt and not to contribute and propose their own answers. A deep and constructive "criticism of modernity," or of "postmodernity," does not seem to be within Muslims' scope; at most, it would be thought to reveal their wish to find pretexts to reject it, or simply, more insidiously, their attempt to "Islamize" it. Some Muslim thinkers have integrated such postulates and keep trying to show how "progressive" they are by constantly "adapting," which, in the end, amounts to wholesale "intellectual assimilation" to the terms of the debate as stated by many Western elites. They thus confuse necessary self-criticism and the surrender of intelligence to the decrees of the prevailing order.

Between the self-enclosure of some *fuqahâ* (with *fatwâ*, which adapt out of necessity and subsequently confirm the existing order) and the self-dilution of some thinkers (through a self-critical approach that sometimes extends to denying oneself and one's own ability to suggest alternatives), there is another way that both disrupts a tradition made so sclerotic by fear that it has become ossified and criticizes the all-out surrender that is often motivated by the same fear, the same lack of self-confidence. Muslims need a new, more coherent balance, as well as new, more stimulating energy, to enable them to contribute and propose their own answers in today's and tomorrow's world.[2]

[New patterns of authority]

I mentioned earlier a shift in the center of gravity of authority in the field of the elaboration of law and ethics, since the balance must be restored between the objects of study (the text and the Universe) and the sciences connected with them. This means that those specialists (scientists or experts) with the best mastery of contemporary scientific knowledge within their specialties and the research techniques related to them must be integrated into the circles of text scholars during their debates and deliberations to formulate legal rulings, the *fatâwâ* about specific issues.

Text scholars who practice *ijtihâd* (*mujtahidûn, fuqahâ'*) in various national or international circles established throughout the world (in Saudi Arabia, Cairo, Damascus, Tehran, Qum, Kuwait, Amman, Djakarta, but also in Washington, Dublin, and other cities) have always admitted that it was imperative for them to be informed and accompanied in their reflections by scientists or doctors who could provide precise information about the state of knowledge or the potential consequences of some particular technique or scientific practice. Moreover, what is accepted in the experimental and medical sciences, because of the precise nature of the expertise involved, has no parallel in the social sciences where such consultations are rare, if not virtually absent. Economists, lawyers, experts, sociologists, or political scientists are often considered as "intellectuals" (*muthaqqafûn*), as "thinkers" (*mufakkirûn*), and sometimes as specialists (*mutakhassisûn*): all those qualifications implicitly fall short of acknowledging the skills of such experts and recognizing their areas of expertise as "sciences," and all the more so in considering them as "scientists." This implicit hierarchy—that is yet so explicit in effect—has the twofold function of clearly defining where "Islamic authority" should reside and, consequently, who can legitimately state opinions and express themselves in the fields of law and ethics.

This begins by acknowledging them as *ulamâ'*, a status established by the Quran itself, as we have seen, as extending beyond the sphere of the knowledge of texts to include that of Nature and the social and human environment. We should therefore recognize that there are not only *ulamâ' an-nusûs*, scholars specializing in texts, but also *ulamâ' al-wâqi*, context scholars. The integration of *ulamâ' al-wâqi* into *fiqh* councils has become imperative and should make it possible to broaden the horizons of *ulamâ' an-nusûs* so that scientific stakes can be perceived both globally and historically.[3]

[Islam and women]

Islamic legal thinking about women is certainly the field that has suffered most from . . . literalist *reduction* and cultural *projection.* We have seen that the Revelations, accompanied by the Prophet's example, represented a divine pedagogy that consisted, over twenty-three years and according to historical circumstances, in changing early Muslims' mind-sets and leading them to consider the issue of women differently. A study exclusively focusing on the texts, their substance, comparison, and chronology . . . shows that this is a continued process of liberation that is accounted for by the message's global vision and by the objectives (*maqâsid*) inferred from the process. Therefore, in addition to reading the texts, one should examine the cultural environment of the time and understand what these texts refer to and which issues are involved in what they say. It appears that in virtually all the fields of women's being and activity in societies, text sequences not only state injunctions but also open prospects that can only be extracted through a holistic, goal-oriented approach. Whether about the relationship to God, to faith, or to the mosque; about necessary education and autonomy, for oneself and toward others; about relating to the body, sexuality, marriage and divorce; about relating to work, money, politics, or even war, one can observe that the Quran and Prophetic traditions take highly innovative positions, which are also very open about their understanding of and dialectical involvement in social environments. The issue, then, is no longer only to know what the texts say about women, but rather to understand what was promoted, defended, and prescribed concerning women's being and power, in relation to the environment of the time. The relationship between texts and contexts must be studied, and this will enable us to extract principles and objectives. Texts do not speak by themselves, and teachings are both synchronic and diachronic: the relation to time is crucial, the relation to the context is imperative. A literalist reading cannot account for those evolution dynamics and their tense relation to time and environments. Specializing in the contents of texts alone, as is required of *fuqahâ'* as a priority, is likely to restrict both the substance of the message and its higher objectives.

Because some existing texts are sometimes read and interpreted without considering chronology and context, it becomes impossible for some *'ulamâ'* to dare express clear legal opinions in the light of higher objectives. They should, for instance, speak out on the fact that keeping women illiterate and forbidding them to work, reach financial autonomy, or play a social and economic role, as well as such practices as female genital mutilation, forced marriages, the denial of divorce, or restraint against domestic violence, are absolutely contrary to Islam's message as shown through its evolution (over twenty-three years) and the Prophet's own attitude.[4]

[Note also Ramadan's comment on the approach taken by classical commentators in this area in the following sentence from just before the above text.]

Reading the early commentaries proposed by such great scholars as at-Tabari, ar-Razi, or al-Qurtubi clearly shows that they were indeed immersed in a specific culture and that their comments about women—their role as well as how they should be treated—stems [*sic*] as much, if not more, from cultural projection as from normative critical reading.[5]

From *What I Believe*

Western Islam: Religion and Culture

Numerous Muslims—*'ulamâ* as well as ordinary believers—have opposed the idea that there could be a "Western Islam" or a "European Islam" different from the one and only "Islam." They have interpreted such terms as attempts at division, adulteration, or perhaps dangerous reform. In other circles, sociologists have claimed that there is not "one Islam" but several very different "Islams" depending on interpretations or societies and that this diversity must be addressed on a circumstantial basis. Confronted by those two contradictory approaches, my position has been to present things from within and in this manner to grasp both the unity and the diversity of the Islamic universe. As regards belief, the pillars of faith (*ʿaqîdah*) and practice (*ʿibadât*), Islam is one and unites all traditions (both Sunni and Shiʿa) on the basis of the Quranic revelation and of Prophetic traditions (Sunnah) that set the common framework and principles. East and West, North and South, Muslims relate to those scriptural sources, fundamentals, and practices, and everywhere this is, palpably and visibly, what nurtures the "faith community" called the *ummah*.

That being said, diversity cannot be denied, and it mainly operates on two levels. First, there is a diversity of readings and interpretations, which accounts for the different traditions, trends, and legal schools (as many as thirty at some periods). This diversity has always existed and, depending on the differences, it has always been more or less accepted (sometimes with difficulty, particularly between Sunni and Shiʿa) by scholars and ordinary Muslims. The other level of diversity is cultural: the principles of Islam regarding social affairs (*muʿâmalât*) have always been very inclusive toward cultures and traditions (recognising *al-ʿurf*, sound custom established before Islam): Muslims in Africa or in Asia have largely kept their way of life and habits while respecting the creed, practices, and principles shared by all Muslims. They have simply been selective and preserved what did not contradict any principle of their faith: it has been so for centuries, and this explains the notable differences in mind-sets and ways of life among Arab, African, Turkish or Asian Muslims. Thus there is one religion, one Islam, with various interpretations and several cultures.

What happened elsewhere in the past is happening in the West today. What we call Western Islam is of exactly the same nature: it is an Islam that respects the common creed, practices, and principles and makes the various Western and European cultures its own. We are witnessing the birth of a Western Islamic culture within which Muslims remain faithful to fundamental religious principles while owning up to their Western cultures. They are both fully Muslim as to religion and fully Western as to culture, and that is no problem at all. The point is not to create a new Islam but to reconnect Islam with its original dynamism, creativity, and confidence, which enabled the faithful to observe and integrate positively all that was good and positive in the cultures they encountered while remaining critical and selective when those cultures could result in insularity, in questionable behaviour and usage, or in systematic discrimination. All cultures, whether Arab, Asian, or Western, require a critical and self-critical mind apt to assess habits in light of principles because habits often erode or blur principles. One should therefore be both open and critical: always remain curious and seek what is beautiful and good, and always remain cautiously alert in assessing what is negative and unfair.

To reach this objective, Muslims in the West and in Europe must perform a twofold work of deconstruction and reconstruction. One must first set out to distinguish what is religious and what is cultural in the way they conceive Islam when they come from Pakistan, Turkey or Arab countries. There is no faith or religion without culture, nor any culture without a religious substrate, but religion is not culture: operating the distinction is not easy but exile makes it necessary and difficult, yet over the course of time, paradoxically, it becomes easier and easier. Initially, of course, migrants always huddle around their religion, culture and community to protect themselves from the foreign environment. They stick to the ways of life of their countries of origin, often confusing religion, culture, and traditions. The second and later generations cannot be content with this attitude and they always (being also more educated) come to question some cultural traits of the countries of origin as they naturally absorb the language and culture of the country in which they live. This transition period is one of natural conflict between generations but also with the surrounding society: what is involved here is doing away with the habits inherent in the parents' culture that are seen as problematic and as not always Islamic, and taking as one's own the positive elements of Western cultures while remaining faithful to Islam's principles. In countries where the Muslim presence is longer established, this transition is already well under way and the stage of cultural integration has already been overcome: the young are now culturally French, British, American, South Africa, Singaporian, or Canadian. In other countries, the process is accelerating, and there are now increasing numbers of Muslim Westerners without this being a problem for the women and men who define themselves as such.[6]

Notes

1. Tariq Ramadan, *Western Muslims and the Future of Islam* (Oxford: Oxford University Press, 2004), 35–36.
2. Tariq Ramadan, *Radical Reform: Islamic Ethics and Liberation* (Oxford: Oxford University Press, 2009), 37–38.
3. Ibid., 130–31.
4. Ibid., 213–14.
5. Ibid., 212.
6. Tariq Ramadan, *What I Believe* (Oxford: Oxford University Press, 2010), 41–44.

Tariq Ramadan's Tryst with Modernity

Toward a European Muslim Tradition

SAJJAD RIZVI

IN THE INTRODUCTION to a significant recent collection of essays on the concept of religion, Hent de Vries writes:

> "Religion" may—or may not—be here to stay. As a "concept" (but which or whose exactly?), from one perspective it might seem to be losing its received reference (the transcendent, the world beyond, and the life hereafter) and its shared relevance (a unified view of the cosmos and all beings in it; a doctrine of the origin, purpose and end of all things; an alert, enlightened or redeemed sense of self; a practice and way of life), if it had not done so already. Yet from another perspective, it continues to claim a prominent role in attempts to understand the past, to grapple with the present, and to anticipate, if not to prophesy, the future.[1]

This sums up the theme of this volume and provides the crucial context for understanding modern Muslim public intellectuals such as Tariq Ramadan, whose thought I will address. Sociologists of religion, and even some specialists in religious studies, have continuously expressed surprise in recent years that the themes of tradition and modernity, once seen as phases within societal and epistemological development, just keep coming back. Traditions most notably expressed in the idiom of religious and cultural beliefs were so many aspects of false consciousness that needed to be overcome. God-talk, once considered obsolete in the social and human sciences, has similarly returned with a vengeance. The Weberian shift from enchantment to disenchantment, from a theocentric reality to an anthropocentric Enlightenment, even post-Enlightenment world, has failed to bring about the secularization that displaces faith from the public and privatized spheres. A number of thinkers have therefore attempted to reassess classical secularization theory and reconsider key features of it.[2] First, what is the role of religion in the public sphere? Following Habermas's most recent position, do we grudgingly allow religion to hold public space to avoid "trouble" as long as it cedes authority to critical and secular reason, or do we concede that faith-based, even fundamentalist and isolationist theocratic positions within a liberal democratic bargain are worthy of our societies, as Swaine argues?[3] Second, to what extent has the condition of modernity actually facilitated the perpetuation of multivocal disciplines and practices of tradition embedded in exegetical communities of meaning?[4] Third, does the overarching monism of modernity give way to disaggregated notions of multiple and alternative modernity?[5]

So much for political theology—and in fact it is precisely a politicized notion of religiosity and soteriology that plagues much modern Islamic thinking and indeed broader thought relating to the category of religion. Alongside this, even in theology, one experiences the return of the messianic and apocalyptic, the God beyond being and within the realm of possibility, concepts that force us to rethink what we even mean by religion, by belief, a stripping away of ontotheology in favor of the immediacy of experience.[6] The basic notion that our fundamental intellectual values are barely veiled and secularized modes of theological thinking has been extensively aired, whether they pertain to the political or to the metaphysical.[7] Even secularism qualifies as a form of religious commitment, while from the opposite direction, European thought on religion and secularity is provincialized by examining the constructed nature of both from the margins.[8] This return with a vengeance of God, expressed within a seemingly secularized idiom with greatest irony, is evident in the work of John Micklethwait and Adrian Wooldridge.[9] Neotheism clashes and finds fertile ground for its ideas due no doubt in part to the fundamentalism of the neo-atheism of the likes of Richard Dawkins and Christopher Hitchens.[10]

The return to God, the revival of tradition, and the calibration of modernity in the imagination are at least partly due to the focus upon Islam. So the question that arises is how Muslim thinkers in the contemporary period (re)think their intellectual traditions, their inherited modes and articulations of *phronesis* (practical wisdom), and their ethical engagements in a world of alternative modernities. In a sense, the themes have changed little in the past two centuries of Islamic modernism and liberalism: a concern with equity, the rights of women, and the oppressed; concerns for social justice; the need to rethink basic texts and approaches to texts; and a reassessment of the sources and methods (and indeed authority) needed for understanding what it means to live the good Muslim life in the world today.

One of the most prominent Muslim thinkers engaged as a public intellectual in these questions is the Swiss-Egyptian thinker Tariq Ramadan (b. 1962). Ramadan was born into the aristocracy of the Muslim Brotherhood and is still deeply marked by the thinking of this movement; he trained in philosophy and the human sciences and is presently professor of contemporary Islamic studies at the University of Oxford.[11] I will not say much about his biography beyond this and will turn to the analysis of themes in his work that relate to tradition and modernity. I shall also attempt to highlight what I consider to be the shortcomings of his approach.[12]

But before analyzing features of Ramadan's discourse, I want to set out some further contexts for understanding his thought. First, notions of minimalist ontology in contemporary analytic philosophy, a distrust of dualism and a reconfiguring of the human as a holistic, physical being prompt us to ask, where does this leave the question of spirituality? Or rather, perhaps we should ask whether the fact that we need to reinject spirituality into our understanding of religion betrays an assumption of the relative significance of mental and extramental states. Can spirituality be confined to inner states? Second, contemporary Kantian and post-Kantian epistemologies evince a rejection not only of the idea of pure experience (just at a time when some reformed epistemologists are forgoing natural theology in favor of justifications for religious belief based on experience) but also of the assumption of rational agents acting to discern ethical issues of the good life and epistemic questions relating to our ability to know truth. Heightened epistemic conflict between peers brings about the process of objectification, the need for believers and indeed for anyone holding a particular type of belief to justify it: according to Dale Eickelman and James Piscatori, this process of objectification is a primary feature of modern Muslim politics and of the efforts of Muslims to understand and belong in the contemporary world.[13] Finally, we must consider the European project and how we define it and more specifically whether there is space in Europe for Islam and for Muslims.

So from the general theoretical issues of ontology and epistemology to the specifics of Muslim ipse identity and Europe, the broad contours within which Ramadan is writing are of critical significance and perhaps stymie his efforts to fulfill the intellectual challenge.[14]

Forging a European Muslim Tradition

We begin with the idea that has made Ramadan famous, namely, the promotion of "European Muslim" as a meaningful theoretical and theological category and his forging of a European Muslim tradition as the context for understanding what it means to be a Muslim in Europe today. This was the topic of perhaps his first important work published in the late 1990s, *To Be a European Muslim*.[15] Now he has shifted the term to "Western Muslim." What does he mean by Western Islam?

Ramadan argues that an understanding of the Western context is critical and requires opening channels of dialogue between Muslims and Western thought (note, not between Muslim thought and Western thought). His focus is, therefore, on arguing that the unity of the global Muslim community is compatible with the existence of culturally and geographically specific communities of Muslims, and that the unified creed and tradition of Islam is capable of absorbing and facilitating the flourishing of minor or localized traditions and forms of vernacularization. Western Muslims are a social fact of the diversity of Europe and of the world of Islam. Muslims in Europe enjoy freedom of religious belief and expression and indeed freedom to proselytize. Hence, Ramadan argues against extremists that, contrary to the legal construct that divides the world into Muslim political territory (*dār al-islām*) and enemy territory (*dār al-ḥarb*), one should regard Europe as a place for proclaiming the faith and bearing witness to it (*dār al-daʿwa* or *dār al-shahāda*).[16] In an extended discussion of ways in which one can calibrate the legal tradition's view of relations between polities and communities, he agrees with Faysal al-Mawlawi (a prominent Lebanese member of the European Council for Research and Fatwa) that Europe constitutes a special case in which one can proclaim one's faith; but Ramadan himself prefers the notion of Europe as *dār al-shahāda* because Muslims can practice their faith, affirm their identity, proclaim God, and act ethically.[17] Importantly, the "European situation" allows Muslims to cooperate for the common good and express their social responsibility, thus blending their universal duty as Muslims with their civic duty as citizens.[18] As such, Ramadan genuflects toward those who proclaim the special minority status of Muslims in Europe and insist upon a jurisprudence of special circumstances appropriate to the situation (*fiqh al-aqalliyyat*) as a necessary evil along the path toward an ethical turn in understanding the moral law.[19] Ramadan therefore seems to think that conceding special rulings for the extraordinary situation of Muslims in non-Muslim jurisdictions is a useful first step toward an ideal situation in which ethical conduct is more uniformly understood in a future in which jurisprudence and ethics are entirely consistent.

Alongside the legal description of the Western context comes an analysis of the lived reality of Muslims in Europe and the ethical framework of the intellectual traditions that they encounter. With respect to the latter, Ramadan argues that Muslims need to embrace a rights-based approach to ethical intersubjectivity. While he fails to establish a systematic theory of justice, his treatment of women's rights indicates some useful directions: a commitment to education and access to texts, an exhortation to women to take ownership of their texts, and a contextualization of patriarchal traditions as limited by what he terms the dual inheritance of "literalist reduction" and "cultural projection."[20] He is somewhat squeamish about using the term "feminism" (although more recently he seems to have shifted[21]), but unlike more radical Muslim theologians such as Amina Wadud, he has yet to state that the text may be forgone or set aside. His approach remains one of "reading the text for liberation" and as such is still scriptocentric.

Adherence to the text and the inability to go beyond the text acts as a restraint to the more liberal elements in Ramadan's thought. His approach is very much one determined to find relevant resources within the Islamic tradition to engage in the project of reform. What are the bases of his rethinking of the faith in the Western context? Ramadan makes much of the fact that he has a traditional seminarian's training (at al-Azhar no less) as well as an academic's and hence claims the credibility and authority to engage in his enterprise.[22] He draws upon some relevant existing modes of analysis in Muslim juristic reasoning that allow one to rethink ethical rules relevant to differing places and times. So the first element of the tradition upon which he draws is the primary slogan of modernist Muslim thought, namely *ijtihād*, or the process of trained and informed independent legal reasoning based on differing hermeneutics of the text. *Ijtihād* constitutes a probabilistic and critical interpretation of texts based on received traditions of hermeneutics and principles of deriving law. Ramadan claims that the call for *ijtihād* is not only essential for each time and place but is consistent with his self-identification within the movement that he terms "salafi reformism."[23] As a tool, it does not lose its foundations in scriptural texts such as the Qur'ān and the Ḥadīth but also engages rationally with them in a nonliteralist manner. The function of *ijtihād* is not only to deduce new rules of comportment based on analogical reasoning from existing texts but also to pursue reform (*istiṣlāḥ*) that is compatible with the pursuit of the objectives of the Sharīʿa (*maqāṣid*).[24]

The second element of the jurisprudential tradition concerns an understanding that the contextual custom (*ʿurf*) and lived actuality or reality (*al-wāqiʿ*) constitutes a significant determinant of what the law is in a particular space and time.[25] It forces one to consider carefully what is essential in the religious message. Ramadan states that since the prime determinant of religious identity as a Muslim is faith, then we need to concede that there is no faith without understanding and knowledge of the text and the context and the free choice to adhere to that faith from which arises responsibility.[26] He argues that in fact the present situation in the West requires a new type of jurisprudence in which a careful synergy is needed between textual and "scholars who understand the context" or the lived reality. A dynamic law therefore must be predicated upon the marriage of two types of expertise and authority, the religious-scriptural and the scientific (whether exact, social, or human sciences).[27] What makes a particular text relevant to a believer in the contemporary context and how can one distinguish what is essential from what is accidental or the immutable from the mutable? Is it clear and decisive texts that are immutable? As with much modernist thinking, Ramadan displays a certain fuzziness over such questions.[28] What defines the essential and the immutable and distinguishes it from the mutable? Ramadan fails to tell us. The commitment to change and transformation of the law and understanding of religion is more striking in his later work, where he argues that, instead of being adaptive and passive, Muslims need to be more proactive in understanding their faith in Europe.[29] They should proclaim the universal principles of Islam in pursuit of justice and human dignity.[30]

Within this element, Ramadan draws out an important distinction often implicit in classical juristic texts: how does one distinguish between rules or principles that are fixed and immutable and those that are transient and changeable? A basic distinction is drawn between the text and its interpretation with the former being innocent of coercive and patriarchal readings perpetuated by men influenced by their cultural context. This amounts to a rather naive hermeneutics. The principles that he argues are immutable derive from basic philosophical conceptions of the law and the aims of the moral law or the Sharīʿa.[31] Like Soroush and others, Ramadan argues that the mutable includes elements of cultural specificity and textual multivocality: the world of Islam is one in which people are united by certain core beliefs and the notion of being part of a corporate whole but divided by cultural differences and diversity in the expression of their faith, which also affect their reading of texts.[32] European Muslims thus can act as bridges of communication and mutual understanding. However, the call for Muslims to give up their immigrant Islam and embrace their European emergent reality is a strange dichotomization that ignores the hybridity of identities that exist in Europe. It also establishes a false distinction between the domains of the "religious" and the "cultural," a common distinction among Salafi reformist preachers. As Ramadan puts it: "Islam is not a culture . . . the essence of Islam is religious."[33] Here, refuting the oft-cited charge that he practices doublespeak, Ramadan says: "I had decided to engage in that process of mediation between universes of reference, cultures, and religions. I fully accepted both my Muslim faith and my Western culture and I claimed that this is possible and that common values and hopes are more essential and more numerous than differences. Conveying that message is difficult in this time of impassioned debates dominated by confusion and mutual deafness. A mediator is a bridge and a bridge never belongs to one side only."[34]

The third element of Ramadan's borrowing from the tradition relates to a rethinking of what one means by Sharīʿa and its instrumentalization through the pursuit and protection of its objectives (*maqāṣid*) and not through adherence to particular rules.[35] This tendency, which is widespread among thinkers influenced by the Muslim Brotherhood but also among many others in contemporary European Islam, is linked explicitly to the notion of the common good cited in its jurisprudential form as *maṣlaḥa*.[36] A primary qualification to practice *ijtihād*, according to Ramadan, is precisely a knowledge of the higher objectives of the moral path or the Sharīʿa, which he defines as "the expression of individual and collective faithfulness, in time, for those who are trying in awareness to draw near to the ideal of the Source that is God."[37] These objectives or *maqāṣid* are translated (and expanded beyond the traditional essential five) by Ramadan into the following values: dignity of life and nature, welfare, knowledge, creativity, autonomy, development, equality, freedom, justice, love, fraternity, solidarity, and diversity.[38]

Ultimately, Ramadan argues that if one understands the Western context and what it means to be Muslim, drawing from the traditional resources, one will find a median integrative path, being neither a Muslim without faith nor a Muslim in the West but not of it, and will arrive at being a Western Muslim who embraces the different elements of his faith and reality.[39]

Whither Reform in Modernity?

Ramadan's program for Western Muslims is one of reform, so it would be useful here to indicate why one needs reform and to what end. First, he argues that at the very least reform is about opening a critical debate.[40] It reflects the need for Muslims in every place and age to make sense of what it means to be faithful based on traditional categories of renewal and reform (*tajdīd* and *iṣlāḥ*) and to understand texts and contexts.[41] Pluralizing understanding is a result of reform and is necessary to distinguish between the mutable and the immutable in the faith.[42] Radical reform requires a transformation of the understanding of the faith and not just some adaptation.

Second, reform demands that Western Muslims are engaged and integrated. Their very engagement is their jihād, their path to faithfulness that requires a balanced effort.[43] This may include forgoing elements of particularism such as the demand for certain types of separate status: he singles out specialist Muslim schools as unhelpful.[44] Integration and a clear and committed sense of belonging require a balance between the universal and the particular, between universal principles and cultural particularities, between an immutable moral path and a commitment to a specific citizenship. He argues that Muslims and others need to move beyond an identity discourse that objectifies people to decide who they are.[45] Thus integration demands a move beyond multiculturalism toward a rather *laïque* notion of citizenship in which individual responsibility and the pursuit of social justice are paramount.

Third, reform requires the integration of two distinct universes of discourse relating to the Muslim and the Western, and entering into dialogue between and within civilizations.[46] Ramadan advocates pluralizing modernity and not

Islamizing it or modernizing Islam.[47] Since he seems to have decided that these are the requirements of the intellectual context, this entails forgoing theology as traditionally understood in Islam as irrelevant. Such an attitude is rather common in much liberal contemporary Muslim thinking in which there is no need to defend God but rather one ought to focus upon the human, a humanizing of theology. Ramadan actually has very little to say about how one understands God, humans, and the wider cosmic reality.

Finally, Ramadan's more recent work reflects a more systematic shift toward engaging critically with the traditions of law and jurisprudence. Reform needs to be transformative and not merely adaptive and hence should address the very principles of legal theory in the Islamic tradition as well—something that was unthought and untouched in his earlier work.[48] In his short apologia *What I Believe*, he sums up the quest for reform in categorizing seven values, or "Cs," that should define the modern Western Muslim: confidence, consistency, contribution, creativity, communication, contestation, and compassion.[49] These are all good ideas and values in themselves but they read rather too much like self-help speak. They also do not strike me as reflecting anything specific to being Muslim, but surely universal values are derived from some meditation upon what tradition produces those values?

For Further Reflection

1. What is the purpose of reform? Is it an attempt to demonstrate that Muslims are modern and normal, that they "fit" in Europe and are capable of advocating shared values? To what extent does Ramadan merely indulge in apologetics and, as suggested by those who would ascribe more sinister motives, a clandestine *daʿwa* or mission?
2. What is the relationship between religion and culture? Where does faith lie within our lived experiences?
3. Who are Ramadan's interlocutors? Who is the audience? Is he caught between placating conservatives and liberals within the world of Islam and without?
4. Does Ramadan's reform with a view to modernity constitute an actual ethical turn or a rethinking of the faith beyond *fiqh*? Or is it another form of political theology centered on ips-identity politics? How does one recapture both moral authority and moral agency in the present?
5. Where is the deep meditation upon the hermeneutics of the text and reality? What are the principles for determining what is immutable and mutable?

6. Is ontotheology truly dead (or even just irrelevant) in contemporary Islam? What implications might our analysis have for the more general phenomenon of religion? What is meant by faith and faithfulness in our world? This leads us back to the fundamental question posed at the beginning: what is religion?

Notes

1. Hent de Vries, "Why Still 'Religion'?" in Hent de Vries, ed., *Religion: Beyond a Concept* (New York: Fordham University Press, 2008), 1.

2. Jose Casanova, *Public Religions in the Modern World* (Chicago: University of Chicago Press, 1994); and David Martin, *On Secularization: Toward a Revised General Theory* (Aldershot, UK: Ashgate Publishing, 2005).

3. Jürgen Habermas, *An Awareness of What Is Missing: Faith and Reason in a Post-Secular Age* (Cambridge: Polity Press, 2010); and Lucas Swaine, *The Liberal Conscience* (New York: Columbia University Press, 2006).

4. One thinks of Alasdair MacIntyre's famous trilogy: *After Virtue* (London: Duckworth, 1981); *Whose Justice? Whose Rationality?* (London: Duckworth, 1988); and *Three Rival Versions of Moral Inquiry* (London: Duckworth, 1990); and Hans-Georg Gadamer's classic works on tradition, history, and hermeneutics: *Philosophical Hermeneutics* (Berkeley: University of California Press, 1976); and *Truth and Method* (New York: Crossroad, 1989).

5. See the special issue of *Daedalus, Multiple Modernities* (Cambridge, MA: American Academy of Arts and Sciences, 2000). This debate has found two different types of Muslim responses: first, an enlightenment-grounded rejection of multiplicity by Aziz al-Azmeh, *Islams and Modernities* (London: Verso, 2009), and an embrace of pluralizing modernity by Amyn Sajoo, ed., *Muslim Modernities: Expressions of the Civil Imagination* (London: Tauris, 2008).

6. Richard Kearney, *The God Who May Be: The Hermeneutics of Religion* (Bloomington: Indiana University Press, 2002); Jean-Luc Marion, *God without Being: Hors-texte* (Chicago: University of Chicago Press, 1991); John Caputo, *On Religion* (London: Routledge, 2001); and Slavoj Žižek, *On Belief* (London: Routledge, 2001).

7. Carl Schmitt, *The Concept of the Political*, trans. George Schwab (Chicago: University of Chicago Press, 1996); and Schmitt, *Political Theology: Four Chapters on the Concept of Sovereignty*, trans. George Schwab (Cambridge, MA: MIT Press, 1985); Giorgio Agamben, *State of Exception*, trans. Kevin Attell (Chicago: University of Chicago Press, 2005); and Agamben, *Homo Sacer: Sovereign Power and Bare Life*, trans. Daniel Heller-Roazen (Stanford, CA: Stanford University Press, 1998); Hent de Vries, *Philosophy and the Turn to Religion* (Baltimore: Johns Hopkins University Press, 1999). More generally, see the collected volume: Hent de Vries, ed., *Religion: Beyond a Concept* (New York: Fordham University Press, 2008).

8. Talal Asad, *Formations of the Secular: Christianity, Islam, Modernity* (Stanford, CA: Stanford University Press, 2003); and Asad, *Genealogies of Religion: Discipline and Reasons of Power in Christianity and Islam* (Baltimore: Johns Hopkins University Press, 1993); Saba Mahmood, "Religious Reason and Secular Affect: An Incommensurable Divide?" *Critical Inquiry* 35 (2009): 836–62; and Dipesh Chakrabarty, *Provincializing Europe: Postcolonial Thought and Historical Difference* (Princeton, NJ: Princeton University Press, 2000).

9. John Micklethwait and Adrian Wooldridge, *God Is Back: The Global Rise of Faith Is Changing the World* (London: Penguin, 2010).

10. Christopher Hitchens, *God Is Not Great: The Case against Religion* (New York: Atlantic Books, 2007); Richard Dawkins, *The God Delusion* (London: Bantam, 2006). This latter has itself spawned a veritable library of refutations.

11. See his official site www.tariqramadan.com.

12. There are a number of studies of Ramadan, mostly hostile, such as Caroline Fourest, *Frère Tariq: Discours, stratégie, et méthode de Tariq Ramadan* (Paris: Grasset, 2004). Andrew Marsh has produced more sophisticated political analyses, such as "Reading Tariq Ramadan: Political Liberalism, Islam and 'Overlapping Consensus,'" *Ethics & International Affairs* 21, no. 4 (2007): 399–413. For a more sympathetic engagement locating Ramadan's public ethics within a Habermasian paradigm of communicative action, see Chi-Chung Yu, "Islam in the West: A Study in the Thought of Seyyed Hossein Nasr and Tariq Ramadan" (Ph.D. diss., University of Exeter, 2008), a study undertaken under my supervision. A sympathetic theological interfaith encounter is Gregory Baum, *The Theology of Tariq Ramadan: A Catholic Perspective* (Montreal: Novalis, 2008).

13. David Basinger, *Religious Diversity* (Aldershot, UK: Ashgate, 2002); and Dale Eickelman and James Piscatori, *Muslim Politics* (Princeton, NJ: Princeton University Press, 1996).

14. Ipse identity relates to the intentionality of the subject and the ability of a self to be an agent. It therefore concerns the assertion of the Muslim self insofar as it is Muslim and in distinction to others. I draw upon the formulation of Paul Ricoeur, *Oneself as Another* (Chicago: University of Chicago Press, 1992).

15. Tariq Ramadan, *To Be a European Muslim* (Leicester, UK: Islamic Foundation, 1999).

16. Ibid., 150.

17. Tariq Ramadan, *Western Muslims and the Future of Islam* (Oxford: Oxford University Press, 2004), 72–75.

18. Ibid., 75–77.

19. Ibid., 53.

20. Tariq Ramadan, *Radical Reform: Islamic Ethics and Liberation* (Oxford: Oxford University Press, 2009), 212–14.

21. Tariq Ramadan, *What I Believe* (Oxford: Oxford University Press, 2010), 65.

22. Ibid., 12.

23. Ramadan, *Western Muslims*, 26–27.

24. Ibid., 46.

25. Ramadan, *Radical Reform*, 101–12.

26. Ramadan, *Western Muslims*, 80.

27. Ramadan, *Radical Reform*, 130–33.

28. Ramadan, *Western Muslims*, 35–36.

29. Ramadan, *Radical Reform*, 37–38.

30. Ramadan, *What I Believe*, 8.

31. Ramadan, *Western Muslims*, 35–36, and Ramadan, *Radical Reform*, 37–38.

32. Ramadan, *What I Believe*, 41–44.

33. Ramadan, *Western Muslims*, 214.

34. Ramadan, *What I Believe*, 14.

35. Tariq Ramadan, *The Quest for Meaning: Developing a Philosophy of Pluralism* (London: Allen Lane, 2010), 57–61.

36. Ramadan, *Western Muslims,* 38.
37. Ibid., 32.
38. Ramadan, *Radical Reform*, 143.
39. Ramadan, *Western Muslims,* 83–84.
40. Ramadan, *What I Believe*, 7.
41. Ramadan, *Radical Reform*, 13–14.
42. Ibid., 17–18.
43. Ramadan, *Western Muslims,* 113.
44. Ibid., 130–33.
45. Ramadan, *What I Believe*, 67–73.
46. Ibid., 20.
47. Ramadan, *Radical Reform*, 145–46.
48. Ramadan, *What I Believe*, 85.
49. Ibid., 88.

Afterword

ROWAN WILLIAMS

MODERNITY AND THE scatter of terms related to it are agreed to be slippery words. They are hardly ever used neutrally, just to describe what happens to be the cultural position at the present moment. They may be used in both positive and negative ways: "modernization" is assumed unthinkingly to be a good thing; "modernism" is a bad thing in the vocabulary of traditional Catholic thought; "modernity" is now commonly used for a cluster of cultural and intellectual habits generated (broadly) by the European Enlightenment and supposedly transcended by the advent of a "postmodern" era. When we discuss tradition and modernity, we need to be careful to acknowledge just what work the word "modernity" is doing in particular contexts—not least so that we avoid building into our discourse an assumption that these two words, "tradition" and "modernity," are in all circumstances natural opposites.

A paradox that several of the essays here hint at is that it is modernity of a certain kind that makes it possible to talk about tradition as we do. In a "traditional" society, there is a sense in which tradition is invisible: habits of mind and spirit are transmitted un-self-consciously, not least because patterns of authority are not open for discussion. Modernity means not only the shrill protest against authority that is beyond discussion but also the awareness that transmission itself is seldom if ever a matter of handing on an unchanged deposit. The events of transmission themselves subtly alter what is being handed over—not necessarily in a sinister sense but simply because reflection on the "deposit" allows new vocabulary to be generated in response to new questions. Intellectual modernity permits us to look at the transmission of habits and beliefs from a bit of a distance, to track the various ways in which tradition works cumulatively. And in a cultural environment where some degree of awareness of change is unavoidable, this means that tradition is not a protected and isolated area of human discourse but is inseparable from the entire organic life of a culture or a social system. Modernity lets us think about tradition in relation to actual history, tradition as a phenomenon, not just a record of repetition. Exactly what is repeated, or rather re-embodied, in what terms, at what point, becomes a matter of interest. And this in turn allows elements of comparative study to enter in: we examine not only our own formation by the transmission of habit and belief but the stories of tradition in the lives of other communities. We have become able to raise the question of authentic and inauthentic transmission with a new intensity and a wider perspective.

As those remarks indicate, such a "modern" approach to tradition doesn't necessarily mean that tradition has become uninhabitable. In religious terms, it is still eminently possible to say that the founding event, the revelatory event, remains decisive yet continues to unfold itself, even establishing its authority by its capacity to respond to new circumstances. In John Milbank's words, "alteration need not betoken distortion." The alternative is what Vincent Cornell calls "epistemological quarantine": sources of knowledge from outside the initial circumstances of the revelation must be shunned. Both Christianity and Islam have at times generated such strategies, arguing for the unique privilege of the first believers and resisting the idea that the language of revelation might sustain itself in dialogue with other kinds of knowing. But—as some of our authors point out—this can have the effect of setting revealed knowledge alongside secular as competitors for the same territory, which implies a lowering of the status of what is claimed for revelation.

The subject is full of such paradoxes; one that recurs often is that to be a "traditionalist" today represents a choice. In contrast to the un-self-consciousness of premodern tradition, the contemporary traditionalist has opted for this rather than that set of habits and beliefs. The much-abused modern individual with supposedly autonomous will has made his or her selection according to criteria that are not themselves part of the tradition. And this means that there is no simple and innocent status for tradition over against modernity: modernity has already insinuated itself simply by offering the concept of tradition as something that can be thought about from the outside.

What is also clear from these essays and extracts is that an opposition between scripture and tradition is just as unhelpful. Scripture, for Christian and Muslim alike, is the central element in what is transmitted. Janet Soskice illustrates this point in relation to Christianity, but, as John Milbank's intriguing reflections suggest, there may be differences between Christian and Muslim approaches depending on how far scripture itself already carries within it a history of rewriting and rereading, as with the Jewish and Christian Bible, and how far scripture is to be seen as a single determinative moment of breakthrough, as seems to be the case with Islam. In the former case, Milbank claims, it is more straightforward to develop a theology of tradition as unceasing variation on canonical themes, while Islam is bound to be more concerned with the purity and "transparency" of the lineage of reading. This deserves more consideration, in the light both of the typical Catholic Christian understanding that there is no single original moment of revelation in textual form and of the Protestant Christian insistence that historical variations have to be brought back to confront a foundational witness that must be allowed to criticize or challenge whatever is generated from it. Whether Milbank's further suggestion that certain strands in Shīʿī Islam stand closer to a Christian and European view of text and tradition is plausible is a complex question but one worth asking in this connection. Other essays—such as that by Abdullahi Ahmed an-Naʿim—underline the fact that in practice Islamic interpretation of scripture and Sharīʿa is capable of "fresh consensus around new techniques of interpretation as well as applying these techniques to develop new or different substantive principles and rules of Sharīʿa." In other words, there are hermeneutical questions for Muslims apart from the apparently simple issue of a lineage of transmission.

Recep Şentürk draws attention to one question that is at once raised by this in the particular social and political context of "modernity." Traditional authorities are generally in eclipse—outside, perhaps, the "private" setting of the devotional circle with a lineage of teaching. In the wider Muslim world what we can call public sacred authority is hard to find; hence, the scale of the contemporary challenge to distinguish between genuinely "traditional" interpretations and frankly arbitrary or ignorant readings of texts by self-appointed sages. Şentürk is clear that this is quintessentially a "modern" situation, tradition both authentic and not-so-authentic bidding for a hearing in the contemporary public (market) square. Polyphony is unavoidable, and this makes new demands on both individual and corporate discernment—for which in turn deeper modes of (traditional) personal and spiritual formation are needed.

And this points us to the deeper epistemological problems at work in this field, problems that are obviously continuous with those we examined when an earlier seminar looked at the relation between religious and scientific understanding.[1] What do we think counts as knowing? What counts as learning? Here the tension between tradition and modernity comes closest to being a straight opposition. Traditional modes of handing on habits and beliefs assume that to know your way in the practice and thought of your faith will lay upon you a number of possibly costly, certainly protracted disciplines. You will not know what you need to learn except by taking time and taking part. The "rationalist ego" (see Stephen Fields's essay on Newman) resists this: knowledge is seen as what can be accessed and confirmed by equally simple sets of procedures operated by the individual mind. The claims of faith will always be disadvantaged in our kind of intellectual world by such a presupposition. So to defend tradition in any way as a serious ground for knowledge is to be committed to redefining knowledge as it is regularly presented to us. This in turn requires a developed understanding of the role that tradition plays in all kinds of cultural activities, whereas it is often discussed as though it were an issue unique to religion. As is hinted in these pages, it is important to see how "modernity" itself is a matter of tradition, a transmitted set of habits and beliefs that shape what is thought to be possible and meaningful.

The discussion represented by these pieces is therefore not one that invites a facile antimodern stance. It accepts that we are now irreversibly (so far as we can see) in a cultural situation where it is not possible to be unaware of the fact that traditions have real and complex histories that are not just about the peaceable unfolding from within of what is implicit in them. But this does not mean either an acceptance that traditional claims to truthfulness are empty or that "modern" accounts of knowledge and certainty are to be taken as beyond criticism. To be able to see one's convictions in historical perspective and still to be committed is an intellectually credible position: any number of factors may have contributed to a belief—in religious faith as in literary judgement or scientific hypothesis—but this does not of itself invalidate the content of such a belief. The location of a belief against its complex social conditioning will not settle its truthfulness. In this context, the "modern" is not to be feared. Where the tension does become something more like conflict is when it is assumed that there is one and only one socially and intellectually credible way of arriving at a belief, and that this is essentially through unaided observation on the part of the individual ego. People of faith are what they are because of a confidence that what I earlier called taking time and taking part are crucial to acquiring beliefs of a particular kind. They assume that what is spoken about and explored in a shared *imaginaire* over time is worthy of trust on the basis of a range of criteria that are not easily reduced to "modern" terms.

The defense of tradition as a credible way of knowing, particularly in the context of claims about revelation, is thus part of the defense of a certain picture of human subjectivity. We are not primarily individual agents left to work out how to find our way in a material world; we are addressed before we speak, we learn slowly how to manage our own identity in what we say, how to shape for ourselves and others a picture of who we are and have been that can be offered as meaningful in the complicated world of linguistic interaction. Revelation, and tradition as a means of transmitting what revelation declares, tell us that our primary posture as human beings is receptive—not passive, an easy mistake to make—but intelligently attentive to an environment that is providing the material for our identity as we sense and think about it. We build our identities, strange as it sounds, on the basis of what has decisively interrupted our self-constructions and self-generated conventions. To be a subject, a self, is to be somewhere where a world encoded in language "lands," settles; and tradition, in the religious and nonreligious context alike, is simply the process by which what we receive becomes also what we give, so as to shape the lives of others.

Ultimately, then, living out of a tradition is inseparable from gratitude, from the basic attitude of acknowledging an initiative that is not ours and that works toward our enrichment and our reconciliation with one another. In our discussions at Georgetown, that focus on gratitude in relation to all we say and do as people of faith was often articulated and became very much part of how we sought to understand one another. Modernity appears in such a context as a good tool for analysis in some ways but a poor framework for thinking about thinking or thinking about knowing. Tradition appears as something rather ambivalent when chosen in order to find a secure corner where modernity's corrosive influence does not permeate, but something profoundly positive when grasped as our embeddedness in a world that moves through time and in a humanity that moves through language and through which language moves. For the believer, that language itself is ultimately grounded in God's own movement outward to what he has graciously made; and that is where our gratitude finds its terminus.

Note

1. See David Marshall, ed., *Science and Religion: Christian and Muslim Perspectives* (Washington, DC: Georgetown University Press, 2012).

Index